# Alive to L

*Perspectives on language awareness for English language teachers*

*Valerie Arndt, Paul Harvey and John Nuttall*

CAMBRIDGE
UNIVERSITY PRESS

PUBLISHED BY THE PRESS SYNDICATE OF THE UNIVERSITY OF CAMBRIDGE
The Pitt Building, Trumpington Street, Cambridge, United Kingdom

CAMBRIDGE UNIVERSITY PRESS
The Edinburgh Building, Cambridge CB2 2RU, UK        www.cup.cam.ac.uk
40 West 20th Street, New York, NY 10011–4211, USA      www.cup.org
10 Stamford Road, Oakleigh, Melbourne 3166, Australia
Ruiz de Alarcón 13, 28014 Madrid, Spain

First published 2000

Typeset in Sabon 10.5/12.5pt

*A catalogue record for this book is available from the British Library*

*Library of Congress Cataloguing in Publication data applied for*

ISBN 0 521 56015 2 hardback
ISBN 0 521 56882 X paperback

Transferred to digital printing 2004

# Alive to Language

# CAMBRIDGE TEACHER TRAINING AND DEVELOPMENT

## Series Editors: Marion Williams and Tony Wright

This series is designed for all those involved in language teacher training and development: teachers in training, trainers, directors of studies, advisers, teachers of in-service courses and seminars. Its aim is to provide a comprehensive, organised and authoritative resource for language teacher training development.

**Teach English** – A training course for teachers
*by Adrian Doff*

**Training Foreign Language Teachers** – A reflective approach
*by Michael J. Wallace*

**Literature and Language Teaching** – A guide for teachers and trainers\*
*by Gillian Lazar*

**Classroom Observation Tasks** – A resource book for language teachers and trainers\*
*by Ruth Wajnryb*

**Tasks for Language Teachers** – A resource book for training and development\*
*by Martin Parrott*

**English for the Teacher** – A language development course\*
*by Mary Spratt*

**Teaching Children English** – A training course for teachers of English to children\*
*by David Vale with Anne Feunteun*

**A Course in Language Teaching** – Practice and theory
*by Penny Ur*

**Looking at Language Classrooms** – A teacher development video package

**About Language** – Tasks for teachers of English
*by Scott Thornbury*

**Action Research for Language Teachers**
*by Michael J. Wallace*

**Mentor Courses** – A resource book for trainer-trainers
*by Angi Malderez and Caroline Bodóczky*

**Alive to Language** – Perspectives on language awareness for English language teachers
*by Valerie Arndt, Paul Harvey and John Nuttall*

**Teachers in Action** – Tasks for in-service language teacher education and development
*by Peter James*

**Advising and Supporting Teachers**
*by Mick Randall and Barbara Thornton*

\* Original Series Editors: Ruth Gairns and Marion Williams

# Contents

# Acknowledgements

We would like to thank all those students, teachers and colleagues who have helped us in the process of being ourselves more 'alive' to language, and who have thus contributed in numerous ways to the coming-into-being of this book.

Our gratitude is also owed to our editor, Tony Wright, for his unfailing help, constructive advice and constant support throughout the project.

The authors and publishers are grateful to the authors, publishers and others who have given their permission for the use of copyright information identified in the text. While every endeavour has been made, it has not been possible to identify the sources of all material used and in such cases the publishers would welcome information from copyright sources.

Collins, A. and J. Atkinson. Smack Dee. *The Sun* 26th October 1996. (News International Newspapers Limited, 26th October 1996), on p. 23; Great Western Timetable (1996), on p. 25; Horoscope by Marjorie Orr, *Daily Express*. 18th December 1998, on p. 26; Addo, M. Are Judges Beyond Criticism under Article 10 of the European Convention on Human Rights? on p. 31; BBC Television Weather Forecast 26th April 1996. (BBC 1996), on p. 36; The Bash Street Kids from *The Beano* (D. C. Thomson: Dundee), on p. 40; Letters from *The Times*, by permission of The Times Newspapers Limited on pp. 42, 83, 85; Letters from the *North Devon Journal* on p. 42; BUAV advert reproduced courtesy of BUAV on p. 46; Netscape Text on p. 52; *The London Gazette* 1685, on p. 53; *Sporting Life* 20th December 1996 (Mirror Group), on p. 53; Eckersley, C. E. 1938. *Essential English for Foreign Language Students Book 1*. Longman, by permission of Pearson Education on p. 64; Richards, Hull and Proctor, *Interchange Student's Book 1*. 1990. Cambridge University Press, on pp. 64, 72; Swan, M. and C. Walter. 1985. *Cambridge English Course 2*. Cambridge University Press on p. 69; Carter, R. and M. McCarthy. 1997. *Exploring Spoken English*. Cambridge University Press on p. 73; BBC Radio 4. Mid-week Choice. 18th February 1985. (BBC 1985), on p. 75; James, B., R. R. Jordan and A. J. Matthews. 1979. *Listening Comprehension and Note-Taking Course*. Collins, on p. 88; Young, D. J. 1984. *Introducing Grammar*. Century Hutchinson. By permission of Routledge, on p. 101; Butt, D. *et al. Using Functional Grammar: 2nd edition*, with permission from the National Centre for English Language Teaching and Research (NCELTR), Australia. (Macquarie University: Sydney), on p. 102; *Guardian Weekly* extract cited in Hudson, R. 1992. *Teaching Grammar: A Guide for the National Curriculum*. Blackwell: Oxford, on p. 102; Marenbon, J. 1987. *English our English*. Centre for Policy Studies: London on p. 103; Clark and Clark. 1977. Child Language, on p. 104; Crystal, D. 1986. *Listen to Your Child*. Penguin Books Ltd., on pp. 105–107; Montgomery M. 1986. *An Introduction to Language and Society*. Methuen, on p. 109; Auerbach, E. R. 1993. *TESOL Quarterly* 27/1. (Copyright 1993 by Teachers of English to Speakers of Other Languages, Inc.) on p. 110, used with permission; Gretz, S. and A. Sage. 1986. *The Bears who Stayed Indoors*. A & C Black Ltd: Huntingdon, on pp. 116–117; Nesfield. 1944. *English Grammar, Past and Present*. Macmillan, on p. 118; Stannard Allen. 1974, on p. 119; Reproduced by permission of Oxford University Press from *Access to English: Starting Out* by Michael Coles and Basil Lord (Oxford University Press 1974), on p. 120; Broughton. 1968. *Success with English*. Penguin, on p. 121; Trudgill, P. 1983. *Sociolinguistics: An Introduction*. Penguin Books Ltd. on p. 132; Jones, L. 1981. *Functions of English*. Cambridge University Press on p. 144; Hinton, M. and R. Marsden. 1985. *Options*. Nelson, by permission of Pearson Education on p. 145;

Bell, J. and R. Gower. 1992. *Upper Intermediate Matters*. Longman, by permission of Pearson Education on p. 145; Jordan, R. 1992. *Academic Writing Course (New Edition)*. Nelson, by permission of Pearson Education on p. 146; Sinclair, J. 1995. *Activate your English*. Cambridge University Press, on p. 147; Reproduced by permission of Oxford University Press from *Advanced Masterclass CAE Student's Book* by Tricia Aspinall and Annette Capel (Oxford University Press 1996), on p. 148; Canale, M. 1983. *From Communicative Competence to Communicative Language Pedagogy*. Longman, by permission of Pearson Education on p. 149; Ivanic, R. 1990. *Critical Language Awareness in Action*. In R. Carter (ed.) 1990. *Knowledge about Language and the Curriculum: The LINC Reader*. Hodder and Stoughton, on p. 149; Crystal, D. 1995. *Cambridge Encyclopedia of the English Language*. Cambridge University Press, on pp. 155–56; McGregor, H. E. 1960. *English for the Upper School*. Whitcombe and Tombs: Sydney, on p. 158; Trask, R. L. 1994. *Language Change*. Routledge, by permission of Taylor Francis Books Ltd, on p. 161; Landale, J. and P. Newton. Spin nurses keep media on message in the holding pen. *The Times* March 1997. (Times Newspapers Limited, March 1997), on p. 163; McJob in *The Independent on Sunday* 22nd June 1997 and 13th July 1997, on p. 165; Banks, I. 1995. Abacus: London (Little Brown and Co.), on p. 173; Cameron, D. 1995. *Verbal Hygiene*. Routledge, by permission of Taylor Francis Books Ltd, on pp. 180–181; Cutts, M. and C. Maher. 1984. *Gobbledegook*. Allen and Unwin by permission of HarperCollins, on p. 187; Hamilton, A. In plain English, Hector you are nothing but a terrorist. *The Times* 15th May 1997. (Times Newspapers Limited, 15th May 1997), on p. 188; Barker, P. 1994. *The Eye in the Door*. Penguin Books Ltd., on p. 197; Hale, S. 1997. Clash of world perspectives: the discursive practices of the law, the witness and the interpreter. In *Forensic Linguistics: The International Journal of Speech, Language and the Law 4(2)*. By permission of the University of Birmingham Press, on pp. 203–204; Maley *et al.* 1997. Orientations in lawyer-client interviews. In *Forensic Linguistics: The International Journal of Speech, Language and the Law 2(1)*. By permission of the University of Birmingham Press, on p. 204; Colney *et al.* 1975. *Duke Law Journal*. North Carolina, on p. 205; Pennycook, A. 1994. *The Cultural Politics of English as an International Language*. Longman, by permission of Pearson Education on pp. 215–216.

# Key terms and transcription conventions

## Key terms

Below are the conventions we have used in this book to refer to some key terms:

EIL English as an International Language – i.e. as the language currently most widely used for international political, business, academic and information technology purposes

EL1 English used as a first or mother-tongue language

EL2 English used in a wide variety of 'second' and 'foreign' language contexts, but *not* as a first or mother-tongue language

ELT English Language Teaching in the context of EL2 teaching and learning

L1/MT a person's first or mother-tongue language

L2 any language which is *not* a person's first or mother-tongue language

▷ This symbol next to an activity indicates that there is a commentary for the activity concerned.

## Transcription conventions

In some cases where we have included spoken texts as examples, we have used a minimal set of transcription symbols to indicate some of the features of spoken language as follows:

↓ or ↑ indicates general downward or upward pitch movement within a 'chunk' of language or an intonation unit, e.g. '↑Can I help you?'

UPPER CASE indicates stressed syllables, e.g. '↓NO, ↓you CAN'T'

+, ++, +++ indicates breaks (or pauses) of varying length in the flow of sound, + being the shortest

[ indicates overlap (two speakers speaking at the same time)

# Introduction

> ... in language study, as in life, if a person is the same today as he [sic] was yesterday, it would be an act of mercy to pronounce him dead, and to place him in a coffin rather than in a classroom.
>
> Rassias, 1967

Our aim in this book is to provide those involved in the teaching and learning of the English language with a wider perspective on language than is often available in English Language Teaching (ELT) reference works. We shall build upon established concepts within the framework of what is known as Language Awareness (LA). The basic premise is that learning more about language and about how language works is a useful, productive and interesting activity: increasing one's awareness – being more 'alive' to language – can bring considerable benefit, both personal and professional. One such benefit, as Eric Hawkins points out in his book *Awareness of Language*, is that Language Awareness provides more room for 'discussion of the phenomenon of language itself: its rule-governed behaviour, its variety and at the same time its universals, its acquisition, and its place in society' (1987:97).

Our book complements a number of other ELT publications by including subject matter which has perhaps not traditionally been considered as the province of English Language teachers, and which is not always dealt with in teacher training courses. Scott Thornbury, in *About Language* (a companion book in this CUP series) notes that his book is 'about language in the narrower sense, that is *the analysis of the linguistic systems that constitute language*' (1997:x, his italics). Our book is intended to present a broader view, based in the main on language seen within socio-cultural dimensions, that is, how people actually *use* the language. Thus, as well as looking at some areas typically thought of as being part of language study (grammar, for instance) we broaden the view by considering other aspects of language in use, including those relating to culture and context, to discourse, to variety, to change and to power. To illustrate the discussion, extensive use is made of samples of authentic language from a range of sources, as well as examples from ELT materials. Key reference works are identified in each of the areas discussed, and there is a wide-ranging bibliography which points readers in the direction of further, more detailed sources of information.

## What is Language Awareness?

Language Awareness (LA) is an approach to language study which draws upon a number of disciplines including language teaching, applied linguistics, and several other related areas such as psycholinguistics, sociolinguistics and anthropological linguistics. It encompasses work undertaken in a variety of contexts: first language learning in schools and higher education; teaching and learning second or foreign languages; and the study of socio-cultural influences upon people's use of language. It involves researchers, teachers, trainers and students from many different backgrounds, of many different ages, and in many different ways.

The unifying principle underlying all these diverse approaches to the study of language is the goal of increased awareness, brought about by examining features of language and studying how language works. Not only does this help to promote a general interest in and knowledge of the subject; equally important is that people's beliefs about language become more informed. That is, becoming more aware enables us to make more competent judgements about what happens, and why, when language is used. This increased awareness helps us, first, to make more sense of the systems that all languages operate within; at the same time, by stressing that language has to be seen as a fundamental and integral part of human culture and society, and not something that can be neatly separated from its context of use, LA confronts us with the flexibility, dynamism and power of language.

## What are the benefits of LA for language teachers?

We believe that teachers can benefit from LA in a number of ways:

- *LA helps us appreciate the complexity and sophistication of communication through language.* As users of our first language (L1), we come to know intuitively how to operate socially, culturally and linguistically in our own socio-cultural setting and we bring to the L1 learning process a great number of skills. But, unless we make the effort to understand how this communicational expertise operates, we are likely to remain unaware of it, and, some would argue, disadvantaged because of our lack of awareness.
- *LA methodology is a productive and rewarding route for exploring the richness and complexity of language.* This is a practical, discovery-based methodology which invites us to come to our own conclusions about language. It emphasises analysis of data drawn from people's actual use of language in a wide range of socio-cultural contexts, with discussion and tasks based on this analysis. It encourages us to think of language with an open mind, not a narrow one.
- *LA helps us think about what is involved when we attempt to transfer L1 skills to another language.* It brings to our attention differences in the ways

people acquire first and second languages; it indicates potential difficulties in acquiring a second language; and it alerts us to differences in socio-cultural expectations and norms in first and second language contexts.

- *LA helps those involved in ELT to understand more about how English works.* It contributes to teachers' ability to explain the language better and to their feeling of being better placed to evaluate teaching materials and approaches. It encourages them to understand more about the cultural contexts of English as an International Language.
- *LA can be considered an important strand of professional development within ELT.* It contributes to the process of moving forward in the quest for a broader and better informed knowledge-base from which to teach, thus boosting confidence, and widening teaching perspectives.

## What does the book aim to do?

We intend the book to be used as an aid or a tool for awareness-raising in the following broad areas:

- how people actually use language
- how language teaching materials choose to present language
- what kinds of language knowledge teachers of language should have

In the process of exploring these general areas, we address other, more specific, pedagogical issues directly relevant to ELT:

- questions relating to the use of 'real' language and 'reduced' language (i.e. the over-simplified language found in many ELT textbooks) for teaching purposes
- the debate over what sort of grammar should be taught
- the future role of English as an International Language
- questions relating to the 'ownership' of English
- implications for ELT of 'empowerment' of teachers and learners
- difficulties of addressing complex areas, such as discourse, in the classroom
- the impact of technology on language teaching

## How is the book organised?

The book adopts an awareness-raising approach: this involves reading the *text* of each chapter, examining the *samples* of language and *extracts* from reference or textbooks which are interspersed throughout the text, and working through the *activities* which are normally based on analysis or discussion of the samples or extracts. Suggestions about the main points to be drawn from this discussion or analysis are given in *commentaries*.

There are six chapters, each with an overview and then a number of major sections relating to particular topics.

## Areas addressed

Chapter 1 looks at a number of general features of *language-in-use* (for instance *structure*, *context* and *flexibility*) and aims to set up an 'awareness' framework for discussions in the chapters which follow. Chapter 2 explores the main elements of *discourse* in both spoken and written English, while Chapter 3 looks at views on, approaches to and examples of *grammar* teaching. Chapter 4 is concerned with *varieties* of English, and attitudes towards them. Chapter 5 deals with language *change* and how it affects English and the way it is taught. Chapter 6 looks at issues relating to language and *power* and the way language is used – and how it can be abused – within social contexts. It is probably useful to read Chapter 1 first, in order to understand the perspective from which the book looks at language, but after that the chapters are not necessarily sequential. It is possible, for instance, to look at *Change* (Chapter 5) before *Grammar* (Chapter 3), or *Power* (Chapter 6) before *Variety* (Chapter 4). In other words, most of the chapters are free-standing. There are cross references in the book within and between chapters but we have tried to keep these to a minimum.

## Language samples and extracts

Throughout, the text is illustrated with language samples, the vast majority of which are from authentic sources including textbooks, language teaching materials, media publications and our own data. In addition, we have sometimes included extracts from key references where appropriate.

## Activities

Interspersed throughout are activities which are intended to reinforce or extend the points made in the text. They include discussion and reflection as well as activities relating specifically to extracts or language samples. In some cases there are follow-up activities such as data-collection or fieldwork.

The tasks readers are asked to undertake include:

- reading extracts and texts and answering focus questions
- summarising and discussing ideas and conclusions
- considering samples of language use and making judgements and decisions about them
- deciding on the relevance or appropriacy of language examples for teaching purposes
- identifying patterns from language examples
- generalising from particular instances or examples
- completing gap-fill or tabular activities
- relating information or ideas to individual teaching situations

- considering the advantages and disadvantages of teaching approaches or teaching materials
- thinking about ways of further using or exploiting ideas and concepts

## Commentaries

There are detailed commentaries for the majority of activities except where these are open-ended or extended, for instance where project work or some sort of mini-research or reflection is suggested. Frequently the commentaries provide further information and discussion on the topic or activities.

## Further reading

The short list of references at the end of each chapter points readers towards sources of more detailed information should they wish to explore further any of the topics covered in the chapter. Most of these references are general rather than technical or highly specialised.

# Who is the book for?

The book is primarily a resource book for use on educational and teacher training courses where the study of the English language is a required element or where some background reading about language is necessary. It can be used by teacher trainees – both those speaking English as their first language (EL1) and those speaking it as a second language (EL2) – on a variety of courses, such as the RSA/UCLES Diploma or Certificate courses, or TEFL/TESOL Diplomas within higher education and at universities. People on in-service training and language awareness programmes may also find it useful, as may those involved in literacy-related work.

The majority of the activities are designed (and have been trialled) with groups of teacher trainees in mind. They often involve discussion and analysis, and readily lend themselves to pair- or groupwork. Thus, trainers involved in teaching areas of language study should find that they can select appropriate topics and activities both for classroom and other use, such as assignments, guided project work or further reading. The book could also be used by groups of language students studying English at advanced levels with a teacher.

At the same time, the book is designed to be accessible to individuals working on their own, with a personal choice of how many of the activities to undertake and how far to investigate the areas discussed. We hope that, in addition to being a resource and activity book for those involved in teaching (and learning) English, it is accessible as an 'interest' book to anyone who enjoys language for its own sake and who wishes to expand or build on their existing knowledge.

## How much language knowledge do we assume the reader has?

We assume that typical readers of this book are familiar with basic grammatical and lexical terminology, including parts of speech (e.g. *noun, verb, adverb*), names of verb forms and tenses (e.g. *gerund, past perfect*) and patterns of sentence-based grammar such as *reported speech* or *conditional* structures – the kind of terms, in fact, that you would find in a modern ELT grammar such as Murphy (1994) or Swan and Walter (1997) or in ELT books on vocabulary such as McCarthy and O'Dell (1994). We also assume some non-technical knowledge of language systems, for instance basic phonology terms such as *intonation* and *stress*, and we assume an acquaintance with what is broadly meant by certain language study terms such as *semantics*, language *change* and *sociolinguistics*. Important content or terminology words are highlighted in the text and where possible examples are given. Where we deal with more complex issues, we have glossed them or provided more information in footnotes. There is also a short glossary at the beginning of the book to explain how we have used certain key terms (e.g. *EL2*) in this particular book.

## Further notes

One of the central themes of the book is that language is complex; there are thus inevitable limitations as to how much can be covered in a book of this size and scope. We have tried to select a coherent and reasonably wide cross-section of information. Others would not necessarily agree on the choices, balance or ordering, but we hope very much that colleagues involved in LA work would support the main premise behind the book, even if they might approach it in a different way.

We anticipate, from trialling the activities and discussing the content matter with groups of our own students, that some readers may find some of the subject matter of the book complicated. Nevertheless, we hope that they will not be overly deterred by this, and we would encourage those who feel less confident to use some of the further references to explore issues that look interesting.

We are aware that the language base of the book is drawn predominantly from British English. This is largely because of the environment in which we, the authors, currently work and teach. Nevertheless, we are of course very conscious – both from personal experience and from our work as trainers, teachers and writers – that there is a much larger world of English beyond Britain. We make reference to some aspects and examples of this in the book. Perhaps someone will be inspired to redress the balance and approach the subject from a different viewpoint.

We are also very much aware that some of the language samples, data and comments may already be dated by the time the reader encounters them, particularly those connected with technology.

Finally, perhaps it is worth spelling out some of the 'non-aims' of the book, i.e. things we are *not* trying to do. We are definitely *not* trying to promote English, either as a narrow British-based language variety or as an international language. Rather, we are saying something about the current situation of English with some possible thoughts on directions in which it might develop. Despite the widespread use of English, we are certainly *not* saying that English is inherently, or in any other sense, richer than other languages, *nor* do we intend to say that learning about the culture associated with English as a first language (EL1) is, or should be, a prime teaching aim for teachers of EL2. Any impressions to the contrary are entirely the responsibility of the authors, as are any other slips, inaccuracies or misleading statements in the book.

# 1   Language-in-use

## 1.1   Overview

The main aim of this opening chapter is to suggest a general framework for considering language from the socio-cultural perspective of *language-in-use* outlined below:

- *Language is dynamic and powerful*: it reflects and is reflected by the changing ways human societies order themselves; it influences and is influenced by people's relationships, activities and communications. Structured, but flexible, it is a vital human tool for getting things done in the world and the ways in which people actually use language to accomplish their various ends are subtle and complex.
- *Language is rarely either straightforward or value-free*: it always springs from the linguistic choices made by participants in any 'language event'. In order for any instance of 'real world' language to be fully understood, its context – including what has gone before it and what is likely to come after – has to be taken into account. This context is the key to decoding the meanings carried in the choices people make. These choices depend partly on the fact that language is flexible, and partly on what people consider to be the most effective way of using language to convey their message. The effectiveness of any communication depends, in turn, upon a whole range of extra-linguistic factors, including the response, interpretation and attitude of the receiver of the message.

The perspective on language outlined above may not necessarily be one which is familiar to language teachers, whose day-to-day work may have much more to do with the linguistic systems that make up a language: grammar, vocabulary, phonology and possibly discourse. In our framework for awareness of language-in-use, therefore, we will introduce eight features of language in general which we hope will, first, support the broader perspective, and second, provide a basis for understanding the discussion in subsequent chapters of the book. A brief summary of these features and their basic characteristics is provided first, and then we look at each feature in greater detail, with examples to illustrate it from a variety of sources.

## 1.2    A basic framework for awareness of language-in-use

Just as language is both complex and complicated, so is its study. It would be very difficult to decide upon a definitive list of language features comprehensive enough to include everything and please everyone. The basic features we list below, each with a short gloss, are among those we consider to be useful starting points for enhancing our awareness of language-in-use. Figure 1 shows how these features can be seen to relate to each other: working out from the centre, we can say that the language people use – the 'what' – depends on their *choices* of words and structures, which in turn are allowed by the *flexibility* of the language; 'how' they put across their message will depend on their choice of form from the huge *variety* available to them, and their choice of *medium*, which will in turn be dictated by the *attitude* and *effect* they wish their message to convey. The recipients of these messages will, consciously or unconsciously, likewise have an attitude towards, and judge the effectiveness of, the chosen words and structures. Finally, at the outer edge of the Figure, all choices and reactions to choices are governed by the specific *context* within which the language is used, and by the 'knowledge of the world' brought to bear upon the interaction by the initiator(s) and recipient(s).

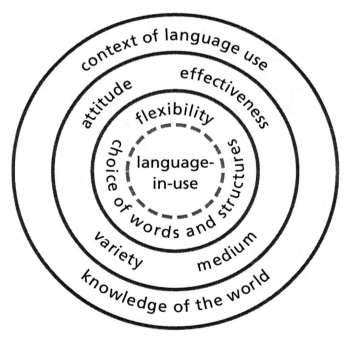

*Figure 1*

The basic language awareness features in the framework above, and briefly described below, are *all* important: it would be hard to say that some are more important than others. Also, we can see that the categories are not mutually exclusive (i.e. things in one category can also quite easily be in another) and that there is often considerable overlap between them.

**knowledge of the world:** the way our use and understanding of language is affected by our specific cultural backgrounds, our learning experience, and the way we view the world

If we did not have this knowledge it would be difficult for us to understand each other; things like railway timetables and phone books would be unintelligible. *Knowledge of the world* helps us in one type of context to interpret correctly what someone is saying to us, or in another, to identify a specific newspaper from its format and typeface.

**context:** the importance of the situation and environment – including the relationship between initiator and recipient – in which people use language, and their purpose in using it

A lecture on thermo-nuclear physics has an identifiable context, as does a family argument or a newspaper sports report. Thus, the language used in each context is likely to be very different.

**variety:** the different forms in which language may appear

One major set of factors here relates to the obvious differences between spoken and written language but there are other equally powerful factors contributing to variety, such as style, source, situation, dialect and accent.

**medium:** the modes or channels through which language is manifested

This not only extends the spoken/written distinction, but is also concerned with the form and style in which meanings and messages are transmitted. For example, the language used in a teenage comic, or in a conversation between friends is very different from the language of a legal document, or that of a telephone enquiry. E-mail is an example of a relatively new medium which is evolving a distinctive form and style of its own.

**attitude:** the fact that people use language to *convey different attitudes* as well as the fact that they *have different attitudes* towards the language they encounter

Letters to newspapers and radio phone-ins are two examples of contexts where the former dimension of attitude can be seen, i.e. people convey opinions through the linguistic choices they make when they write or speak, as the case may be. The judgements we make about other people's use of language illustrates the latter dimension.

**effectiveness:** the degree to which users of language successfully achieve their purpose

Warnings, prohibitions, advertising and advice are examples of areas where effectiveness can be relatively easily judged. In other areas, such as political propaganda or literary criticism, judgement is much less straightforward, and possibly controversial.

**structure:** the basic ways in which language is organised and structured

This feature enables us to understand how a language works and how the various components interact with each other. The systems and rules of grammar, vocabulary and pronunciation are all important aspects of structure, as are other less obvious ones such as regional variations, or discourse (interwoven stretches of language or sequences of utterances beyond discrete sentence level).

**flexibility:** the way language is dynamic and able to adapt to changing circumstances

In English, technology contexts provide a wide range of instances where new words have appeared (*interface, internet*) and existing words have taken on new meanings (*mouse, web*). Changes in social attitudes and mores influence usage, e.g. in Britain, the increasing acceptance of the word *partner* in preference to *wife/husband, spouse* or *girl/boyfriend* in the context of a personal relationship.

## 1.3    Features of language-in-use

We now look in closer detail at the eight features in the framework, starting with the broadest constraints on language use – *knowledge of the world* and context of communication.

### 1.3.1  Knowledge of the world

The way each of us views the world is dictated by our socio-cultural background(s) and our learning experiences. The more similar our backgrounds and experience, the more likely it is that we will have similar interpretations of what is going on when we encounter any instance of language-in-use. These interpretations will be both linguistic (such that we understand the language) and socio-cultural (such that we recognise the significance of the language behaviours which are part of the society and culture we inhabit). This interrelation in interpretation is inevitable, and as language teachers, we are constantly aware of it.

When a language is an international property, as in a sense English is, the interface between linguistic and cultural interpretations becomes an extremely sensitive issue. This is perhaps why ELT coursebooks often attempt to go for the culturally 'lowest common denominator' approach by producing materials that hopefully will offend nobody and appeal to a wide (world-wide) audience. The truth is, though, that nothing is value-free. Even something as apparently straightforward as greetings and leavings (which often appear in the introductory units of coursebooks), may be more complicated – and even treacherous – than they seem. Is it possible, for example, to learn from an English language textbook when or whether you should shake someone by the hand as you greet or leave them? What is the assumed cultural context in which this greeting or leaving takes place and are there in fact any norms which govern this particular behaviour? If there are, do they depend more upon the cultural context within which the language is being used than upon the language itself? What right has the original cultural context of the language to impose its norms (if indeed they exist) upon anyone else using the language in a different cultural context?

It is, of course, certainly possible for learners of a second language to produce the forms of the language accurately without ever having had any first-hand contact with the culture(s) or societies in which it is spoken as a first language. At the same time, though, any claim to be able to operate effectively in a language involves much more than just manipulating the forms successfully. An important pedagogical question, therefore, is: *How and to what extent should language teachers attempt to include the socio-cultural dimension and teach the 'knowledge of the world' associated with the target language?* We could expand upon this basic question with others such as:

- Whose version of this 'knowledge' might be taught?
- Why should it be taught?
- What use do learners wish to make of the target language, and thus what knowledge do they need?
- What cultural context is the language being taught in?
- Can we expect coursebooks to cater for the huge diversity of student backgrounds, needs and expectations?

Another important question is: *To what extent do people wish to participate in the culture of the language they are learning?* This in turn raises yet more questions:

- What are the goals of people learning the language? (commercial? scientific? academic? political? diplomatic? educational? personal?)
- Are there reasons – political, social or religious – why association with the culture of the language may not be attractive or appropriate?
- To what extent can the learner's own culture mesh with the L2 culture without a conflict developing?
- Might it be easier for certain learners (e.g. children, who are generally less inhibited than adults about cultural niceties) to integrate cultural knowledge than others?

Our first four examples illustrate the extent to which all texts (including spoken 'texts') are grounded in the culture which produced them. These particular examples happen to have originated in the culture of late 20th century Britain, and understanding of these texts, both linguistic and cultural, is based to a large degree on shared experience of that culture.

## Activity 1 ▷

> ▶ Look at Examples 1.1, 1.2, 1.3 and 1.4 on pages 23–26. What 'knowledge of the world' do you need to bring to bear on these texts in order to be able to understand them? Does your 'knowledge of the world' allow you to identify or place these texts easily in their cultural context?
>
> ▶ Would you say there are aspects of this 'knowledge' which are reasonably 'teachable'? How far do 'textual' features (i.e. layout, typeface, graphics and so on) of the texts in Examples 1.1, 1.3 and 1.4 help in this respect?

**Example 1.1**

# SMACK DEE

Comic Jack …
street brawl

## Raging comic flattens TV critic over 'Cockney' taunt

## EXCLUSIVE

**By ANDY COULSON and JANE ATKINSON**

**FURIOUS comic Jack Dee flattened a TV critic in an amazing street brawl yesterday.**

The star – famous for his deadpan expression – was getting into a taxi when university-educated Victor Lewis-Smith yelled: "You Cockney commoner."

Jack, 34, **LEAPT** from the cab, **THREW** several punches at the dreadlocked critic – and had to be **PULLED AWAY** by his own manager.

The manager was left nursing a bruised face after one of the comic's blows missed and landed on him. Two passing policemen intervened in the 1am punch-up outside a London club.

Teetotal Jack, and Lewis-Smith – who is five inches taller at 5ft 11in – were both spoken to but no action was taken.

Sulky loudmouth Lewis-Smith is consulting lawyers over the incident – but defiant Jack has vowed to fight any action. He fumed last night: "Victor is a very poor heckler."

*Before the bust-up the pair were spotted angrily shouting at each other in the bar of the trendy Groucho Club in Soho.*

Lewis-Smith, who has often savaged

**Continued on Page Seven**

## Example 1.2

D is a senior house officer in a hospital; P is a patient. Turns in the interaction are numbered.

1   **D**    Hello, Mr X?

2   **P**    Yes, that's right.

3   **D**    I'm Dr Y. Now I'd like to check a few of the details of your problem.

4   **P**    Right, doctor.

5   **D**    This is Mr N from the University. He's looking at doing some of the things we get up to in hospitals.

6   **P**    Oh yes.

7   **D**    Now, what's the main thing that's been worrying you lately?

8   **P**    Well, I've had a bit of shortness of breath.

9   **D**    Does this happen at any particular time?

10   **P**    Well, after walking a fair way I get a bit …

11   **D**    How about at night?

12   **P**    Well yes I wake up feeling a bit …

13   **D**    Yeah any other problems?

14   **P**    No, I've been fine in myself.

15   **D**    No headaches?

16   **P**    No.

17   **D**    Now when you wake up is it because of shortness of breath, or is there something to bring up?

18   **P**    Well it's the shortness of breath mainly I think.

19   **D**    D'you feel very short of breath?

20   **P**    It's difficult to say really, sometimes it's quite severe.

21   **D**    How many pillows do you use? D'you feel uncomfortable if you lie flat?

22   **P**    Well not really, if I wake up feeling this … I usually get up then and …

23   **D**    Yeah OK, now you were being treated by Dr A for blood pressure, weren't you? What happened? Did it clear up?

24   **P**    Well, he as good as told me to stop taking the tablets.

25   **D**    I see. D'you look after yourself at home? Do you do your own cooking?

26   **P**    Oh yes, that's fine.

27   **D**    Appetite OK?

28   **P**    Well, you know …

29   **D**    Well, we're just going to take some blood off you. Just sit back and the Sister'll be along to see you in a minute OK?

30   **P**    Yes, thank you doctor.

31   **D**    Right.

*(Authors' data)*

## Example 1.3

| Mondays to Fridays | | | | | B |
| | | | | MX WW | SO TT |
|---|---|---|---|---|---|---|
| London Paddington | d | 2245 | 2335 | 2345 | 0045 | 0045 |
| Slough | d | 2229 | 2329 | 2329 | 0052 | 0052 |
| Heathrow Terminal 🚌 | d | 2145 | 2215 | 2215 | 2315 | 2315 |
| Gatwick Airport | d | 2124 | —— | 2224 | 2317 | 2317 |
| Reading | d | 2309 | 0008 | 0017 | 0123 | 0124 |
| Didcot Parkway | d | 2323 | 0024 | 0032 | 0141 | 0140 |
| Swindon | d | 2341 | 0046 | 0055 | 0208 | 0202 |
| Chippenham | d | 2354 | 0058 | —— | —— | —— |
| Bath Spa | d | 0009 | 0111 | —— | —— | —— |
| Bristol Parkway | d | 0037v | —— | 0122 | —— | —— |
| Bristol Temple Meads | a | 0022 | 0125 | —— | —— | —— |
| Weston-super-Mare | a | —— | —— | —— | —— | —— |
| Newport | d | —— | —— | 0142s | 0313 | —— |
| Hereford | a | —— | —— | —— | —— | —— |
| Cardiff Central | a | —— | —— | 0203 | 0332 | —— |
| Bridgend | a | —— | —— | —— | —— | —— |
| Port Talbot Parkway | a | —— | —— | —— | —— | —— |
| Neath | a | —— | —— | —— | —— | —— |
| Swansea | a | —— | —— | —— | —— | —— |

Notes for this and opposite page:
A    Service continues to Taunton.
B    Does not run 17 January to 21 February.
C    Service continues to Carmarthen. Table 4
D    Refreshments are not available.
b    Change at Redhill and Reading.
c    Change at Maidenhead and Reading.
e    Arrival time. Change at Bath Spa.
f    Service travels via Bristol Temple Meads before Bristol Parkway.
g    Arrives 0830.
k    Change at Oxford.
v    Arrival time. Via Bristol Temple Meads.
MX   Monday mornings excepted.
SO   Saturday mornings only.

For standard notes see inside back cover.
Light printed timings indicate a connecting service.    See page 5

18

*(Great Western timetable)*

**Example 1.4**

# STARS
## By Marjorie Orr *Britain's top astrologer*

**IF IT'S YOUR BIRTHDAY TODAY:** Then your year ahead will be very focussed with a strong sense of mission, hard working, extravagant and rather romantic. You will feel you have turned a corner. Keeping fit is a priority in a fast moving, rather challenging year. DOES YOUR BIRTHDAY FALL UNDER THE CURRENT STAR SIGN? PHONE 0894 707 319 TO HEAR MARJORIE'S SPECIAL FORECAST.

## Sagittarius (November 23–December 22)

The New Moon in your sign only comes round once a year and this is definitely your day to make resolutions for the next 12 months. What kind of image do you want to project? Does this mean clearing out the wardrobe? Or will you be mixing and matching the old with the new. Whether it is clothes or a deeper aspect of your personality you are determined on a makeover.
More details: ☎0894 707 342

## Capricorn (December 23–January 20)

Shining light on hidden places is not always easy for a practical rather ambitious sign like yourself. You much prefer flying ahead producing solid results and ambitiously scaling the heights. But try to find the time when you can. After Tuesday, when the Sun moves into your own sign, there will no chance for calm reflection since a busy schedule lies ahead.
More details: ☎0894 707 343

## Aquarius (January 21–February 19)

Keep an eye around for any encounters with new acquaintances. They could become firm friends in the days ahead if you make the effort to pull them into your circle. You are sifting and sorting through different options at the moment and may need different company to travel with. What is important, for whatever begins now, is that you are committed, no ifs and buts.
More details: ☎0894 707 344

## Pisces (February 20–March 20)

The seed of a project, plan, idea or new venture is planting itself firmly in your head now at work. It will take time to flourish, but it is good to have a dream which you can follow over the next year. Now you can begin to see where you can rally the support behind you. The more hands on deck and shoulders to the wheel the less effort it will take to get it all rolling.
More details: ☎0894 707 345

## Aries (March 21–April 20)

Whatever you want to do in terms of travelling further afield, or maybe just painting your life on a broader canvas, now is the time to get cracking. Being fiery and highly imaginative, you are never short of grand visions of what you would like. Make sure that at least one of them gets pushed slightly further down the road to reality now. Do not hold back. Fortune favours the brave.
More details: ☎0894 707 334

## Taurus (April 21–May 20)

By next Tuesday you will be out of this rather intense, slightly confrontational phase but do not think that all your pushing has been in vain. Your perseverance of the past weeks will pay off over the next few months in ways you cannot imagine. But one more building block needs to be put in place now to get new financial ventures or agreements off on a good footing.
More details: ☎0894 707 335

## Gemini (May 21–June 21)

You can decide to wipe the slate clean in long running relationships and see whether you can get off to a new start. Or maybe you just want to start afresh altogether by making new connections that you feel can bring you much fulfilment. Whichever way you lean, you know you need to take the initiative and be clear about what your renewed commitment means.
More details: ☎0894 707 336

## Cancer (June 22–July 23)

Never was there a better day to start a new health regime. Get out the diet sheets and choose whichever suits your mood. This is about feeling more energised, not getting slimmer. You need to start treating your body like a racing machine, that needs good fuel, sensible maintenance and pit stops every so often. If you keep running without recharging your batteries you will feel flat.
More details: ☎0894 707 337

*(The Express 18.12.98)*

## 1.3.2 Context

In the 'real world', as distinct from the often controlled and constricted world of many language teaching materials, language always occurs in specific contexts, involving *people* (their personalities, relationships, socio-economic status) and *situations* (the purpose(s) and importance of the communication, social and cultural expectations about it, what came before it and what is likely to come after). These contextual factors, especially when several participants are involved, give rise to language which is often much more complex than controlled teaching materials would suggest, not only because of its unpredictability, but also its inevitable link with situational and personal circumstances. Our notion of context is represented graphically in Figure 2.

*Figure 2*        Contextual factors (constraints on context)

People speaking a language as their first or mother-tongue language do not always need to think consciously about the contexts of their language use, unless these contexts demand a particular effort for successful or effective communication (preparing for an important interview, for instance, or writing a book). However, for second language learners, context may present a number of difficulties:

• different conventions govern use of language in different cultural contexts

- contexts may be misinterpreted by learners, and thus communication may break down
- conventions associated with a context may be deliberately flouted (e.g. for humour) or manipulated (e.g. for asserting or maintaining power) – learners may not easily recognise this
- many language coursebooks pay lip service to context, but in fact find it difficult, if not impossible, to present language in truly meaningful contexts – except of course the context of language learning itself
- the natural language of many real-world contexts is too difficult for a language learning context

Nonetheless, learning about contexts is an essential part of any language learning process, be it first or second language, and part of this learning involves developing a sense of what we need to do, socially and linguistically, in a variety of situations. This is often what linguists mean when they talk about language being appropriate rather than language being right or wrong.

Although it is hard to see how learners can learn what they need to know about a language without developing a sense of context, actually providing a real sense of context in most teaching situations is very difficult. Thus, learners who have not had much – or indeed any – opportunity to experience language in contexts other than the language learning classroom, and who have perhaps spent a lot of time studying 'decontextualised' language, will find the 'real thing' very daunting. It is not surprising that learners often find informal conversation between groups of L1 speakers hard to understand. We shall take this point up in more detail in Chapter 2 when we examine some discourse features which relate closely to the question of context, and their implications for teaching and learning.

## Activity 2

> ▶ Look at the two spoken texts transcribed in Examples 1.5 and 1.6 on pages 29–30 and the two written texts reproduced in Examples 1.7 and 1.8 on pages 31–32.
> ▶ Describe and compare the different contexts in which you think the language used in these four examples might have occurred. Can you specify any language features (e.g. degree of formality, degree of explicitness, topic, layout, format, etc.) which help you to identify the contexts? (You could make a grid, along the lines indicated below, to help you do this).

| Example # | Context | Language Features |
|---|---|---|
| | e.g. who? to whom? where? when? why? how? about what? | e.g. formality? explicitness? topic? layout? |

> ▶ Do you think these four examples could be used for language teaching purposes? If so, what kinds of purpose might they serve? If not, why not?

**Follow-up:** Think of some ways in which language teachers can provide their students with opportunities for experiencing language in 'real-world' contexts.

**Example 1.5**

Characters as follows: A is mother; B is father; C is houseguest; D is small daughter of A and B (*For transcription conventions, see page* x.)

|   |   |   |
|---|---|---|
|   | A: | ↓isn't her ↑CHOP done yet |
|   | B: | well I don't ↑KNOW have a ↑LOOK at it + |
|   | C: | ↑you know we + ↑you know how we + discovered |
|   |   | we had the same caSETTE player we've got that one TOO + |
| 5 |   | (*phone rings*) [THAT's the one that nearly set us on ↑FIRE |
|   | B: | [oh GOD that's the TELe + ↓can you ↑GET it |
|   | D: | yes |
|   | C: | OURS had a PROBlem + the wire went RIGHT THROUGH |
|   |   | HERE and it started ↑SMOKing |
| 10 | B: | oh god |
|   | C: | so I've got to buy a new ↑WIRE ↓but it's ↓STILL GOing |
|   | B: | hang on ↑who's that on the PHONE |
|   | D: | can you tell ↑DAD it's JACKie |
|   | A: | oh it's ↑JACKie |
| 15 | C: | did you ↑KNOW your tape was reCORDing |
|   | B: | ↑yeh |
|   | C: | oh that's ok then++ |
|   | B: | ↓erm ++++ |
|   | A: | Liz + when did you put this ↓CHOP ON |
| 20 | B: | oh god I don't know + erm it ↑SHOULD be done what |
|   |   | ↑TIME is it |
|   | C: | quite a long [↑TIME ago |
|   | B: | [have a ↑LOOK at it |
|   | C: | ↑WOH + ↑CRUNCHing [aWAY + it's a BIG one though |
| 25 |   | [mum dad + it's ↑COLin |
|   | B: | oh god + look it's ↑COLin ↓can you go and TALK to him |
|   | C: | it's ↑VEry ↑BIG though + it might [take a bit more to cook |
|   |   | ↑THROUGH I think |
|   | B: | [YEH + hang ON a |
| 30 |   | MINute |
|   | A: | erm |
|   | B: | you'd better go Carolyn |
|   | C: | [this might be |
|   | A: | [can you + ↓can you put HER + it's ↑REAdy I think + ↓can |
| 35 |   | you put the ↑SWEETcorn on |
|   | B: | ↑YEH can you send her ↑IN here + ↓can I put the ↑WHAT |
|   | C: | do you think it ↑IS ready + I wonder if [it's a very ↑THICK |
|   |   | chop if it ↑WAS ready |
|   | A: | [sweetcorn on |
| 40 | B: | what did she ↓SAY |
|   | C: | can [you put the ↑SWEETcorn on she said |
|   | A: | [helLO + how are ↓YOU |

*(Authors' data)*

## Example 1.6

*(For transcription conventions, see page x.)*

---

...what we're going to DO is to try and ↓ LOOK at ↑++ what do we mean by this idea of myth↓ OLogy what is myth↓OLogy ++ um is it any ↓DIFferent + to + some of the things that we see going on in the media these ↓DAYS or is it↑ in ↓FACT + the very ↓BASis on which + er the media ↓WORKS ++ ↑I'm going to ↑START by looking at some kind of er theoRETical ideas a↓BOUT + myth↓OLogy + what do we actually ↓MEAN by this ↓TERM what ↓COULD it mean + um ↑+ IN this lecture I'm ↓NOT trying to put across to you the ideas that you'll go a↓WAY from here and think to yourself well + I ↓NOW know ex↓ACTly what mythology ↓IS I know how it works in the MEDia↑+ um + I have ↓ LEARNT all this + I'm not trying to ↓DO that ++ ↑what I'm trying to ↓DO is to↑ sugGEST some i↓DEAS to you a↓BOUT how you might start to think ↓DIFferently + about the ↓MEDia + and the way that it interacts in ↓YOUR ↓LIFE + um because we're for all of us the media is an important + ASpect + um of our LIVES ++ OK ↑so let's START with some of the more theor↓ETical stuff +++ um↑ the first thing about mythOLogy is is that is A ↓STRUCTured ↓SYSTem ++ ↑you can look at ↓MYTHS ++ and UM +++ find that in ↓ALL of them there is a kind of ↓STRUCture going on ++ now what do we mean by ↓MYTH + let me give you an ex↓AMple + um↑+ in ↓BUDDHism there's a story of um + a um a teacher who ++ finds + a + an + en↓LIGHTenment ++ if you like ++ and ↑spends + and deCIDES to spend the next THREE months + um + in the ↓LOTus position looking at a ↓WALL + FINDS enlightenment and decides to look at a ↓WALL for three months now st↑+ a number of students ↓COME to him + and ↓ASK him + all kinds of ↓QUESTions about + en↓LIGHTenment + and er↑+ the TEACHer + says + ↓NOthing +++ er↑ and then ↓FINally ONE student comes to him who is ↓ DESperate to um + find+an answer to his ↓QUESTion + and ASKS the TEACHer who is still looking at the WALL↑ ++ um the question ++ um + how do I find my ↓SOUL +++ and the teacher doesn't ↓ANSwer so he ↑asked him the question aGAIN↑ and again the teacher doesn't ↓ANSwer ++and then ↓FINally + in + fru↓STRAtion the student↑ + CUTS +OFF + his +LEFT+ARM ++ and pre↓SENTS it to the ↓TEACHer in order + for him to try and get some kind of re↓SPONSE Im not suggesting that's something ↓YOU might like to do (laughter) ++++ and the teacher ↑THEN says + um + what is your ↓ QUESTion ++ and he says um + the student says ++ the question IS↑ um + how do I↑ ++ REConcile my ↓SOUL I am in ↑TOR I am in ↑TURmoil trying to ↓FIND my ↓SOUL + um + the teacher says↑ +++ if you ↓SHOW me your soul↑ + I will reconcile it ↓FOR you ++++ ↓now + er that's a kind of + er + straightforward STOry↑ and if you ↓LISTen to the STORy↑ you ↓MIGHT think that that what the story is about is ++ teacher looking at a ↑WALL and + student cutting off his ↑ARM and + trying to find an answer to the ↓ QUESTion but of course +++ the under↓LYing MEANing of the ↓STORy ++ is that as far as the ↓TEACHer is concerned↑ ++ the ↓SOUL +++ may not e↓XIST ++++ this this this iDEA of preSENTing the ↓SOUL to the teacher to be reconCILED in some way ++ can't HAPpen because the soul can't be i↓DENTified so↑ with↓IN the story there is a kind of↑ MORal ↓TALE if you like there's something under↓LYing the story which is ↑MUCH MORE im↓ PORTant ++ than the PEOPle in it + or the actual STRUCTure of the story it↓SELF +++ um↑ + so ↓MYTHS all MYTHS have this kind of structured SYSTem ↓IN them they work on TWO ↓LEVels one level is ++ the very sim↓PLISTic level of let's see who's IN it↑ + let's see what ↓HAPpens to them ++ and then the ↓ OTHer level is↑ what is this ↓ACTually a↓BOUT + what's the + um + what is the ↓ MESSage that is in ++ enCAPsulated in ↓MYTH ++++ so↑ + firstly it's a STRUCTured SYSTem and ↓SECondly ++ it has an ef↓FECT + on its ↓AUDience ++...

---

*(Authors' data)*

**Example 1.7**

# Are Judges beyond Criticism under Article 10 of the European Convention on Human Rights?

## I. Introduction

On the premise that democratic government is founded *inter alia* on the accountability of public bodies and their officials, as well as on the popular participation and collective decision-making by the governed at all levels of government, there is merit in the proposition that it is improper to curb open debate, especially in matters which are of public interest. The European Court of Human Rights (the Court)[1] has endorsed the importance of this principle of open debate and the unrestrained exchange of views on matters of public interest[2] in its decisions relating to Article 10 of the European Convention on Human Rights (the Convention)[3] which guarantees freedom of expression. The Court has been particularly unyielding in upholding this freedom when it rejects requests to support restrictions on critical comment about public affairs[4] other than judges, about whom there is evidence to suggest that the Court is unwilling to apply its rigorous standard of supervision.

This article assesses the standard of supervision relating to the criticism of public officials generally and of judges in particular. It is argued that the differences in the Court's case-law relating to judges are not inconsistent with the policy of upholding democratic ideals which underlies the interpretation of Article 10.

---

[1] The supervision of Contracting States' compliance with the Convention is presently undertaken by the European Commission of Human Rights (Articles 19–37 of the Convention), the European Court of Human Rights (Articles 38–56 of the Convention) and the Committee of Ministers (Articles 31, 32 and 54 of the Convention), although in practice the Court's responsibilities are the most important (see Article 45 of the Convention). In any case, with the recent adoption of Protocol No. 11 to the Convention (text *reprinted* in Vol. 15 (1994) *Human Rights Law Journal*, p. 86) the Court and the Commission are expected to be merged into a single Court with the coming into force of the Protocol. On Protocol No. 11 see, A. Drzemczweski and J. Meyer-Ladewig, "Principal characteristics of the new ECHR control mechanism as established by Protocol 11, signed on 11 May 1994", vol. 15 (1994) *Human Rights Law Journal*, p. 81; H.G. Schermers, "The Eleventh Protocol to the European Convention on Human Rights", Vol. 19 (1994) *E.L. Rev.* p. 367; A.R. Mowbray, "A new European Court of Human Rights", 1994 *P.L.*, p. 540.
[2] *Handyside v. United Kingdom*, Eur. Ct. H.R., Series A.24 (1976), 1 E.H.R.R. p. 737; *Sunday Times v. United Kingdom No. 1*, Eur. Ct. H.R. Series A.30 (1979), 2 E.H.R.R. p. 245; *Lingens v. Austria*, Eur. Ct. H.R. Series A.103 (1986), 8 (1986) E.H.R.R. p. 103; *Oberschlick v. Austria*, Eur. Ct. H.R., Series A.204 (1991), 19 E.H.R.R., p. 389
[3] Convention for the Protection of Human Rights and Fundamental Freedoms (Rome 1950), text *reprinted* in Brownlie, *Basic Documents on Human Rights*, (Oxford. 1992) p. 326
[4] See *Lingens v. Austria, loc. cit., Scwabe v Austria*, Eur. Ct. H.R. Series A.242-B (1993), (politicians); *Thorgeir Thorgeison v. Iceland*. Eur. Ct. H.R., Series A.239 (1992), 18 (1994) E.H.R.R. p. 843 (police); *Castels v. Spain*, Eur. Ct. H.R. Series A.236 (1992), 14 (1992) E.H.R.R. p. 445 (government policy)

**Example 1.8**

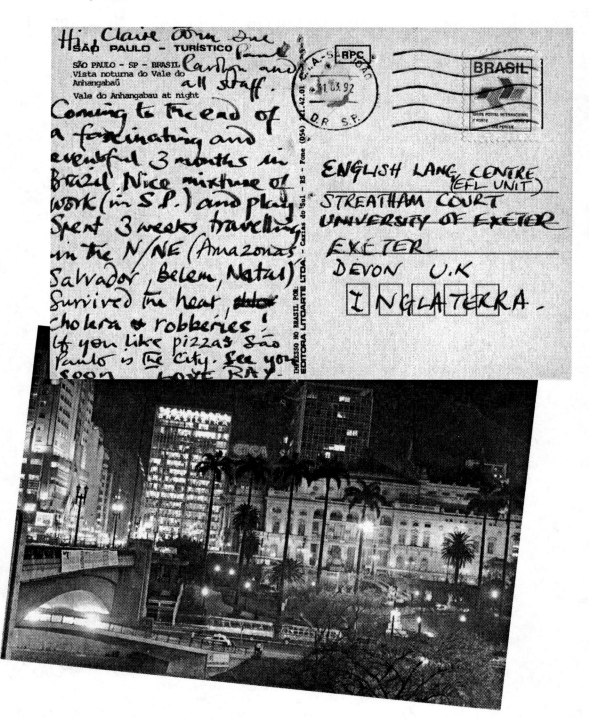

### 1.3.3 Variety

Two major questions for language teachers and writers of language teaching materials are:

- Which language items from the huge diversity available should be selected for learners to learn?
- How can one reduce the endless options to a manageable and accessible framework?

These questions stem from the enormous variety any language is capable of generating. Within the space of any given timeframe (a day, an afternoon, an hour, or an even shorter unit) we may call upon many different sorts of language, depending on who we are talking to, the subject we are dealing with and a whole host of other contextual factors. Among the kaleidoscope of influences on this range and richness, some of the most conspicuous and fundamental are the following:

- *form* (e.g. written/spoken)
- *style* (e.g. formal/informal, assertive/tentative)
- *source* (e.g. newspaper, novel, TV chatshow, telephone conversation)
- *purpose* (e.g. to advise, inform, warn, amuse)
- *context* (e.g. courtroom, classroom, home, company boardroom, factory floor)
- *speaker/writer origin* (e.g. speaker using Scots dialect or Liverpool accent; 19th-century American novelist)
- *social factors* (e.g. age, gender, social group)
- *personal usage* (e.g. the varieties we use at different times to different people)

One problem in describing these parameters is that some of them are hard to define. If we take style, for example, what some people might regard as merely informal might be considered rude by others. Another problem is that we can identify different levels of variety: *broad differences*, as for example between spoken and written language categories; or more *specific differences* within categories, such as those between the pronunciation, grammar and vocabulary of someone from Glasgow and someone from New York, or, at an even finer level of distinction, people from different parts of a large metropolitan area.

In some senses, dealing with the variety of language-in-use is becoming ever more complex because boundaries between categories are becoming increasingly fluid, partly as a result of the changing nature of some communication channels and the widespread influence of the media. For instance, we can see that some (though not all) features often associated with the *form* distinction are not as straightforward as might first appear and each is inevitably affected by the context of use:

| *Spoken language* | *Written language* |
| --- | --- |
| - *less formal* than written language (though not always – what about public lectures?) | - often used for *formal* purposes (but what about a scribbled telephone message?) |
| - *not permanent* (but what about when it's recorded spoken language?) | - *relatively permanent* (but only if preserved – what about e-mail messages?) |

| *Spoken language* | *Written language* |
|---|---|
| • often *less clearly structured*, with hesitations, false starts, etc. (but what about the TV news?) | • often *more structured* with clear segmentation conventions (but what about a 'stream-of-consciousness' novel?) |
| • spoken interactions often conducted *face to face* (though not if via the telephone) | • written interactions usually conducted *at a distance* (but how 'distant' is e-mail?) |
| • speakers have *identifiable accents* (but they can change them, if they want) | • writers have *no accents* (but often clearly recognisable styles) |
| • spoken interactions are *usually synchronous*, where speaker and listener interact within the same immediate timeframe (e.g. telephone conversations) | • written interactions are *usually asynchronous*, where writer and reader interact over a period of different, non-immediate timeframes (e.g. a correspondence by letter) |

## Activity 3 ▷

Look at Examples 1.9–1.12 on pages 34–36.

▶ Use the list of contextual and formal factors at the beginning of this section to help you characterise each of these examples as a variety of language. What features of the examples enable you to guess their source and identify them as a variety of language-in-use? (The actual sources of the four examples are noted in the commentary.)

**Follow-up:** Try keeping a record of the various kinds of language you come into contact with within the course of a specified period – say a working day, or a weekend. Note the diversity, and try to account for it, using the categories in the contextual and formal factors list at the beginning of this section.

If you are a teacher, think of the varieties of language-in-use you consider to be useful for your students, and justify your decisions.

## Example 1.9

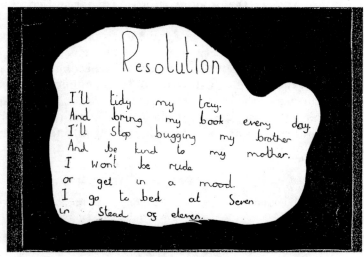

**Example 1.10**

Mrs. Todgers laughed immensely at the dear love's humour, and declared she was quite afraid of her, that she was. She was so very severe.

'Who is severe?' cried a voice at the door. 'There is no such thing
5  as severity in our family, I hope!' And then Mr. Pecksniff peeped smilingly into the room, and said, 'May I come in, Mrs. Todgers?'

Mrs. Todgers almost screamed, for the little door of communication between that room and the inner one being wide open, there was a full disclosure of the sofa bedstead in all its monstrous impro-
10  priety. But she had the presence of mind to close this portal in the twinkling of an eye; and having done so, said, though not without confusion, 'Oh yes, Mr. Pecksniff, you can come in, if you please.'

'How are we to-day,' said Mr. Pecksniff, jocosely, 'and what are our plans? Are we ready to go and see Tom Pinch's sister? Ha, ha,
15  ha! Poor Thomas Pinch!'

'Are we ready,' returned Mrs. Todgers, nodding her head with mysterious intelligence, 'to send a favourable reply to Mr. Jinkins's round-robin? That's the first question, Mr. Pecksniff.'

'Why Mr. Jinkins's robin, my dear madam?' asked Mr. Pecksniff,
20  putting one arm round Mercy, and the other round Mrs. Todgers: whom he seemed, in the abstraction of the moment, to mistake for Charity. 'Why Mr. Jinkins's?'

'Because he began to get it up, and indeed always takes the lead in the house,' said Mrs. Todgers, playfully. 'That's why, sir.'

25  'Jinkins is a man of superior talents,' observed Mr. Pecksniff. 'I have conceived a great regard for Jinkins. I take Jinkins's desire to pay polite attention to my daughters, as an additional proof of the friendly feeling of Jinkins, Mrs. Todgers.'

'Well now,' returned that lady, 'having said so much, you must
30  say the rest, Mr. Pecksniff: so tell the dear young ladies all about it.'

**Example 1.11**

(*For transcription conventions, see page* x.)

**Martin:** *(referring to previous report from India)* ↓no sub-continental weather HERE ↓Isobel Lang can tell us what's going to happen + ↓ good MORNing Isobel

**Isobel:** ↓good morning to YOU + ↑well NO not really because things ARE looking a bit ↓COOLer over the coming weekend although it will end on a rather WARM note today + in southern parts + ↑of course in EURope's + ↓REALly unsettled weather through the Mediterranean heavy showers there + in fact if we take a look at the EURopean summary for THIS weekend + ↓well some really HEAVy showers through IBERia and the WESTern Mediterranean + some rather HAZy conditions for the ↓eastern MED as well as the WINDS strengthen up ++↑for the British Isles well a rather ↓CLOUDy start to the day + ↑even here in WEST London a good deal of rather MISTy HIGH cloud but + SOME ↓SUNshine nonetheless and I think MANy southern parts of Britain will actually have quite a NICE and warm DAY + ↑some rain to the northeast once again that'll gradually weaken as it slips SOUTH + a little bit of rain around ↑eastern parts of ENGland TOO but that'll WEAKen + ↑so I think the ↓PROspects really are for a somewhat ↓BRIGHTer week end to the DAY for the far northWEST of Scotland SHOWERS there but still ↓QUITE a lot of rain for these WESTern areas + ↑but down to the SOUTH + it should remain ↓DRY and BRIGHT + ↓that's IT ++

**Martin:** ↓thank you very MUCH Isobel

**Example 1.12**

| | |
|---|---|
| A | hi it's ↓ME again |
| B | ↓mm |
| A | forgot to ask you take the dogs' ↓MEAT out of the freezer |
| B | ↓OK ↑anything ELSE ↓THREE EGGS today |
| A | ↓GOOD++ ⌈↑OK |
| B | ⌊↓what time'll you be HOME? |
| A | don't ↓KNOW+ ↓USual probably |
| B | ↓OK |
| A | ↓OK+ ↓CIAO |
| B | ↓CIAO |

## 1.3.4 Medium

Using language always entails making choices of structure, vocabulary, pronunciation (in spoken language) and format, and these choices are, to a large extent, dictated by the *medium* we use to convey the message. Hymes (cited in Coulthard 1985:50) argued that '*how* something is said is part of *what* is said', an observation which extends to written language too. Thus, the language we might choose for the following two sample pairs of spoken and written mediums is likely to be different in each case:

- face-to-face communication/communication via the telephone
- e-mail/a hand-written letter

And choices dictated by medium are, of course, further constrained by the specific type of text and context – whether we are writing an important business letter or a shopping list, whether we are being interviewed on television or chatting to an old acquaintance at a party.

For any given *medium* context we have conventional ideas about how language is used and organised. But some medium contexts present us with interesting challenges. One such challenge is the difficulty we encounter when we examine spoken forms of language. Not only is it very hard to represent spoken language in a written form (evidence of the basic differences between the two mediums) but the closer we get to the phonetics (i.e. the aural details in transcribed symbolic form) of what is actually said, the harder it becomes for unskilled users without specialised training to understand the message (see the 3rd version of the utterance in Example 1.14).

Another challenge is that technological developments may require us to question and adjust our ideas about conventions associated with certain mediums. E-mail for example, while it is obviously a written medium, looks as though it may have some of the typical features of spoken language. Because e-mail could be said to straddle the spoken/written divide, we might at first find ourselves confused over which linguistic choices we should make when we use this medium. However, e-mail has rapidly become widely accepted as a new medium of communication, with its own distinctive style and format, largely on account of the convenience, speed and efficacy with which it conveys messages and facilitates a written dialogue or discussion.

## Activity 4 ▷

> ▶ Which types of medium are represented in Examples 1.13, 1.14 and 1.15 on pages 38–40?
> ▶ Look at the list of mediums at the beginning of this section and add any more you can think of. What kinds of effects might these mediums have on the kind of language people use when they communicate through them?

## Example 1.13

Received: from cen by hermes via ESMTP (JAA10553); Wed, 6 Mar 1996 09:43:18 GMT
Received: from ws500.ex.ac.uk by cen; Wed, 6 Mar 1996 09:43:16 GMT
Date: Tue, 5 Mar 1996 22:39:59 PST
From: Niki Davis <N.E.Davis@exeter.ac.uk>
Subject: Re: May day in Sofia
To: Paul Harvey <P.D.Harvey@exeter.ac.uk>
cc: Niki Davis <N.E.Davis@exeter.ac.uk>,
   Rachel Powell PA <rachel.a.powell@exeter.ac.uk>
Message-ID: <ECS9603052259A@exeter.ac.uk>
Priority: Normal
MIME-Version: 1.0
Content-Type: TEXT/PLAIN; CHARSET=US-ACII

               addressor
               &
               addressee(s)

Rachel
Please could you follow up the travel agent on this: when would we be flying
to
Sofia in Bulgaria for this meeting and when back?
Niki

               message #4 in
               response to
               message #3 (no arrows)

On Fri, 1 Mar 1996 17:09:35 PST Paul Harvey wrote:

>From: Paul Harvey <P.D.Harvey@exeter.ac.uk>
>Date: Fri, 1 Mar 1996 17:09:35 PST
>Subject: Re: May Day in Sofia
>To Niki Davis <N.E.Davis@exeter.ac.uk>
>
>Niki
>Yes. I shall have to do a bit of negotiating but Yes. Any idea what date
we would
go
>out?
>
>Paul
>
>

               message #3 in
               response to
               message #2
               (one set of arrows)

>On Fri, 1 Mar 1996 06:03:31 PST Niki Davis wrote:
>
>>From: Niki Davis <N.E.Davis@exeter.ac.uk>
>>Date: Fri, 1 Mar 1996 06:03:31 PST
>>Subject: Re: May Day in Sofia
>>To: Paul Harvey <P.D.Harvey@exeter.ac.uk>
>>Cc: Nick Birbeck <N.Birbeck@exeter.ac.uk>
>>
>>Paul
>>Will you be able to make the 1st May OK?
>>
>>I felt our meeting went well today and have asked Paul Thornton to help
us with
>>WWW at our 'course' on 28/3/96.
>>Niki
>>
>>

               message #2 in
               response to
               message #1
               (two sets of arrows)

>>On Fri, 1 Mar 1996 13:43:13 PST Paul Harvey wrote:
>>
>>>From: Paul Harvey <P.D.Harvey@exeter.ac.uk>
>>>Date: Fri, 1 Mar 1996 13:43:13 PST
>>>Subject: May Day in Sofia
>>>To: Niki Davis <N.E.Davis@exeter.ac.uk>
>>>Cc: Nick Birbeck <N.Birbeck@exeter.ac.uk>
>>>
>>>Niki, Nick,
>>>
>>>After Roumen's latest message it will have to be the 1-3 May for Copernicus,

>>>Bulgaria. There's no point in trying to change it now.
>>>
>>>Paul
>>>
>>
>>
>
>

               message #1 – earliest of
               four related messages
               (three sets of arrows)

**Example 1.14**

Version 1
Transcription: 'standard' written English symbols.

This is quite beyond me. I I I've I'm rather
overawed. I mean everybody's on a different
level to me. I I I feel very inferior.

Version 2
Transcription: broad phonemic, including word stress, weak vowels (e.g. [i]) and
elision (e.g. [dɪfrə·nt].

ðɪs ɪz kwaɪt biˈjɒnd miː aɪ aɪ aɪv aɪm
ˈraːðər ˌəʊvəˈrɔːd aɪ miːn ˈevribɒdiz
ɒn ə ˈdɪfrənt ˈlevəl tə miː aɪ aɪ aɪ
fiːl ˈveri ɪnˈfiːriə

Version 3
Transcription: slightly less broad than Version 2, showing some allophonic
variation e.g. devoicing [w̥], velarisation [ɫ], aspiration [dʰ], syllabic consonants,
assimilation, palatised links, elision and glottalisation [ʔ]. Also shows stressed
syllables with step up in pitch, tonic syllables with direction of tone, tone unit
boundaries. Does not show changes in speed or loudness, or amount of pitch
variation. Transcription remains as if representing separate words. In reality there
is little separation between words.

ˈðɪsɪs ↑kw̥aɪʔ bjɒ↘nn miː | aɪʲaɪ ʔaiʏ aim ↑raːðə
ˈʔəʊvəʔɔ↘.dʰ | aɪ min eˀvribɒdiz | ɒn ə ↑dɪfrnʔ le↘vɫ
tʰ mi | ʲaɪʔʲaɪ aɪ ˈfiːɫ ↑veriʲ ɪŋfiːrjə |

*(Authors' data)*

## Example 1.15

## 1.3.5 Attitude

If we think of the range of socio-cultural and contextual influences on people's use of language, we could say that attitude is as multi-dimensional as the individual user. At the same time, we can approach the connections between attitude and language use from two opposite, but complementary directions:

- an *individual's* ability to express and convey a wide range of feelings through the way they use the language
- the judgements people make about how *other people* use language

Taking the first of these two directions to start with, we can say that expressing and conveying attitudes involves both what is being talked about and who is being addressed. In spoken English, in addition to choice of vocabulary and structure, i.e. *linguistic* elements, there are many other devices for transmitting attitude. These are known as *paralinguistic* elements and, where spoken language is concerned, include intonation, tone, voice quality, pitch, loudness, speed and silence – the very features of speech which, as we said in 1.3.4, are the hardest to capture in any way other than via the ear. Even with apparently simple utterances such as 'yes' or 'thank you', the range of attitudes that can be conveyed with these paralinguistic elements is enormous. For example, the different ways in which 'yes' or 'thank you' can be said might indicate:

| | | |
|---|---|---|
| thoughtfulness | sarcasm | irony |
| anger | puzzlement | interest (mild, or strong) |
| sympathy | threat | gratitude |

In written mediums, where there is no recourse to the paralinguistic features of spoken interaction, different kinds of language resources are exploited to express attitude. Choice of vocabulary and structure are, clearly, major contributors to style and tone – and thence to attitude. Other devices such as use of metaphor, rhetorical questions, juxtaposition of ideas, arrangement of text on the page, and choice of punctuation are equally valuable as means of expressing attitude through written forms. Newspaper letters provide a readily available source for looking at how people convey a variety of attitudes in writing, common ones here including:

| | |
|---|---|
| complaint | support |
| ridicule | congratulation |
| disapproval or anger | approval |
| disgust/outrage | praise |
| irony (serious) | irony (flippant) |

Turning to the second dimension of attitude – judgements made on other people's use of language[1] – the following list of emotively-charged words illustrates some of the common kinds of evaluations, both positive and negative, people make on how other people speak or write:

| | | |
|---|---|---|
| articulate | eloquent | fluent |
| fractured | lazy | posh |
| slovenly | sloppy | uneducated |

[1] a theme to be developed at greater length in Chapter 4

## Example 1.16

**a**
### Heart to hub

*From Ms Laura Lewis*

Sir, We were delighted to hear that your correspondent whose hubcaps were stolen (letter, November 28) did not require counselling.

However, other victims are not in such an advantageous position and can find even what to some would be considered the most minor crimes very distressing. They are grateful for the emotional support and practical help that Victim Support can offer.

Yours faithfully,
LAURA LEWIS
(Co-ordinator), South Westminster Victim Support Scheme,
38 Ebury Street, SW1.
November 28.

**b**
*From Mr Barrie N. Davies*

Sir, Some years ago, my wife and I were shopping in a supermarket when our trolley was taken from behind us by a leggy young man who ran off with it, somehow evading the checkouts. The trolley held a dilapidated and empty briefcase, a rented video and a pound of onions.

The supermarket reported the theft and the following week we were offered counselling. We wondered what could possibly be said to comfort us.

Yours sincerely,
BARRIE N. DAVIES,
22 Grange Road, Ealing, W5.

**c**
### Bread on the waters?

*From the Reverend Dr Peter Whale*

Sir, In these days of moral confusion, what hope do our young people have when the largest branch of Dillons in Birmingham sells cards inscribed "to the one I love" in packets of five?

Yours sincerely,
P. R. WHALE,
83 Chaddesley Court,
Nod Rise, Coventry, Warwickshire.
December 19.

**d**
## Keep dignity in soccer debate

WHILE I respect the right of Mr Thomas (Letters, Nov 21) to make his views felt about football pitches at Sandymere, Northam, there are inaccuracies in his letter.

His "guesstimates" at financial outlay were wildly inaccurate. The football club has spent considerably less than the costs he quotes.

I am saddened when he states the project is led by businessmen, implying a commercial venture. The decision to aim at extending facilities for local youngsters was taken at the well-attended annual meeting of the club. It was voted for unanimously.

Money spent on the project has *not* come out of membership fees; these cover running costs. Any outlay towards Sandymere has been through a committee established for the sole purpose of raising funds for it.

Make your views felt, by all means, but at least have the decency to back them up with honest facts rather than exaggerations, financial mistruths and innuendo.

At all times throughout these procedures the officers and committee of the club have behaved with dignity and no matter what the outcome of the planning meeting this will continue to be the case.

PETER EVANS, on behalf of Bideford Blues and Appledore Junior FC committee

**e**
## 'Mature' folk cause trouble, too

REFERRING to comments (*Journal*, Nov 14) about plans to open the nightclub in Lower Gunstone, I can sympathise with the elderly residents in the New Street flats, but it is not only the elderly that will be affected should the plans for the club go ahead.

My fiancé and I are in our early 30s, live in Lower Gunstone and have witnessed men urinating and people vomiting outside our house. This, coupled with shouting and screaming into the early hours, can make a night's sleep impossible at the weekend. Also, like the residents of New Street, we too have had our car and house vandalised on several occasions.

I had only just read that Mrs Linda Rockey was going to have strictly over 21 year-olds, and I quote "so there won't be any teeny-boppers and you'll get a mature kind of person", when I heard smashing of glass. Looking out of my window I saw a group of men aged between 25-30 kicking a traffic cone down the road. Is this the kind of "mature" person Mrs Rockey is referring to?

NAME AND ADDRESS SUPPLIED

**f**
*From Mrs Ann Taylor*

Sir, How infuriating are the smug people who claim that early retirement can "set you free" — as if we are not able to work that out for ourselves.

Being forcibly retired (ie, redundant) in one's early 50s with three months' salary as a "cushion" and ten years' loss (not just of earnings but of pension contributions) does not make one feel free. Of that you may be sure.

Yours faithfully,
ANN TAYLOR,
5 The Meadows,
Drinkstone, Suffolk.
November 25.

**g**
### Lessons from the case of Mary Bell

*From Mr Richard Voelcker*

Sir, The Mary Bell case confirms that if children suffer undue cruelty, they can develop fear and hate, and may kill. If the publication of the book enables that to be understood it will have been worthwhile.

Yours faithfully,
RICHARD VOELCKER,
Avils Farm,
Lower Stanton St Quintin,
Chippenham, Wiltshire SN14 6DA.
May 3.

**h**
*From Mrs Sharon De Blanc*

Sir, I would like to applaud you for the courage it took to serialize a book that was bound to incur so much criticism. As someone who is currently studying law, and has worked for many years in the mental health field, I believe that it is vital for us to understand why children are killing other children. The problem has escalated recently in America, to previously unheard of levels.

It is only by studying what went wrong with child killers, such as Mary Bell, that we will be able to make the kinds of corrections in our societies and services to prevent these horrors. It is unfortunate that Ms Sereny had to pay Ms Bell, as this will shift the focus away from the author's unblinking examination of the inner life of a child who committed the most serious crime possible.

However, it is certainly understandable that Ms Sereny would feel that Ms Bell deserved some recompense for going through the agonizing process of examining memories of past abuse, as well as her own heinous acts. I have the utmost sympathy for the families of the two children so tragically and horribly murdered by Ms Bell, and regret that the greater good provided to society by the examination of these issues adds to their pain.

Yours etc,
SHARON DE BLANC,
3801 Galleria Court,
Plano, Texas 75075.
pdeblanc@ix.netcom.com
May 2.

*(Newspaper letters – various sources)*

**Activity 5** ▷

> ▶ Try saying the word 'yes' to indicate the various attitudes listed in the second paragraph of this section. Notice which paralinguistic features (i.e. intonation, pitch, loudness, speed, voice quality, etc.) have to be manipulated in order to convey each type of attitude.
>
> ▶ What attitudes are being expressed in each of the newspaper letters in Example 1.16 on page 42? Choose one of the letters and identify devices used by the writer to express their attitude. Say how these devices contribute to expression of attitude.

## 1.3.6 Effectiveness

As language users wishing to communicate with others, we aim to choose language which will be effective. How consciously we choose it will depend very largely on the specific context of the communication: we are more likely to try to choose our words carefully in an important job interview, for instance, than when we respond to a friend's enquiry about what kind of day we have had (if we interpret the enquiry as being of the routine 'How are you – had a good day?' type, that is).

However, it is one thing to *aim* to be effective when we communicate, and quite another to say precisely what constitutes effective communication. This is partly because judgements in this respect are always subjective and governed by factors such as age, gender, personality, mood, emotional state, tiredness, context of communication and so forth. But there are some basic parameters around which we can form judgements of effectiveness:

• ostensible purposes of speakers or writers, and whether or not these are fulfilled
• attitudes and likely interpretations of intended audience
• relationships between those involved in the communication
• extent of knowledge shared between people involved in the interaction

Certain types of basic messages such as warnings or prohibitions are relatively straightforward. Signs such as *Danger: Overhead High Tension Cables* or *No Parking* or *No Smoking* are effective communications where we rarely question – or even notice – how the message is conveyed. Similarly, communications such as party and wedding invitations are usually highly functional and achieve with little difficulty what they are designed to do. In spoken interactions, when someone says 'Thank you' we do not usually question whether this is an effective way of expressing appreciation (though we might start to worry if there were no response to an act or utterance for which we would expect some appreciation).

It seems, then, fairly easy to judge the effectiveness of communications involving basic messages of warning, prohibition, invitation or appreciation – though even here, of course, some messages may be more effective than others in given circumstances: compare a standard *No Parking* prohibition (relatively neutral) with a *Don't Even Think of Parking Here* sign (relatively impolite and unexpected, and thus attention-drawing, and thus effective?), or a standard *No Smoking* prohibition with a *Thank you for not smoking* sign (relatively polite, and thus attention-drawing, and thus effective?). In other more complex and subtle types of communication, we might find it much harder to judge effectiveness.

## Activity 6

▶ Consider the following types of message and list some criteria we might use for judging their effectiveness.
  a) a legal document
  b) a business letter
  c) an advertisement
  d) a university or college lecture

  e) a safety routine in-flight announcement
  f) a CV
  g) a dictionary entry

In fact, it might often be easier to say whether something is *ineffective* than effective. The ineffectiveness might result at one extreme from language which is unjustifiably complex or explicit, or at the other unjustifiably simple or cryptic.

## Activity 7

▶ Consider the following recipe for baked mackerel, offered to customers in a local supermarket, and decide how effective you think it is as an instance of communication:

**FISH**

### *Baked Mackerel*

- Mackerel
- Garlic

- Ginger
- Spring onion

- Almonds

Mix together the garlic, ginger, onion and almonds and place it inside the mackerel. Rub garlic onto the outside of the mackerel and wrap individually in foil. Bake Gas 4/350F for approx 30 minutes.

▶ Now consider the texts in Examples 1.17, 1.18, 1.19 and 1.20 on pages 45–46. Do you think they are effective or ineffective as instances of communication, taking into account their purposes and intended audiences? Give some reasons for your opinion about each text. (You might like to refer back to the four parameters mentioned in the second paragraph of section 1.3.6 as a guideline for this.)

**Example 1.17**

**Example 1.18**

**Example 1.19**

**Example 1.20**

**campaigning to end
animal experiments**

300/301/303/305/310-41/315

NAME.................................................................................

ADDRESS..........................................................................

## HELP US TO HELP LABORATORY ANIMALS

Millions of animals die every year in painful and unnecessary experiments. We are working hard to stop this suffering - and, at last, our campaigns are getting through - but we can only continue this vital work with the help of people who give their support.

Join the BUAV and receive our magazine and the latest campaign news. If you would like to become a member please complete the MEMBER'S AGREEMENT & GUARANTEE and PAYMENT DETAILS sections below.

### MEMBER'S AGREEMENT & GUARANTEE

I/we agree to become a member/s of BUAV. Should the company be wound up, I/we promise to pay the sum of £1 towards its debts if asked to do so. I/we confirm that I am/we are opposed to all animal experiments. I/we acknowledge that acceptance of my/our application is on the express understanding that no previous application by me/us has been refused.

| Subscription Rates | Please tick | | First Member |
|---|---|---|---|
| **Waged** | £12.00 ☐ | | *Full name* _____ |
| **Unwaged** | £8.50 ☐ | | *Signature* _____ |
| **Couple** (at one address) | | | *Date Of Birth* _____ |
| *Please include names of both persons** | £18.00 ☐ | | **Second Member** |
| **Life** | £200.00 ☐ | | *Full name* _____ |
| | | | *Signature* _____ |
| | | | *Date Of Birth* _____ |

*Please amend your address/postcode, above, if incorrect, and add details of second person, if appropriate.

I would like to support the BUAV and send the following donation to help the campaign for laboratory animals:

Please tick:                           Please complete the PAYMENT DETAILS section,
£75☐   £50☐   £25☐   £15☐   other £☐   below

### PAYMENT DETAILS

I enclose a cheque/postal order for £ _____ payable to BUAV.

To pay by Access or Visa fill in your card number and details:

☐☐☐☐☐☐☐☐☐☐☐☐☐☐☐   Expiry date _____

Cardholder's signature _____        Date _____

*Laboratory animals need our help - thank you for caring about them.*

Please return this form and your remittance to:
BUAV, 16A CRANE GROVE, LONDON N7 8LB

## 1.3.7 Structure

All language is, by nature, structured: it would be hard to understand what people said or wrote if it were not. It follows from this that the structure of a language is supported by the existence of rules which allow us to say whether something is acceptable or unacceptable within the structural framework of the language concerned. These rules can be used, for example, to say why the following are not acceptable in English: *we must to go there; *sprhrdny; *two sheeps.* Traditionally, ELT materials have often been constructed around the rules associated with readily identifiable structured language areas such as grammar, pronunciation and vocabulary, as illustrated in the above three instances.

A problem for language teachers and learners arising from the inherently structured nature of any language is that a certain amount of over-simplification is inevitable in teaching and learning it. This is because teachers and writers of language teaching materials need, pragmatically, to select and grade language according to levels, needs and interests of specific or (which is more likely to be the case) idealised groups of students. Thus, not surprisingly, structures often chosen for learning and teaching purposes are selected because:

- they are considered relatively 'easy' to acquire
- they are relatively easy to identify and formulate 'rules' about
- they are useful for practical communication contexts

So, in English, structural systems such as those relating to verb tenses, plural forms of nouns, or distinctions between mass and count nouns, to name but a few of the most common structural elements, form the basic matter of many coursebooks.

Activity 8 below illustrates one area of structure – expressing condition – which often appears as a neat unit in coursebooks, but may often be over-simplified by being reduced to the 'rules' for the three types of conditional sentences exemplified in the first three exponents in the list below.

## Activity 8

> ► Look at the exponents below of some possible ways English has for expressing conditions. The first three are examples of what are often referred to in ELT materials as 'Conditional Sentences Types 1, 2 and 3'.
>
> 1. We won't sit outside if it rains. (Conditional Sentence Type 1)
> 2. We wouldn't sit outside if it rained. (Conditional Sentence Type 2)
> 3. We wouldn't have sat outside if it had rained. (Conditional Sentence Type 3)
> 4. We don't normally sit outside if it rains.
> 5. We're not sitting outside if it rains.
> 6. Don't sit outside unless it's fine.
> 7. It's foolish to sit outside if it's raining.
> 8. If it was raining we usually stayed indoors.
> 9. We normally couldn't sit outside unless it was fine.
> 10. If it's raining you shouldn't sit outside.

11. You can't imagine how unpleasant it is to sit outside when it's raining.
12. You can sit outside if you like.
13. If it should rain we'd have to go inside.
14. If it were to rain, we'd have to change our plans and go inside.
15. Were it to rain, we'd have to go inside.
16. Had it rained, we could not have sat outside.
17. With rain, no way could we have sat outside.
18. We are to sit outside, if possible.
19. We are to sit outside, provided it's fine.
20. Rain, inside; no rain, outside!
21. Outside it is, rain or no rain!
22. It's outside we go, never mind the rain!
23. Whether there's rain or not, we're outside!
24. Whatever the weather, we sit outside!
25. It didn't rain – otherwise we'd have been inside.

- Look at exponents 1, 2 and 3 above. What are the so-called 'rules' for conditional sentences we can draw from these three exponents?
- Now look at the range of structures used in exponents 4–25 to express condition. How many of them actually conform to the 'rules' of exponents 1, 2 and 3?
- Do you think it is helpful or misleading for learners if the 'rules' for expressing conditions in English are presented only through the three traditional types of conditional sentences (as in 1, 2 and 3)?

Although a 'rule-based' approach may be practical for teaching purposes, it has some drawbacks:

- it is based predominantly on *sentence-level* grammars of *written* English
- it ignores or treats as 'exceptions' other types of structure which are more difficult to identify, e.g. the types of structure that can occur in *spoken* English – "E haven't got nothing'
- it often fails to deal with the interrelationship of one area of structure with another, e.g. using an adverb as a response to a question – 'Do you agree with me?'/'Absolutely'
- it often fails to deal with the structures which occur in 'chunks' of language made up of more than one utterance, e.g. the structure of narratives or arguments or conversational exchanges

Such drawbacks may mean that the subtleties of relating choice of structure to context of utterance can easily be overlooked or ignored in the language teaching context; consequently, many learners may remain unaware of the true possibilities of the language and the more opaque, less accessible structures may remain undiscovered.

With the advent of data retrieval, processing and storage facilities on scales unthinkable a few years ago, the questions over the limitations of approaches to language description and analysis described above are gradually being addressed. Projects such as COBUILD[2], for example (whose slogan incidentally

[2] The Collins Birmingham University International Language Database project

is *Helping Learners with <u>Real</u> English*), have had, and are continuing to have, a considerable impact on helping us to look in alternative ways at how language is structured. This particular project has resulted in a series of new reference books for language learners based on how the language is actually used in a very wide range of contexts in the contemporary world, rather than simply on categories of language organisation and description springing from academic analysis. Other projects, such as CANCODE[3], also based on large corpora of language as it is actually used by people in 'real' contexts in the 'real' world, are leading us to a clearer understanding of the grammar of spoken English[4] and the importance of considering language as interactive communication rather than isolated sentences.

Such projects are also helping to expand our notion of structure to include the patterns which occur in language use beyond sentence level – at discourse, 'genre' or text-type level. This notion will be taken up again in Chapter 2, but meanwhile, you might like to try out the tasks in Activity 9 as an illustration of this more expanded conception of 'structure'.

## Activity 9

> ► Look at the two short texts below – each consisting of more than one utterance – where the components have been jumbled. Put them into what seems to you to be a more appropriate order, according to your notions of the structures you expect in conversational exchange (Jumbled text 1) and narrative (Jumbled text 2).
>
> **Jumbled text 1**
> (i) You're welcome.
> (ii) Thank you.
>
> **Jumbled text 2**
> (i) Miraculously, none of the drivers in the cars involved in the collision was seriously injured.
> (ii) Police and ambulance services were soon at the scene, though it took several hours before traffic returned to normal.
> (iii) A maroon Renault, driven by a local businessman, swerved out of control, crossed the highway divider, and crashed head-on into the oncoming traffic.
> (iv) There was severe traffic congestion yesterday during morning rush hour, following a serious accident.
>
> ► What sorts of 'structural' rules were you following when you put the two jumbled texts into a more 'normal' or 'appropriate' order? What do you understand by 'normal' or 'appropriate' in this case? What situational context might you expect each of the unjumbled texts to occur in?
> ► If the two jumbled texts remain in their jumbled order, could we still make sense of them? If so, would we have to adjust our idea of the contexts in which they might occur? If so, what might possible new contexts be? Would we need to make any grammatical changes to the original language?

[3] The Cambridge-Nottingham Corpus of Discourse in English
[4] See, for instance, Carter and McCarthy 1997; Carter 1997; Biber *et al.* 1999.

## 1.3.8 Flexibility

Unlike some other languages, English is allowed to be as flexible as it likes, in the sense that there is no regulatory body to limit the number of loan words coming into the language, e.g. *horde* – from Polish; *glasnost* – from Russian[5]; *cobra* – from Portuguese; *toboggan* – from Canadian French, and originally from Algonquian. Nor is there anything to restrict the invention of new terms to deal with new technology, e.g. *informatics, to download, modem, website*, or the extension of meanings of existing words, e.g. *file, mouse, network, snail mail*.

Widespread access to mass media, together with the global use of English as a language of international communication, provides the means for such items to enter the language, though the ways in which the structure of English allows us to create new items relatively easily may vary. Some common ones are:

- via prefixes and suffixes (*disinform, roughish*)
- via the mechanism which allows nouns or adjectives to metamorphose into verbs (*to rubbish, to stench, to remainder, to pulp, to supersonic, to card, to leaflet*)
- via the invention of euphemistic, association-free terminology to disguise unpleasant realities (*to downsize = to fire staff*)

Other areas where English readily illustrates its flexibility and adaptability include the following:

**brand-names** (some of which enter the language as nouns or verbs )
e.g. inventor's name *Hoover* → noun for invention *hoover* → verb for using invention *to hoover*

**acronyms** (nouns formed from the initial letters of a group of words, which then take on some of the characteristics of 'normal' nouns)
e.g. *AIDS, pre-Aids*; *TEFL, TEFLers*; *UNESCO, UNESCO-related*; *MP, ex-MP*; *CDROM*, 'How many **CDROMs** have we got?'

**newspaper headlines** (which often use their own idiosyncratic grammar systems)
e.g. 'Sado-masochist film *Crash* banned'; 'Licensed to scribble: lottery to give funds to graffiti artists'; 'Outrage over deal to make film about killer West'; 'Tory call over OAPs'; 'Saudi leaks reveal new evidence in nurses' case'

**advertising slogans** (which are often based on the use of words with double meanings, and word-play)
e.g. 'Go to work on an egg'; 'A diamond is forever'; 'Heineken refreshes the parts other beers cannot reach'

**literature** (where writers manipulate forms and flout conventions for creative purposes)
e.g. '... It is spring, moonless night in the small town, starless and bible-black, the cobblestreets silent and the hunched, courters'-and-rabbits' wood limping invisible down to the sloeblack, slow, black, crowblack, fishingboat-bobbing sea ...' (*Under Milk Wood*, Dylan Thomas)

---

[5] We might note here that this word has ceased to be in widespread current use, probably because the immediate context of its borrowing (the breakup of the Soviet Union) is no longer relevant.

'... Sir Tristam, violer d'amores, fr'over the short sea, had passencore rearrived from North Armorica on this side the scraggy isthmus of Europe Minor to wielderfight his penisolate war: nor had topsawyer's rocks by the stream Oconee exaggerated themselse to Laurens County's gorgios while they went doublin their mumper all the time: ...' (*Finnegan's Wake*, James Joyce)

Some people regard this flexibility and adaptability of English as a positive feature: it ensures that the language lives and moves with the times, and can be used by people to serve their specific purposes. On the other hand, it may also give rise in certain circles to constant despair at 'declining standards': people may rebel against new words in everyday usage as 'ugly' or 'meaningless' and many people find the change in meanings of words or their pronunciation objectionable[6]. However, the capacity of language to adapt to new realities and social mores is stronger than the desire amongst certain members of the community to preserve what was once perceived to be the 'standard', or 'acceptable' (see Chapters 3 and 4 for more detailed discussion of this issue).

## Activity 10

> ▶ Look at Example 1.21 on page 52. Can you identify some 'new' language items? How 'new' are they? Is there anything in this text you do not understand? If so, what might be some of the reasons for your failure to understand? (Bear in mind what has been said so far in previous sections about the importance of contexts and culture-specific knowledge.)
> ▶ Example 1.22 on page 53 contains two press announcements relating to horse-racing, but the language is very different. What are some of the differences between the two? Can you think of possible reasons for the differences?
>
> **Follow-up:** The three texts in Examples 1.21 and 1.22 on pages 52–53 illustrate aspects of the flexibility of English as a language. How appropriate do you think it is for teachers of the language to alert students to this aspect of the language they are learning?

---

[6] This situation is much less likely to occur where literature is concerned, when creative manipulation of form and structure is much more readily accepted.

**Example 1.21**

N   DESTINATIONS

# WHAT'S COOL?

Someday, we'll all agree on what's cool on the Net. In the meantime, the Netscape cool team will continue to bring you a list of select sites that catch our eye, make us laugh, help us work, quench our thirst. ... you get the idea. **This list was last updated June 7, 1996.**

Be sure to also check out the growing list of Netscape Server sites in our <u>Customer Showcase</u>.

### $495. a small price to be heard.

NARRATIVE COMMUNICATIONS

No more waiting for graphics and audio files to download – Narrative's Enliven viewer, a Netscape Navigator plug-in for Windows, gives you streaming multimedia on the Web.

**Example 1.22**

Text A

THIS is to give notice to all Gentlemen, that the Ormskirk Plate in Lancaſhire, which heretofore hath been Run for upon the ſecond Tueſday in May, is now put off to the firſt Tueſday in Auguſt next.

THE Plates at Doncaſter Old-Horſe-Courſe in Yorkſhire, mentioned in the Gazett on Monday June the 1ſt. will be Run for the 25th of July next.

Text B

JAMES FANSHAWE yesterday warned punters to hold fire on Champion Hurdle wagers about Bold Gait until the gelding's introduction at Newbury on Monday week.

The Newmarket trainer, who saddled Royal Gait to Champion Hurdle glory in 1992, will have his fingers firmly crossed when the five-year-old attempts timber for the first time in the two-and-a-half-mile Wantage Novices' Hurdle.

# Key references

Van Lier, L. (1995). *Introducing Language Awareness*. London: Penguin.
Wright, T. (1994). *Investigating English*. London: Edward Arnold.

# 2   Discourse

## 2.1   Overview

In Chapter 1 we proposed a basic framework for considering how we use language in a range of communicative contexts. Now, in this chapter, we look in more depth at some of the systems and structures underlying language-in-use – or, as we shall call it here, discourse. Awareness of these structures helps us to understand *how* we communicate with each other in speech or writing. We consider some of the key concepts associated with the study of language at discourse level, focusing on those we feel to be particularly relevant to language teachers:

- the role of *context* in any instance of communication
- the importance of *choice* of lexis and structure
- the relationship between *linguistic form* and *communicative intention*
- the consequences of *shared knowledge*
- the *organisation of information* in discourse
- the centrality of *purpose*

## 2.2   Some definitions and key concepts

Our main aim in this section is to come to an understanding of what is meant by discourse and what is involved in the study of discourse. We also need to establish why it is helpful for language teachers to be aware of discourse studies and what the relevance of such studies is to the teaching of language.

### What is it that language teachers actually teach?

Language teaching classrooms are places where teachers and learners try to get to grips with an enormously complex entity: how people in a certain cultural community (or communities) communicate with each other through the language of that culture. In the teaching/learning process, we have to deal with *forms* and *functions*. The *forms* in which the language appears (*sounds* – combinations of which create words, which represent meaning, and which in turn combine in structures – and *written symbols* – important additional devices for representing meaning in many languages) are the tools we need to carry out the basic *functions* of language, namely, to communicate meanings to other human beings. The most crucial part of the process, though, is teaching and learning about *links between forms and functions*, i.e. choices and combinations of words to fulfil specific purposes (see Figure 3 below).

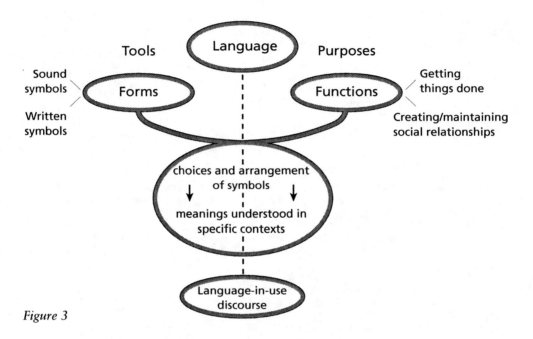

*Figure 3*

At one level, we could interpret the notion of 'combinations of words' as referring simply to combinations allowed by the grammatical, phonological, lexical and semantic systems of the language. At a far more complex level, however, we have to account for all the ways in which contexts of language use influence how the users *choose* to combine words and chunks of language in their interactions with each other, and how listeners or readers interpret and react to these choices. This is essentially what discourse studies are concerned with:

- the coherence of stretches of language used and understood in specific contexts
- the language choices people make when they interact
- the effects these choices have on those involved in the interaction

## What do we mean by the term 'discourse'?

The concept of 'discourse', although fundamental to the teaching of language, is rather difficult to define in a succinct and concise way. Perhaps the best way to understand it is to look at some of the key notions associated with discourse studies.

## Activity 11

> ▶ Look at the definitions below relating to discourse.
> ▶ Note or highlight what seem to you to be some of the key notions involved.
>
> *meaning in interaction ... the different contributions of both speaker and hearer as well as that of utterance and context to the making of meaning* (Thomas 1995:23)
>
> *a dynamic process in which language [is] used as an instrument of communication in a context by a speaker/writer to express meanings and achieve intentions* (Brown and Yule 1983:26)
>
> *discourse arises not as a collection of decontextualised units of language structure, but as a collection of inherently contextualised units of language use* (Schiffrin 1994:39)
>
> *the subtle ways in which language orders our perceptions and makes things happen and thus ... how language can be used to construct and create social interaction and diverse social worlds ... the way talk is meshed together ... language in its social and cognitive context* (Potter and Wetherall 1987:1,6)
>
> *language in use ... it cannot be restricted to the description of linguistic forms independent of the purposes or functions which these forms are designed to serve in human affairs* (Brown and Yule 1983:31)
>
> *language above the sentence or above the clause ... [in] larger linguistic units, such as conversational exchanges or written texts ... language in use in social contexts* (Stubbs 1983a:1)
>
> *the language of communication – spoken or written ... an interlocking social, cognitive and linguistic enterprise* (Hatch 1992:1)
>
> *a way of perceiving, talking about and acting upon the world, particularly in different social contexts or as part of different social practices* (Maley et al. 1995:43)

You will probably have noted some or all of the following:

*interaction, dynamic process*
*language for communication, language in use*
*relationships across utterances, language above the sentence*
*language in its social and cultural context*
*the meshing together of talk*

As we shall see in later sections, these notions are all central to an understanding of human discourse, the study of which is a multi-faceted and extremely complex field of investigation. Crystal (1997a:116) describes some of the different approaches taken by scholars from various academic disciplines. He argues that despite the differences in focus and emphasis there is a common concern, namely 'the need to see language as a dynamic, social, interactive phenomenon' where 'meaning is conveyed not by single sentences but by more complex exchanges, in which the participants' beliefs and expectations, the knowledge they share about each other and about the world, and the situation in which they interact, play a crucial part.'

When we use the term *discourse*, then, we have in mind a dynamic, language-mediated process of interaction between people in specific social, cultural and situational contexts: a casual conversation between friends round the dinner table, a consultation between doctor and patient, a newspaper editorial, a political speech, a letter of condolence, an urgent telephone message. Any language-mediated interaction is constrained by purposes and circumstances, and if we have acquired 'discourse competence' (see below) in the language in question and are familiar with the circumstances of the interaction, then it is likely to be meaningful for us. At even further levels of complexity, we recognise that discourses can be 'embedded' within each other. For example, what is ostensibly a political speech can – for effect – become conversational.

## Discourse competence

As competent users of our first language, whatever that may be, we are experts in its discourse, though, because of our specific personal circumstances and experience, our expertise will always be restricted. That is to say, without sufficient exposure to specific 'worlds' – the legal world, the medical world, the factory shop-floor world or the train driver's world – we are unlikely to be experts in the discourses of those worlds.

Our ability to recognise, respond to and produce appropriate choices and arrangements of language items results partly from formal education. This exposes us to a range of spoken and written *genres* and *text-types* (we looked at some of these in Chapter 1), making us consciously aware of the conventions associated with them, and enabling us to operate within – and when necessary to flout or manipulate – these conventions. But this ability also results from our having been born and brought up in a particular socio-cultural environment, where, as we acquire our first language, we spontaneously acquire with it knowledge about the attitudes, expectations and preconceptions our society and culture has towards the world and how it is represented by our language. We construct mental representations of existence, as we experience it through our particular social, cultural and linguistic environment. These mental representations are in turn reflected in the way we use our language – or, in some cases, languages.

We have, in short, acquired what has been termed *discourse competence* (Canale and Swain 1980). We have learned to distinguish between coherent and garbled messages; we are sensitive to contexts and purposes in communication; we take part in conversation, understanding when to speak, when to let others speak, how to respond appropriately, and how to recognise an inappropriate response; we make sense of what we read and hear, often at levels which are not made explicit by the language. Most of us are probably quite unaware of the enormous communicational complexity of our language use in all the various circumstances of our daily lives, and it is only when we try to explain it that we start to appreciate its sophistication.

A self-evident goal for language teachers is to help people acquire and hone the basic tools (sounds, structures and words) they need to communicate in the language they are learning. Another goal, which might not necessarily appear to be so evident, is to help learners develop L2 discourse competence. Of course, L2 learners have already acquired discourse competence in their L1, and there are those who argue that there is little point in attempting to 'teach' L2 discourse[1]. There may indeed be discourse 'fundamentals' which could be said to be universal. Three obvious areas are:

- *sequence* (the systematic ways in which *utterances* – stretches or chunks of language, occuring in actual language use – are created, structured and ordered)
- *coherence* (how sequences of language 'hang together' and how users of the language create, interpret and 'make sense' of these sequences)
- *force* (the effects utterances, or sequences of utterances have, i.e. how they are interpreted and reacted to)

Nevertheless, we would contend that it is the differences in the ways these fundamentals are realised in different languages which is the challenge for language teachers and learners. Thus, an understanding of the discourse conventions of the L2 in question is not only relevant, but, we would argue, essential. The more teachers understand about how people communicate successfully with each other in the language they are teaching, the greater the help they are able to give their students. Not least among the legacies of communicative language teaching methodology has been the realisation that teaching a language involves far more than simply dealing with its syntactic, lexical and phonological components, because language-in-use results from the ways people *choose* to manipulate these components in discourse.

## 2.3  Aspects of discourse

Having established a broad conception of what we mean by the terms *discourse* and *discourse competence* we now examine some discourse components in more detail. We focus on six aspects of discourse and discourse competence which seem to us to have particularly important implications for language teachers:

- relevance and choice
- structures of spoken interaction
- meanings
- shared knowledge
- organisation
- purposes

These six features are illustrated with examples from both spoken and written discourse in English, and together they contribute to the understanding of the fundamentals of discourse mentioned above: sequence, coherence and force.

[1] See, for example, Swan 1985a and b.

## 2.3.1 Relevance and choice

### The importance of context and purpose

Example 2.1 below contains a scenario, immediately recognisable to people who know what a typical country pub in Britain is, what sort of food is likely to be served at lunchtime, and how many people are likely to be in the pub on a Sunday, particularly if it is in a popular location. These specific contextual details may not, of course, be universally familiar, but the basic situation – or a similar one – probably is.

### Example 2.1

> *(Friends are having lunch on a Sunday in a crowded pub. A has gone to the bar to order the food, but because the pub has run out of what B (one of the present authors) originally requested, has taken the liberty of replacing the original order with something he (A) considers reasonably similar, and accept-able to B. Having started eating, B finds the food far from satisfactory. A enquires whether B is enjoying her lunch.)*

> A: How's yours, ↑OK?
> B: ↓Yes, ↓fine.

> *(Authors' data)*

First, let us think about this short exchange from the perspective of someone who interpreted only the *forms* of the language. Such a person might well recognise the question form of A's contribution, and taking it at its face value, understand that A wants to know whether B's food is OK – assuming, that is, that the context will enable 'yours' to be interpreted as the food that B is eating. They might hear B's response, and assume that B was satisfied. However, understanding the language forms alone would not, in this particular case, have led to an accurate interpretation of the *meaning* of this interaction. The *force* of both A's question and B's response would have been missed. For in fact, A's question was an appeal for reassurance that the choice he had made on B's behalf was acceptable, and B's response was the outcome of a decision that to tell the truth would have been too great a threat to A's 'face', and indeed to her (B's) own interests, given that the pub was very crowded – if A had not chosen on her behalf, acting as he believed in her best interests, she might still have been waiting for any food at all.

Now let us look at this exchange from a discourse perspective. First, how did B know that A's real intention was not to find out if her food was OK? Then, why did the words she chose for her response bear no relation to the truth? Why did she not say what she meant? What hint as to the real situation might A have picked up in B's choice of the word *fine* (as opposed to, say, *absolutely wonderful/great; I'm really glad/thank goodness/just as well they'd run out of what I ordered, etc.*) – which in fact is exactly what did happen, as it soon became obvious to A that a white lie had been told! And how did neither participant need any more information than the word *yours* to understand that what was referred to was the plate of food that A had ordered for B, which B did not really want to eat, but was nevertheless consuming?

We can go some way to arriving at the answers to these questions by looking at two principles, or sets of maxims, which have been proposed as a basis for understanding certain aspects of spoken interaction: the *co-operative principle* and the *politeness principle*. These principles have been suggested as ways of understanding norms[2] of conversational interaction, which are assumed by the interactants to apply as the interaction evolves – unless they are deliberately flouted for some special purpose. They help us to understand how hearers infer what is meant from what is said, acting as a kind of explanatory bridge between 'expressed meaning' and 'implied meaning' (Thomas 1995:56).

## The co-operative principle

According to the *co-operative principle* (CP), as formulated by the philosopher Paul Grice (1975) to explain how we interpret what he termed 'conversational implicatures', or 'implied meaning', speakers will normally obey four maxims:

- they will not knowingly give false or untrue information (Grice's maxim of *quality*)
- they will give as much or as little information as required by the context of interaction (Grice's maxim of *quantity*)
- they will not include irrelevant information (Grice's maxim of *relevance*)
- they will make every effort to be clear, unambiguous, and not unnecessarily long-winded (Grice's maxim of *manner*)

## The politeness principle

One version of the maxims of the *politeness principle* (PP), formulated by Leech (1983), is as follows:

> Minimize (all things being equal) the expression of impolite beliefs
> Maximize (all things being equal) the expression of polite beliefs

and another, put forward by Lakoff (1973) and later termed *the rules of rapport*, suggests that speakers often speak as they do:

- to avoid imposing on others (i.e. to keep a suitable distance)
- to give options for response (i.e. to act with deference)
- to make the receiver feel good (i.e. to establish/maintain friendly relations)

---

[2] We should note that there are linguists who point out that these 'norms' are not necessarily applicable to all types of conversational style (especially those identified as typically feminine), and that in any case 'conversation' is an extremely flexible notion (see, for instance, Cameron 1985:39ff; Coates 1994).

## Activity 12 ▷

> Look again at the conversation in Example 2.1 in the light of the co-operative principle (CP).
>
> ▶ Which maxims are being obeyed by the speakers?
> ▶ Which maxims are being flouted by the speakers?
>
> Then look at the conversation in the light of the politeness principle (PP).
>
> ▶ To what extent does this principle help to explain the CP flouts you have identified?

You can probably think of lots of situations where the CP and PP conflict or clash with each other – either stock situations (such as having to compliment people on their choice of clothes/hairstyle/house decor and so on, which to you are in appallingly bad taste, or having to lie about the quality of someone's cooking, or giving in to an opponent in an argument where to prolong it would not be worth the effort) or situations you personally often find yourself in where you compromise with the truth. Decisions to make such compromises often relate to the need for *tact* (see Leech 1983) and the importance of *face* (see Brown and Levinson 1987; Gumperz 1982). However, not only do we constantly flout the co-operative maxims on these kinds of grounds; we often do so because we are, consciously or unconsciously, aware of and sensitive to *power and status relations* between participants. Furthermore, it is often the need to create, maintain or safeguard these social relationships which dictates to a very great degree the ways in which people choose to interact with each other through language.

### Relevance theory

Once again, as we saw in Chapter 1, we recognise the absolute importance of context and purpose in understanding how discourse works. The fact that both context and purpose *are* so important is one of the grounds on which Sperber and Wilson (1995) argue that of all the Gricean maxims, *relevance* is the one which really matters, precisely because we do so frequently flout the others in the interests of context and purpose. Their notion of relevance, and the relevance theory they derive from it, is complex. In simple terms, however, they claim that communication depends ultimately on what participants understand as being relevant to the interaction. 'Relevant' here means relevant not merely in terms of the superficial topic, but much more importantly in terms of the whole agenda (i.e. the purposes of the interactants and what they hope to achieve):

- the assumptions made about the context and purpose(s) of the interaction
- the shared knowledge of the interactants
- the power, familiarity and status relations between the interactants
- the way the agenda is adjusted and redefined as the interaction develops

All these considerations lead people to make language choices which are relevant to the immediate context and purpose of the interaction.

## Activity 13 ▷

If you have never considered your own use of language before, in terms of the co-operative, politeness and relevance theories, you might like to try keeping track of your own interactions during a specified period – say an hour, a morning or evening, or even a whole day. You could do this by:

(i)   making brief notes in a *field diary*: try to remember the exact words which were used in a particular interaction – like the pub exchange in Example 2.1. Think about the context and purpose of the interaction and relations between the participants. Note how these things influenced the choice of language. Note which principles were being obeyed or flouted, and what kinds of conflicts between the principles arose.

(ii)  using a *'buddy' tape*: get together with another person and record on tape your interpretations of a particular interaction. You can then use the recording as a data record and/or as a basis for discussion.

(iii) using a *checklist* (see commentary for an example).

**Follow-up:** Observe and reflect upon how the language you used in various interactions was influenced by the principles we have been discussing above, e.g.

▶ Did you give untrue information? If so, why?
▶ Did you withhold relevant information or say too much? If so, why?
▶ Did you say things in a roundabout or unclear way? If so, why?
▶ Were you conscious of difference in status between you and the person(s) you were interacting with? If so, how did this affect your use of language?

## *Do language teachers have to compromise?*

One route to acquiring a second language is total immersion in the real life and culture from which it springs. This route to active understanding and participation in the language may involve little or no 'reduction' or simplification, but it may be long, circuitous, and not particularly easy. For these reasons it is an option neither practically feasible, cost-effective or context-appropriate in most L2 teaching/learning situations. Quite probably it would not be the most efficient, either. The route for most L2 learners involves classrooms, limited amounts of time, and recreation or simulation of contexts of language use (apart from the actual teaching/learning context).

Language teachers and writers of language teaching materials, therefore, always have to 'reduce', to a greater or lesser extent, the subtleties of spoken interaction in the interests of what we might call *inducting* learners into the language. Samples of language have to be provided for classroom use, either as models to illustrate what is likely to happen in given situations, or as exponents of structure, or as launching points for tasks and activities. They will always be artificial in terms of conversational interaction, because they will always be divorced from a live context which has its unique agenda, though clearly they will be real enough in terms of a teaching agenda.

Questions arising from this classroom route to L2 acquisition are:

- to what extent do we need to compromise (i.e. reduce the language for teaching purposes?)
- how do we decide what is an appropriate compromise?

Example 2.2 contains two extracts, both of which come from the early stages of coursebooks designed for L2 learners of English at beginning levels. Text A was published in 1938, Text B in 1990. If you compare them you can see just how much the focus of language teaching materials has changed, but nevertheless they both, even the relatively up-to-date sample, remain artificial in terms of the CP and PP maxims, because they are invented by materials writers who are not part of, or party to, the interactions represented in the dialogue, nor to any interactions which might arise in the course of the use of the dialogues in the classroom.

## Activity 14 ▷

> ▶ Find as many instances as you can in the samples of language presented in the two texts in Example 2.2 on page 64 which flout the CP and PP maxims. Analyse the grounds on which the maxims are flouted.
> ▶ To what extent do you think the flouts are justified for the purpose of teaching the language?

## *Cultural aspects of relevance theory*

As we saw above, the notion of relevance is a powerful general tool for understanding the choices people make about the language they use in interactions with others. One central consideration for language teachers, though, is the *cultural* aspect of relevance, precisely because the interface between relevance and politeness is so crucial.[3]

It has been suggested (see Brown and Levinson 1987) that consideration for the 'face' of other people is a universal politeness phenomenon: we normally work on the basis that if we respect others' feelings and sensitivities, they will in turn respect ours. But although the *notion* of face may be universal, the *nature* of face may vary widely from culture to culture. The challenge, therefore, is to learn the specific constraints of face in a culture which is not one's own. Learners bring to their L2 learning contexts their L1 concepts of politeness and respect for face, but these may not necessarily match: behaviour and language which may be polite in the L1 equivalent situation – and therefore relevant and appropriate – may be subject to misunderstanding and misinterpretation in the L2 context, and vice versa.

---

[3] See Thomas 1995, Chapter 6, for an extensive discussion of theories of politeness in the discourse framework.

## Example 2.2

### Text A

|   | Teacher: | I am the teacher. I am Mr (Miss, Mrs) —. What are you? |
|---|---|---|
|   | Class: | We are students. |
|   | Teacher: | Are you a student, Mr A? |
|   | Mr A: | Yes, I am a student. |
| 5 | Teacher: | Are you a student, Miss B? |
|   | Miss B: | Yes, I am. |
|   | Teacher: | Are you in the classroom, Mr C? |
|   | Mr C: | Yes, I am in the classroom. |
|   | Teacher: | Are you a man, a woman, a boy or a girl? |
| 10 | Student: | I am a —. |
|   | Teacher: | What are you, a man, a woman, a boy, or a girl? |
|   | Student: | I am a —. |
|   | Teacher: | Who are you? |
|   | Mr D: | I am Mr D. |
| 15 | Teacher: | How are you, Mr D? |
|   | Mr D: | I am very well, thank you. |
|   | Teacher: | Who are you? |
|   | Miss E: | I am Miss E. |
|   | Teacher: | How are you, Miss E? |
| 20 | Miss E: | I am very well, thank you. |
|   | Teacher: | What are you all? |
|   | Class: | We are all students. |
|   | Teacher: | Are you all men? |
|   | Students: | Yes, we are. |
| 25 |   | No, we are not. |

(Eckersley, C.E. (1938). *Essential English for Foreign Students Book 1*. London: Longman, p. 37)

### Text B

|   | Noriko: | Hi! My name is Noriko Sato. |
|---|---|---|
|   |   | I am from Osaka, Japan. What is your name? |
|   | Chuck: | I'm Chuck O'Brien. |
|   | Noriko: | And where are you from, Chuck? |
| 5 | Chuck: | I'm from Austin, Texas. |
|   | Noriko: | Oh, really? Nice to meet you. |
|   | Chuck: | Nice to meet you, too. |
|   | Noriko: | By the way, what do you do? |
|   | Chuck: | I'm a sales manager. |
| 10 |   | And how about you? |
|   | Noriko: | I'm a dance instructor. |
|   | Chuck: | Hey, Noriko, can I join your class? |

(Richards, Hull and Proctor. (1990). *Interchange. Student's Book 1*. Cambridge: Cambridge University Press, p. 3)

## Activity 15 ▷

▶ Look at the brief scene in Example 2.3. in the light of the cultural aspects of relevance we have been considering. Note that this particular incident is grounded in the culture of late 20th-century Britain.

### Example 2.3

*(Two 6-year-old primary school children are playing football in the school field. One kicks the ball out into the road. The other starts to run down the field to retrieve it. Meanwhile, a passerby – at least two generations older than the boys, and not known personally to them – stops, retrieves the ball and throws it back to the boys.)*

Boy A: *(to Boy B)* Don't worry, he's getting it.
Boy A: *(to passerby)* Cheers, mate.

*(Authors' data)*

▶ Imagine the scene in Example 2.3 taking place in a cultural context that you are familiar with, either your own or another you know well. To what extent do you think A's use of the reference word *he* to refer to the passerby, and his acknowledgement of the passerby's action with the expression *Cheers, mate* would infringe politeness maxims in that culture?

▶ Would you say these two usages infringe politeness maxims in terms of British cultural norms – i.e. could Boy A be considered rude in referring to the passerby as *he*, and why doesn't he say something like *Thank you very much* or even *Thank you very much, sir* in acknowledgement?

▶ If you think politeness maxims have been infringed, how could this, nevertheless, be explained?

Sensitivity to cultural variation in interpreting politeness phenomena is a quality, we would argue, that language teachers – and learners – need to cultivate, not only on the grounds of awareness of 'face' considerations, but also in practical terms. Example 2.4 below contains a sentence which a Japanese (female) learner wanted to include in her CV:

### Example 2.4

I am said to be responsible and hard-working.

*(Authors' data)*

A structure which appeared to the student to indicate an appropriate modesty (*I am said to be ...*) does not fit comfortably into the register required for a CV in English: such a structure could be misconstrued as indicating doubt, and in any case goes against the 'immodest' principle of CV writing, i.e. that for CV purposes in Anglo-American cultures[4] one needs to be as immodest as pragmatically possible about achievements and personal qualities.

---

[4] An unsatisfactory term, but one meant to indicate cultures such as those of Britain, the USA, Australia, New Zealand, where English is the predominant first language.

## 2.3.2 Structures of spoken interaction

### Order in disorder

Our focus in this section moves now to the 'orderliness' of spoken interaction. To illustrate some of the points we want to make, we will use the random snatch of domestic interaction we encountered earlier in Chapter 1 (Example 1. 5). When we look again at the transcription of this spoken interaction, an initial reaction might be to think that this is anything but orderly, and to wonder whether anyone could make any sense of it. There are four participants, all of whom have different 'agendas'; there are at least three different 'conversations' going on simultaneously; and there is constant overlap and interruption.

### Activity 16 ▷

Look again at the transcription of the domestic interaction, reproduced in Example 2.5 on page 67.

▶ Can you identify three different 'conversations'?
▶ What seem to be the individual agendas of the four participants, i.e. why are they talking to each other? what do they want to achieve?

Despite the apparent incoherence of the above sample of 'real-world' speech interaction, with its false starts, interruptions and overlaps, we can see sophisticated mechanisms in operation – mechanisms of taking turns, of relating utterances to each other, and of opening and closing sequences of turns *as the discourse is actually unfolding*. These all contribute to the underlying coherence of the interactions, making them meaningful to the four participants, who do manage to keep track of the various conversations whilst at the same time keeping to their own agendas.

### Four structural features

Let us now take a closer look at four features of spoken interaction which help to give it structure: turn-taking; adjacency pairs; speech events and topic.

**Turn-taking**
Classic conversation analysis claims that, unless they have a good reason for doing so, people do not overlap with each other when they speak, nor do they leave long pauses between turns.[5] Turns normally pass from one speaker to another in a co-ordinated manner; each speaker allows the other(s) adequate opportunity and time to 'hold the floor', which is both socially and personally 'valued'; and there are clearly recognisable cues prompting participants to add their contributions to the evolving interaction. This is true even in the apparently quite disorderly interaction of Example 2.5. People use various devices to signal their intention to take part in, or get out of an interaction – the type of signal depending very much upon the context of the interaction; similarly, they signal that a turn is starting or coming to an end. These signals can be *linguistic* (e.g. syntactic completeness or use of a formulaic expression), *paralinguistic*

[5] See, for instance, Sacks *et al.* 1974.

## Example 2.5

A is mother; B is father; C is houseguest; D is small daughter of A and B.

The notes in the right-hand column indicate some of the common features of naturally occurring speech interaction.

| | | |
|---|---|---|
| 1 | A: | ↑isn't her ↓CHOP done yet |
| 2 | B: | well I don't ↓KNOW have a ↓LOOK at it + |
| 3 | C: | ↓you know we + ↓you know how we[1] + discovered we had |
| 4 | | the same casSETTE player we've got that one TOO [2]+ |
| 5 | | (*phone rings*) [THAT's the one that nearly set us on ↓FIRE |
| 6 | B: | [oh GOD that's the TELe + ↑can you ↓GET it |
| 7 | D: | yes |
| 8 | C: | OURS had a PROBlem + the wire went RIGHT THROUGH |
| 9 | | HERE and it started ↓SMOKing |
| 10 | B: | oh god[3] |
| 11 | C: | so I've got to buy a new ↓WIRE ↑but it's ↓STILL GOing |
| 12 | B: | hang on ↓who's that on the PHONE |
| 13 | D: | can you tell ↓DAD it's JACKie |
| 14 | A: | oh it's ↓JACKie |
| 15 | C: | did you ↓KNOW your tape was reCORDing |
| 16 | B: | ↓yeh |
| 17 | C: | oh that's OK then++ |
| 18 | B: | ↑erm ++++[4] |
| 19 | A: | Liz + when did you put this ↑CHOP ON |
| 20 | B: | oh god I don't know + erm it ↓SHOULD be done what |
| 21 | | ↓TIME is it |
| 22 | C: | quite a long [↓TIME ago[5] |
| 23 | B: | [have a ↓LOOK at it |
| 24 | C: | ↓WOH + ↓CRUNCHing [aWAY + it's a BIG one though |
| 25 | D: | [mum dad + it's ↓COLin |
| 26 | B: | oh god + look it's ↓COLin ↑can you go and TALK to him |
| 27 | C: | it's ↓VEry ↓BIG though + it might [take a bit more to cook |
| 28 | | ↓THROUGH I think |
| 29 | B: | [YEH + hang ON a |
| 30 | | MINute |
| 31 | A: | erm |
| 32 | B: | you'd better go Carolyn |
| 33 | C: | [this might be |
| 34 | A: | [can you + ↑can you put HER + it's ↓REAdy I think + ↑can |
| 35 | | you put the ↓SWEETcorn on |
| 36 | B: | ↓YEH can you send her ↓IN here + ↑can I put the ↓WHAT |
| 37 | C: | do you think it ↓IS ready + I wonder if [it's a very ↓THICK |
| 38 | | chop if it ↓WAS[6] ready |
| 39 | A: | [sweetcorn on[7] |
| 40 | B: | what did she ↑SAY |
| 41 | C: | can [you put the ↓SWEETcorn on she said |
| 42 | A: | [helLO + how are ↑YOU |

Right-hand column notes:

[1] false start

[2] sentence boundaries not clearly marked

[3] filler shows listener participation and appreciation

[4] filler and pause mark a boundary in the conversation

[5] turn 'miscue' – B answers A's question to C

[6] grammatical 'inconsistency' – speaker uses past form, not present

[7] sentence fragment – answer to B's question in l.36

(e.g. direction of intonation, rise or fall in pitch level, change in volume or speed), or *kinesic* (e.g. eye-contact, gesture, body position). Listeners are sensitive to them and respond accordingly, either by taking a turn, or encouraging the speaker to continue. Sometimes people simply indicate that they are attending to what is going on by 'back-channel' responses – words like *yeh, woh, right, mm* and laughter or breath intake and so on (ll. 10, 24, 26, 31 in Example 2.5).

When interaction is not smooth, we seek explanations. For instance, when overlaps and interruptions occur, they might signal meanings such as annoyance or impatience (B's contribution in l. 23, and A's contribution in l. 39 of Example 2.5) or a contextual distraction (B's contribution in l. 6, D's contribution in l. 25). When pauses occur, they often signal meanings such as the importance or significance of the information to come; or they may be interpreted as non-co-operation; or they may mark boundary points in a conversation (ll. 17,18). Although recent research on conversational analysis has questioned the universality of such claims for how conversation works, drawing attention in particular to gender-based differences and preferences in styles of spoken interaction, the basic principle of underlying system and orderliness remains valid.

Spoken interaction as it is often reconstructed or invented in ELT materials can appear strange simply because it is *too* smooth. Example 2.6 on page 69 contains a fairly typical instance of a scripted coursebook 'conversation'[6].

## Activity 17 ▷

> Look at the language of Example 2.6 on page 69. Does it strike you as natural, in terms of the common features of authentic spoken interaction noted in Example 2.5 and discussed above?

### Adjacency pairs

In trying to account for coherence in naturally occurring discourse, the notion of *adjacency pairs*[7] is useful – at least as far as short sequences of utterances are concerned. As the term suggests, utterances often occur in pairs, with the first being followed by a matching response, which is either *preferred* (or expected) or *dispreferred* (or unexpected). We have an example of a preferred response in l. 7 of Example 2.5:

    6 B: (*phone rings*) oh god that's the tele + can you get it
    7 D: yes

---

[6] It is a 'conversation' (the context and purpose of which is not specified) between two 'people' (about whom we know nothing except their names), which forms the basis of a listening activity. The coursebook rubric asks students first to *read* the conversation, i.e. they process what is represented as spoken language through decoding a written script. Then they are asked to *listen* to a (performed) recording of it. The object of the activity is to find differences between what is heard and what is written.

[7] See Schegloff and Sacks 1973.

## Example 2.6

JAN: Hello, Kate. What's the matter?

KATE: Hello, Jan. Oh, dear. I'm going out with Tony tonight, and I haven't got anything to wear.

JAN: What about your blue dress? That's lovely.

5  KATE: That old thing? No. It makes me look like a sack of potatoes.

JAN: Well, why don't you borrow something of mine?

KATE: Could I really?

JAN: Yes, of course. Would you like to?

10  KATE: Well, I'd love to. If you really don't mind.

JAN: What about that green silk thing?

KATE: Green silk?

JAN: Yes, you know. The dress I wore to Andy's birthday party.

15  KATE: Oh, yes. I remember.

JAN: You'd look great in that.

KATE: Oooh!

JAN: And I'll lend you my new shoes to go with it.

KATE: My feet are bigger than yours.

20  JAN: I don't think they are, Kate. Anyway, try the shoes and see. What about a jacket? Have you got one that will do?

KATE: Not really.

JAN: Well, have one of mine.

25  KATE: Oh, Jan. I feel bad, borrowing all your things.

JAN: That's all right. What are friends for? I'll borrow something of yours one of

30    these days.

KATE: Well, thanks a million, Jan. I'd better get moving. Tony's coming in half an hour.

35  JAN: OK. Wait a second. I'll go and get the dress. Shall I iron it for you?

40  KATE: Oh, Jan.

*(Swan, M. and C. Walter. (1985).* Cambridge English Course 2, Student's Book. *Cambridge: Cambridge University Press, p. 24)*

B's *request* is followed by D's *acceptance*, i.e. the preferred response. Had D refused, the response would have been dispreferred. In contrast, the exchange in ll. 15–16 of Example 2.5 contains an example of a dispreferred response:

15 C: did you KNOW your tape was reCORDing
16 B: yeh

C *warns* B about a possibly negative situation she thinks he is unaware of. Her good intention falls flat when he *fails to thank* her for it.

## Activity 18

▶ Below are some common first parts of adjacency pairs. What would be the preferred or dispreferred response in each case? You might find it interesting to look for examples of these six types of adjacency pairs in the interactions in Examples 2.5 and 2.6.

| | preferred response? | dispreferred response? |
|---|---|---|
| question offer accusation greeting apology assessment | | |

▶ What do you suppose the response to the greeting in Example 2.5, l. 42 might have been?

**Follow-up:** How useful do you think the 'adjacency pairs' notion is in language teaching? Can you suggest ways in which it could be brought to the notice of learners?

### Speech events
Another notion which helps us understand structure and coherence over longer stretches of discourse is *speech event*. This term is sometimes used to refer to a sequence of utterances recognisable as a stock routine in a given context or setting, where the pattern of exchanges is reasonably predictable. What scholars of discourse are interested in is how we mark the boundaries of events and sub-units of events: how do we know that one has closed and the next opened? In formal settings, such boundaries are often more clearly marked than in casual conversation.

## Activity 19 ▷

Below are some common settings for speech events. Can you suggest openings and closings which are often used to mark the boundaries of these events?

|  | opening? | closing? |
|---|---|---|
| **a lesson** | | |
| **a service encounter** | | |
| **a telephone enquiry** | | |
| **a GP/patient consultation** | | |
| **a TV newscast** | | |
| **a job interview** | | |

There are certainly some stock expressions which people have recourse to in such situations, and they are a useful basis for language teaching materials using a situational or context-based syllabus ('At the post office', 'At the check-in desk' and so on). But these speech events in real life quite frequently bear little resemblance to how they are imagined and presented in textbooks, as the work of McCarthy and Carter (1994) and Carter and McCarthy (1997) on spoken discourse extensively demonstrates. Example 2.7 on pages 72–73 contains two versions of the 'Ordering a meal' speech event: Text A is a textbook model, while Text B is a transcription of an authentic interaction.

## Activity 20 ▷

▶ Compare the language choices made in Text A and Text B in Example 2.7 at the following points:
  a) the opening of the ordering sequence (A/1 and B/16–17)
  b) the closing of the ordering sequence (A/12 and B/46)
  c) the ordering of the food (A/2, 5 and B/21–22, 29, 33)
  d) the ordering of the drinks (A/10–11 and B/17–20, 37–45)
▶ Compare who initiates the various exchanges in (a)–(d) above – the waiter/waitress or the customer.
▶ Would you say the two texts differ in degree of formality? What linguistic pointers can help us to answer this question?

## Example 2.7

### Text A

---

5  **CONVERSATION:** Ordering a meal

Listen and practice.

| 1 | Waiter: | May I take your order, please? |
|---|---------|-------------------------------|
| 2 | Customer: | Yes. I'd like a hamburger and a large |
| 3 | | order of french fries, please. |
| 4 | Waiter: | All right. And would you like a salad? |
| 5 | Customer: | Yes, I'll have a small salad. |
| 6 | Waiter: | OK. What kind of dressing would you |
| 7 | | like: We have Thousand Island, Italian, |
| 8 | | and French. |
| 9 | Customer: | Italian. |
| 10 | Waiter: | And would you like anything to drink? |
| 11 | Customer: | I'd like a large Coke, please. |
| 12 | Waiter: | Thank you. |

---

(Richards *et al.* (1990). *Interchange 1*, Cambridge: Cambridge University Press, p. 84)

### Text B

Speakers and setting

<S 01>   customer: female (24)
<S 02>   customer: female (24)
<S 03>   female waitress: (20s)

Two old schoolfriends from South Wales meet up to have lunch in London, in a very informal restaurant, the type that serves hamburgers and other fast-food. At the start of the extract, they are looking at the menu. While they are discussing what to choose, the waitress comes up and stands silently, waiting for them to order.

| 1 | <S 01> | I'm gonna have er ... an Old Timer with cheese, I am |
|---|--------|------|
| 2 | <S 02> | What's that? |
| 3 | <S 01> | The Old Timer burger, but I'm gonna have cheese with it. |
| 4 | <S 02> | Oh right, I'm gonna have, I think I'm gonna have a |
| 5 | | veggy one with barbecue sauce on it |
| 6 | <S 01> | Mm, are you gonna have a starter, what you gonna have? |
| 7 | <S 02> | Yeah ... I'm trying not |
| 8 | | to have nachos [5 secs] |
| 9 | <S 02> | I'm either gonna have nachos, buffalo wings or potato |
| 10 | | skins |
| 11 | [11 secs] | |
| 12 | <S 01> | I'm gonna have the deep fried mushrooms, you like |

| | | |
|---|---|---|
| 13 | | mushrooms, don't you? |
| 14 | [3 secs] | |
| 15 | <S 02> | I'm gonna have to have nachos. I'm addicted to it ... |
| 16 | | I want, they don't do cider, and I don't want a beer. [< S03> Hi] |
| 17 | | don't do cider, do you? |
| 18 | <S 03> | Sorry |
| 19 | <S 02> | Don't do cider |
| 20 | <S 03> | No |
| 21 | <S 01> | I'll have the deep fried mushrooms with er, an Old |
| 22 | | Timer burger, can I have cheese on it? |
| 23 | <S 03> | What cheese? |
| 24 | <S 01> | What's the difference? |
| 25 | <S 03> | Swiss. Monterrey Jack is an American cheese [inaudible] how would |
| 26 | | you like it cooked? |
| 27 | <S 01> | Erm well done |
| 28 | <S 03> | Yes |
| 29 | <S 02> | Can I have the, er, nachos and erm, I was wondering |
| 30 | | whether to have a veggy burger or the normal burger, erm, are the |
| 31 | | veggy burgers nice? |
| 32 | <S 03> | Yeah they're okay, they're not made on the premises though |
| 33 | <S 02> | All right I'll have, er, I'll have a normal burger then, with |
| 34 | | barbecued beans |
| 35 | <S 03> | How would you like it cooked? |
| 36 | <S 02> | Erm medium |
| 37 | <S 03> | And drinks |
| 38 | <S 02> | Er, d'you have, er have you got pineapple juice? |
| 39 | <S 03> | [nods her head] |
| 40 | <S 02> | Can I have pineapple juice mixed with white wine? |
| 41 | | Mixed together |
| 42 | <S 03> | White wine |
| 43 | <S 02> | Yeah, in a big glass with loads of ice |
| 44 | <S 01> | [laughs] Erm can I have, erm, mineral water, sparkling one? |
| 45 | <S 03> | Okay |
| 46 | <S 01> | Thanks |

*(Carter, R. and M. McCarthy. (1997). Exploring Spoken English,*
*Cambridge: Cambridge University Press, pp. 97–99)*

### Topic

Casual conversation is much more fluid and flexible than the exchanges expected in 'standard' speech events such as those in Activity 19 above, and in casual conversation it is often *topic,* or what is being talked about, that binds larger stretches of discourse together. Here discourse analysts are not only interested in the very notion of topic, but also in how people start, develop and close topics; how they move on to new ones; and how they keep track of topics when several are going on at the same time – as in Example 2.5.[8]

Example 2.8 on page 75 illustrates how participants develop, embroider, tack digressions onto, and eventually move away from the nominated topic (in this case, *reincarnation*) into a new area (*superstition*). The extract in Example 2.8 is from a radio chatshow – a rather specialised form of speech event in that, though unrehearsed, it is not casual conversation: participants have been invited to speak, in order to entertain an unseen audience, and they are aware that their interactions are being recorded for public consumption. The extract contains many smaller sub-events like *the joke* (ll. 13–16) and *the personal anecdote* (ll. 27–31), which are 'embedded' in the larger 'chatshow' speech event. What is relevant in terms of topic is how people make conscious efforts to link their contributions to the previous one (e.g. D's remark in ll. 8–9) and how the chair of the proceedings sees his responsibility to keep people on topic (e.g. A's interruption in ll. 38–40 to curtail B's digression in ll. 32–36).

### Activity 21 ▷

> ▶ How many topics can you identify in the data in Example 2.5 and how many in Example 2.8?
> ▶ Could you say that either of the examples was more coherent than the other in terms of topic? If so, why?

## 2.3.3 Meanings

We move now to looking at the relationship between form, function and meaning. This is a central concern of *pragmatic* and *speech act theory*[9] which seeks to explain how users of language do things with words, and get other people to do things. It also helps us to understand *how* we are able to infer the function of an utterance from the form it has in its particular context – or in other words, how we interpret meanings in interaction.

[8] See Brown and Yule 1983, Chapter 3, and McCarthy 1991, Chapter 5, for fuller discussions on this.
[9] See Grundy 1995, Chapter 5; Thomas 1995, Chapter 2; and Schiffrin 1994, Chapter 3, for extensive discussions of pragmatic and speech act theory.

## Example 2.8

The topic of discussion at the start of this extract from a radio chatshow is *reincarnation*, one of the guest participants having recently published a book on this subject.

Characters as follows: A is chair of the discussion, B (a well-known racehorse breeder), C and D are invited guest participants.

The notes in the right-hand column indicate common features of naturally occurring speech interaction.

| | | | |
|---|---|---|---|
| 1 | A: | ↓Now I want I want[1] to JUST bring in Alex Bird who's | [1]repetition (to assert claim to a turn) |
| 2 | | sitting ↓QUITE quietly at the end of the table ↑INterested in | |
| 3 | | all this Alex | |
| 4 | B: | This is ↑QUITE beyond me I'm rather overAWED I mean | [2]turn consists of sequence of short chunks not connected with logical markers |
| 5 | | everybody's on a DIFferent ↑LEVel to me I I feel VEry | |
| 6 | | ↓inferior[2] | |
| 7 | C: | Only 'cos we've read the ↓BOOK however [(laughter) | |
| 8 | D: | [↑Could I could I[1] | |
| 9 | | bring it back to + to ↓MY level I mean[3] I think I've been | [3]filler (*I mean*) |
| 10 | | corRUPted by the ↑WHOLE subject because <u>from the age of</u> | |
| 11 | | er + <u>six or seven I</u> was given[4] Fulsham's or Faversham's | |
| 12 | | ↑FUN book + and the joke that stuck in my ↓MIND + was + | [4]false start – speaker changes structure in mid-'sentence' (from *from the age of 6 or 7 I have ...* to *at the age of 6 or 7 I was given ...*) |
| 13 | | ↑GIRL saying to professor + is it right for me professor to be | |
| 14 | | sitting on your KNEE + while you talk to me about | |
| 15 | | reinreincarnation and he said well HEAvens above girl we | |
| 16 | | only live ↓ONCE (laughter) and er er [after that I've ↑NEver | |
| 17 | | been able to take it quite so ↓SERiously | |
| 18 | A: | [well I ↑WONder you | |
| 19 | | see[3] whether you have you have such an such an intimate | |
| 20 | | knowledge of of ↓HORses and the way their minds work at | |
| 21 | | least so it ↑SEEMS that perhaps you were a ↑HORSE at some | |
| 22 | | time or another do you ↑think | |
| 23 | B: | Maybe maybe ↓YES | |
| 24 | C: | Do you have a fondness for ↑OATS or + anything | [5]laughter indicates listener participation and encouragement |
| 25 | | <u>(laughter)</u>[5] | |
| 26 | B: | No not really ↓NO I'm a NAture cure eater really anyway the | |
| 27 | | ↓FACT is that er + that I + don't know ↑<u>anything aBOUT</u> | |
| 28 | | <u>↑horses ACTually at one time I had</u> + TWELVE horses of | [6]'sentence' boundaries not clearly marked |
| 29 | | my OWN[6] + and when my TRAINer took me round to SEE | |
| 30 | | them I would pre preTEND I ↓KNEW which horse it ↓WAS | |
| 31 | | and er you know I mean it's quite unbe↓<u>LIEVable</u>[7] and er | [7]imprecise reference – what does *it* refer to? what is *unbelievable*? |
| 32 | | ↑ACTually I think the only HORSE <u>that I've ever rode in my</u> | |
| 33 | | ↓<u>LIFE</u>[8] was er + my father's CART horse he was a ↓COAL | [8]grammatical inconsistency (*rode* not past participle to complete present perfect structure) |
| 34 | | merchant + as well as a ↓BOOKmaker it + ↓SEMI semi legal | |
| 35 | | bookmaker you know in the DAYS when it was ready money | |
| 36 | | BETting and er + police turned a blind eye to everything[9] | |
| 37 | | ↑[and er | [9]non-premeditated change of topic – the aside (about speaker's father) turns into new topic |
| 38 | A: | [but when ↑in ↑IN your activities have you ever been + er + | |
| 39 | | GOVerned by er + the the movement of the ↑MOON or the | |
| 40 | | ↑STARS or by + super↑STItion in any way at ↑all | |
| 41 | B: | Not in the [↓SLIGHTest but | |
| 42 | D: | [well you do ↓SAY in your book you think you | |
| 43 | | have a guardian angel you're speaking ↓FLIPpantly there are | |
| 44 | | you | |
| 45 | B: | Well ↓YES [yes | |
| 46 | D: | [Yes I ↓see | |
| 47 | | ... (*another extended turn by B on topic of superstition*) ... | |
| 48 | A: | ↑Well now ↓let's give Joe Fisher another WORD ... | |

*(Extract from Mid-week Choice, BBC Radio 4)*

## Forms and functions

Teachers of language will be familiar with the fact that the *forms* which have to be taught as basic tools for communication cannot be exclusively linked with specific *functions* people need language for. On the one hand, we can use one form to carry out a range of functions (see the first part of Activity 22 which explores the versatility of the question form). On the other, we can choose from a whole range of forms, or *exponents*, to perform one function. Think, for instance, of all the exponents we might use to perform the function of offering our services (you can probably add many more to the list below):

- Might one be of asssistance?
- Perhaps I could help you?
- Can I help you?
- Want any help?
- You in trouble?
- You OK?
- Let me do it.
- I'll do it.
- If you need us, just give a ring.
- We can solve all your problems.

Awareness of the lack of straightforward correlation between form and function might lead us to question the usefulness of materials which, at one extreme, simply provide lists of functional exponents without any hints about appropriacy of use or reasons for choice, or, at the other, fail to make clear that a range of possibilities exists. The art is knowing which particular exponent to choose to fit the particular discourse situation, and being able as a participant to interpret the *force* of that choice.

Take, for instance, the opening two turns in Example 2.5:

1  A: ↑isn't her ↓CHOP done yet
2  B: well I don't ↓KNOW have a ↓LOOK at it

When A says 'Isn't her chop done yet' she is not asking for information, although she chooses a question *form*. Rather, she is *expressing surprise or irritation* that the chop is taking so long to cook, and even implying that B is to blame for this state of affairs because he should have put it on earlier – or at least that would be one interpretation, in view of B's somewhat petulant response. We should note here, once more, that much of this meaning is conveyed not only through linguistic features (structure and lexis), but equally important, through paralinguistic features (intonation, stress, pitch, tone of voice and so on). This underlines for teachers the limitations of listening materials (and tapescripts) which make no effort to draw attention to the huge importance of such features in conveying meaning in spoken language.

Activity 22, based around the data of the domestic interchanges in Example 2.5, invites you to explore the complexity of the relationship between form and function.

**Activity 22** ▷

---

▶ Look at all the question forms which occur in Example 2.5 on page 67 and suggest what function they might be being used for in this interaction:

| | |
|---|---|
| l. 1 | l. 26 |
| l. 6 | ll. 34/35 |
| l. 12 | l. 36a |
| l. 13 | l. 36b |
| l. 15 | l. 37 |
| l. 19 | l. 40 |
| ll. 20/21 | l. 42 |

▶ Look at all the instances of the modal verb *can* (ll. 6, 13, 26, 34, 36a, 36b). Note how many different functions this exponent is used for.

▶ Finally, look at all the places where the speakers are requesting someone to do something, and compare the exponents for this function.

| | |
|---|---|
| l. 2 | l. 26 |
| l. 6 | l. 29 |
| l. 12 | l. 32 |
| l. 13 | l. 34 |
| l. 23 | l. 36 |
| l. 25 | l. 40 |

---

## Surface meaning and underlying meaning

Connected with the lack of direct and predictable correlation between form and function is the fact that people often either do not mean what they say, or mean a lot more than they actually say. In other words, the *surface* meaning (sometimes called *sentence meaning*, or *sense*) of an utterance may not be identical with its *underlying* meaning (*speaker's meaning* or *force*). This is because of the *intention* interface between the various levels of meaning.

Let us look again at the interaction in Example 2.3.

> Boy A: (*to Boy B*)  Don't worry, he's getting it.
> Boy A: (*to passerby*)  Cheers, mate.

When A says to B 'Don't worry' the surface meaning is an *instruction* not to worry; and the surface meaning of 'he's getting it' is *a statement* describing what the passerby is doing. However, at the underlying level of meaning, A is *advising* B not to bother running to the end of the field to get the ball, and *giving an explanation* why he should not do so. The force of the utterance is that A *stops B from carrying out the action* he was about to perform.

An ability to distinguish between these different levels of meaning in their contexts is vital in our comprehension of messages. It makes us able to understand as coherent exchanges which are superficially incoherent[10]. It enables us to know, for example, when someone asks *'Have you got some money?'* whether they are concerned for our wellbeing in a potential emergency, or whether they are reminding us not to forget to take some money, or whether they are asking for a loan, or whether they are offering to lend us money.

This ability to go beyond surface meaning in both spoken and written contexts is fundamental to the development of proficiency in a language. It depends upon our capacity to draw inferences from implied meaning and contextual clues. Example 2.9 contains an instance, in the written mode, of how we often need agile inferencing skills to decipher meaning. It is part of an e-mail message received by one of the present authors, notifying potential British participants about details of a linguistics workshop to be held in Holland. The apparent contradictions in the message caused initial perplexity, and it took some time before contextual inferences about academic conferences and workshops made the message coherent.

## Example 2.9

The format of the workshop allows for a restricted number of 20 non-speaking participants who are expected to participate actively in the discussions. Participance will be accepted on a 'FIRST COME, FIRST GO' basis.

*(Authors' data)*

## Activity 23 ▷

▶ There are at least two places in Example 2.9 above where the surface meaning of the language used is at odds with the underlying meaning. Can you identify them?
▶ Can you use your general background knowledge of academic conferences and your knowledge about the specific circumstances of the workshop mentioned in Example 2.9 to make the message coherent?

## 2.3.4  Shared knowledge

The ways in which we bind ideas together with language are enormously complex, as are the ways in which we infer or mentally 'unwrap' meanings from their bindings. How we do this depends to a great extent on the degree to which knowledge of background, context and textual conventions is shared between participants in the discourse. Being party to knowledge shared with people we are talking or writing to – or conversely, not having knowledge in common with them – has a significant effect upon the language choices we make. Knowing when we have to clarify, and to what extent, is a crucial element of discourse competence.

---

[10] See Widdowson's classic "That's the telephone"/"I'm in the bath" example (1978:29) where sentence meaning is several moves behind speaker's meaning –"You'd better answer it because I can't".

## *The need to refer to things*

One important means we have of making what we say or write meaningful and coherent is using various kinds of linguistic referring devices to tie our ideas together. We keep the listener or reader on track by referring back to things we have already mentioned and forward to things we are going to mention, or by referring to aspects of the immediate context of the interaction. Use of these kinds of referring devices – words like *here* and *now*, *this* and *that*, or *come* and *go* – is technically known as *deixis*[11]. But, although such deictic expressions are very convenient shortcuts for long-winded specifications of details, we always have to ensure that knowledge about the context is sufficiently clear to all participants.

Activity 24 focuses on three different means for referring to things in discourse: *deixis*, *shared assumptions* and *inference* (deducing meaning from linguistic clues) and highlights the importance of shared cultural knowledge and assumptions in our understanding of discourse.

[11] See Extract 7 in Chapter 3, page 127, and footnote 3 on page 105 for further details on *deixis*.

## Activity 24 ▷

Look back at the charity appeal in Chapter 1, Example 1.20 on page 46. (As we noted in the commmentary to Activity 7 Chapter 1 on page 44, the organisation actually fails to specify its name – the British Union Against Vivisection – which in itself points to a huge assumption about shared knowledge.)

▶ Without reading the text, but simply looking at the layout of the appeal and using your knowledge of charity appeals in general, what can you predict about the *purpose* of this discourse?
▶ What can you predict about the intended *audience*?
▶ What can you predict about the sort of *language* which is likely to be used?

Below is the opening section of the appeal. It contains examples of three different channels of reference: *deixis* (i.e. using the immediate context of the discourse to take linguistic shortcuts); *shared assumptions* (i.e. relying on the audience's prior knowledge and experience of the topic) and *inference* (i.e. assuming that the audience will deduce unspecified meanings from linguistic clues).

HELP *US*[1] TO HELP LABORATORY *ANIMALS*[2]

Millions of animals die every year in painful and unnecessary experiments. *We*[3] are working hard to stop *this suffering*[4] – and at last our campaigns are getting through – but we can only continue *this vital work*[5] with the help of people who give their support.

▶ Use the headings below to note how you understand the meanings of the highlighted and numbered items in the text above. Think about what channel of reference helped you to understand them – a deictic reference? a shared assumption? an inference?

| Item in text | Channel of reference | Meaning(s) | What helps us to infer the meaning |
|---|---|---|---|
|  |  |  |  |

► Who are 'us' (1) and 'we' (3)?
► What are 'laboratory animals' (2)? Why do they need help? What sort of help?
► Which 'suffering' is meant (4)?
► Which 'work' and why is it 'vital' (5)?

**Follow-up:** Imagine the charity appeal in Example 1.20 (page 46) appeared as a reading text in a coursebook you were using with your learners. Think of some activities you could use with this text to help learners bridge any possible shared knowledge gaps.

## How explicit do we need to be?

One aspect of the 'shared knowledge' dimension of discourse which is important for language teachers is the degree of explicitness required in writing, compared with that required in speech. This takes us back to the centrality of the 'relevance' maxim: often, in speech, referring expressions can be left less explicit than in writing, simply because the context of the spoken interaction will make meanings clear without explicit reference. Also, listeners are actually part of the context of the interaction and can always ask for clarification if necessary. Writers, in contrast, have to anticipate problems of reference for readers, decide which knowledge can be assumed to be shared and which needs to be made explicit, and ensure that the referent of any referring expression is clear. Compare the examples of spoken and written interaction in Activity 25 below to see how we can often afford to be less explicit in speech than in writing.

## Activity 25 ▷

Look at the highlighted referring expressions (a–z) in the two examples of discourse below (Text A is spoken discourse, part of Example 2.5 and Text B is written discourse, part of Example 1.7 in Chapter 1). In the table below the examples, say what each referring expression refers to (i.e. what its referent is) and whether the referent is made explicit by the text itself, or whether it is implied from the context and shared knowledge of the participants.

Text A

C: (a)**you** know (b)**we** + you know how we discovered we had the same cassette player + (c)**we've** got (d)**that** one too + *(Phone rings)* (e)**that's** the one that nearly set us on fire

B: oh god (f)**that's** the tele + can you get (g)**it**

D: Yes

C: (h)**ours** had a problem + (i)**the wire** went right through (j)**here** and (k)**it** started smoking

B: oh god

C: so I've got to buy a new wire but (l)**it's** still going

Text B

On (m)**the** premise that democratic government is founded *inter alia* on (n)**the** accountability of public bodies and (o)**their** officials, as well as on (p)**the** popular participation and collective decision-making by (q)**the** governed at all levels of government, there is merit in (r)**the** proposition that (s)**it** is improper to curb open debate, especially in matters (t)**which** are of public interest. The European Court of Human Rights (the Court)[1] has endorsed the importance of (u)**this** principle of open debate ... in (v)**its** decisions relating to Article 10 of the European Convention on Human Rights (the Convention)[3] (w)**which** guarantees freedom of expression. (x)**The Court** has been particularly unyielding in upholding (y)**this** freedom when (z)**it** rejects requests to support restrictions on critical comment about public officials ...

| A | Referent? | Referent explicit? | Referent implicit? |
|---|---|---|---|
| a | | | |
| b | | | |
| c | | | |
| d | | | |
| e | | | |
| f | | | |
| g | | | |
| h | | | |
| i | | | |
| j | | | |
| k | | | |
| l | | | |

| B | Referent? | Referent explicit? | Referent implicit? |
|---|---|---|---|
| m | | | |
| n | | | |
| o | | | |
| p | | | |
| q | | | |
| r | | | |
| s | | | |
| t | | | |
| u | | | |
| v | | | |
| w | | | |
| x | | | |
| y | | | |
| z | | | |

**Follow-up:** If you look back at the complete version of Example 1.7 in Chapter 1, you will see that the writer, in referring to The European Court of Human Rights and The European Convention on Human Rights has used two devices often found in academic writing of this kind to make sure that readers are able to understand his references to these two entities. What are these two devices?

It is particularly important for teachers of writing to help learners make sure that reference expressions are clearly related to identifiable referents, and that any entities (particularly culture-specific ones) likely to be unfamiliar to readers are adequately explained. Example 2.10 is an extract from an EL2 learner's written text about arranged marriages in Japan, and illustrates typical problems posed both by the 'shared knowledge' dimension of discourse and the intricacies of the reference system – including appropriate use of determiners – in English.

## Example 2.10

In arranged marriage, parents find a consort instead of the person oneself. In such a case that people eager to get married but there is no lover, people go to agent of arranged marriages. Some people are forced to see each other and they have to marry him/her. I agree with an arranged marriage is good in thinking that seeing each other with a view to marriage. Arranged seeing each other is a good occasion to meet new person. Recently group meetings are on increase. Some of group meetings have a purpose to get his wife or her husband. However other are also just entertainments like dance parties. I approve that if they can make good relationship, there is no problem in an arranged marriage.

*(Authors' data)*

## Activity 26 ▷

> Imagine you had to give feedback to the learner who wrote the text in Example 2.10 above. Which items would you identify as needing further clarification:
>
> (i)  because of unclear reference
> (ii) because of failure to take lack of shared knowledge into account?

Although, generally speaking, writers need to make things clear for readers, and readers expect that they will do so, there are times when *depending upon* assumptions about shared knowledge is the most effective way to make a point. This kind of flouting of co-operative principles (see 2.3.1 above) is often the basis of irony and sarcasm, as in the two letters in Example 2.11.

## Activity 27 ▷

> Think about the two letters in Example 2.11 from the perspective of a teacher of EL2 reading skills.
>   How could the teacher help learners understand the force of the message in each case? What aspects of shared 'knowledge of the world' and knowledge of textual conventions could be highlighted?

## Example 2.11

A

### Wonder pills

Sir, My wife has been prescribed pills. According to the accompanying leaflet, possible side-effects are: sickness, diarrhoea, indigestion, loss of appetite, belching, vertigo, abdominal cramps, dizziness, stomach ulcers, bleeding from intestine or bloody diarrhoea, ulcerative colitis, sore mouth and tongue, constipation, back pains, inflammation of pancreas, mouth ulcers, skin rashes, hair loss, sensitivity to sunlight, drowsiness, tiredness, impaired hearing, difficulty with sleeping, seizures, irritability, anxiety, depression, mood changes, tremor, memory disturbances, disorientation, changes in vision, ringing in ears, bad dreams, taste alteration, allergic reactions, swelling due to water retention, palpitations, impotence or tightness of the chest.
    Should she take them?

Yours faithfully,

*(Newspaper letter: source unknown)*

B

### Happy ending

*From M. Tudball*

Please convey my thanks to Lucy Pinney for telling me the ending of *The English Patient* (Diary, April 12). I had planned to see it soon, and she has saved me the time and expense.
    I was also planning to see *The Mousetrap* one day. If she could just let me know who the murderer is I can avoid a trip to London.
Yours sincerely,
M. TUDBALL,
6 Fair Field, Romsey, Hampshire.

*(Newspaper letter:* The Times Magazine 26.4.97)

We saw in Activity 25 that as speakers, we can often afford to be rather lax about explicit referencing. Sometimes, however, we may assume too much of our listeners, as the following example shows. One of the present authors (A) was engaged in a long-distance telephone conversation with a former student (B), who was asking A to supply a testimonial by completing certain forms. A wanted to make sure that B knew the address of the English Language Centre to which she (B) should send the relevant papers. This was how the conversation went at that point:

## Example 2.12

    A: Do you have the address?
    B: Yes, my address is Room 2055, Yin Yam Building ...
                *(Authors' data)*

Here, A's failure to be precise about which address was meant (as well as possible misinterpretation of article usage on B's part) led to the misunderstanding.
    Nevertheless, it is still the case that a common feature of spoken discourse is precisely the kind of lack of explicitness that we see in Example 2.12. Speakers do not need to be precise because, as we have noted, they use paralinguistic

devices of intonation, pitch, silence and gesture to convey meaning. They also often rely to a far greater extent than writers can afford to on the deft inferencing skills of their audience (partly because of the shared immediate context). We can see this in Example 2.13 below (part of the radio chatshow conversation which appeared previously as Example 2.8).

**Example 2.13**

> anyway the ↓FACT is that er + that I + don't know ↑anything aBOUT ↓horses ACTually at one time I had + TWELVE horses of my OWN + and when my[1] TRAINer took me round to SEE them I would pre preTEND I KNEW which horse it[2] ↓WAS and er you know I mean it[3]'s quite unbe↓LIEVable and er ↑ACTually I think the only HORSE that I've ever rode in my ↓LIFE was er + my father's CART horse he[4] was a ↓COAL merchant + as well as a ↓BOOKmaker

**Activity 28** ▷

> Imagine that an EL2 teacher is contemplating using Example 2.13 above as possible 'authentic' listening material:
>
> ▶ What inferences would have to be made by students before they could understand the four numbered referring expressions?
> ▶ Which items would require culture-specific knowledge in order to be understood?
> ▶ Would the fact that the speaker speaks with a fairly broad northern English accent bring anything to bear upon our appreciation of the anecdote? What problems might this pose for the EL2 learner?

## 2.3.5 Organisation

We saw above, in 2.3.2, that there is order and structure in spoken discourse, even though it may appear superficially chaotic and undisciplined. The organisational patterns which operate at varying levels of the discourse hierarchy, in both spoken and written discourse, and from smaller units (or micro-levels) to larger ones (or macro-levels), make significant contributions to the overall coherence of discourse.

Appropriate, or expected, organisation of information helps us to understand messages, whilst inappropriate, or unexpected organisation may result in misunderstanding, or at least difficulty of understanding.

### Some micro-level features

Four micro-level features are considered here: organising information at sentence level; providing 'signposts' to make logical connections between ideas clear; providing 'signposts' to divide a text into 'chunks' of information; and drawing attention to themes and meanings by choice of vocabulary.

**Sentence-level organisation**
The letter in Example 2.14 illustrates how misinterpretation can arise from inappropriate organisation of information at the relatively low level of the sentence.

**Example 2.14**

> **In gear for Marathon**
> Sir, Are there really 25 women planning to walk Sunday's London Marathon, as your Diary reports (April 10), "wearing nothing but a Wonderbra above the waist"? Or would it be fairer to say that they will be wearing nothing above the waist but a Wonderbra?
>
> Yours faithfully,

(*Newspaper letter:* The Times *10.4.97*)

**Signposting logical organisation**
In addition to putting the right bits of information in their right place in a sentence, we also use all kinds of *signposts* to help listeners and readers know where they are in the discourse. Logical 'markers' are one type of signpost which underscore the logical organisation of what we are saying or writing. They are more obvious and formalised in certain types of text (academic genres, for instance) than in others (casual conversation or tabloid newspaper reports, for instance). It is evident, too, that we tend to use a more restricted range of such markers in spoken language than in written language (limiting our choice of connective expressions in speech to 'core' words like *so, but, and, because* and *or*) though this depends, as always, on the context of the discourse.

## Activity 29 ▷

> Choose one (or more) of the logical markers mentioned above – *so, but, and, because, or* – and make a list of other words or expressions which mark the same logical relation(s), but which you would expect to find more frequently used in formal written contexts than spoken.

Not only do we tend to use a more restricted range of exponents to mark connections and link ideas together in speech than in writing, but also such connections are often implicit in spoken language. If you look at the spoken text (Text A) in Activity 30 on page 86, for example, you will see that there are no explicit markers (at the points in the text marked 1–3) to show us the relations between the four ideas. By contrast, the author of the written text (Text B) has littered it with language devices – both lexical and graphic – to ensure that we are clear about the connections between ideas (at points 4–9 in the text).

## Activity 30 ▷

Look at spoken extract A and written extract B below. Say what the logical connection is between the parts of the texts at the points indicated (1–9) e.g. *result, contrast, reason*. Then say how this relation is marked by completing the table below the two texts. A1 has been done as an example.

**Text A**
This is QUITE beyond me[1] I'm rather overAWED[2]
I mean everybody's on a DIFferent ↑LEVel to me[3] I I feel VEry ↓inferior
*(from Example 2.8, p.75, ll. 4–6)*

**Text B**
*(The writer has been discussing objective features of alienation at work)*
... These can be considered the objective features of alienation. Much discussion, however,[4] extends to considering how far the objective features of alienation result in subjective feelings of deprivation or estrangement:[5] a sense of a lack of wholeness,[6] a sense of frustration or[7] of a loss of humanity. Thus[8] many people come to feel that their lives and work are controlled by material things rather than[9] by processes which are ultimately of human origin.
*(Adapted from Worsley, P. (Ed.) 1977.* Introducing Sociology. *Harmondsworth: Penguin:288, 289)*

| Point in text | What is the relation? | How is the relation marked? | | |
|---|---|---|---|---|
| | e.g. result, example, contrast, alternative | not explicitly marked | marked with a punctuation symbol | marked with an explicit logical marker |
| A1 | result | ✓ | | |
| A2 | | | | |
| A3 | | | | |
| B4 | | | | |
| B5 | | | | |
| B6 | | | | |
| B7 | | | | |
| B8 | | | | |
| B9 | | | | |

## Signposting 'chunks' of discourse

Other kinds of signposts indicate beginnings and endings of 'chunks' or sections of text. Again, it is evident that the context of the discourse will determine how clear such signposts are, and again it is often the case that signposting is more consciously considered in written contexts than spoken ones, though not necessarily. In spoken contexts where the interaction needs to be kept 'on course' – job interviews, or hearings in a law court, for instance – signposting is expected to be clear and prominent. The quasi-casual conversation of the radio chatshow in Example 2.8 contains two clear signposts – in line 1 (↓*Now I want I want to JUST bring in Alex Bird ...* ) and line 48 (↑*Well now* ↓*let's give Joe Fisher another WORD...*) – which signal a turn being offered to participants, and new chunks of the interaction opening.

Example 2.15 on page 88 contains two extracts, both from spoken language. Both texts have a similar purpose (to explain what is meant by certain terminology) and audience (learners); both occur in an 'academic' context; and both belong to the same genre (formal academic lecture). However, Text A is authentic spoken language in a formal academic context, and Text B is a tapescript of simulated spoken language in a formal academic context for teaching purposes. In the attempt to draw learners' attention to signposting devices, the simulated speech (Text B) ends up resembling written rather than spoken language. Because much of the inbuilt redundancy of natural speech is lost, and because speakers have different means of signposting than writers, written language read aloud is often much harder to process aurally than graphically. This is frequently the case with speeches or papers or presentations which are pre-prepared in written form and then delivered orally.[12]

## Activity 31

> ▶ Identify different kinds of 'signposts' in the two texts in Example 2.15 on page 88.
> ▶ Identify features of the organisation of Text A which enable us to recognise it as spoken discourse.
> ▶ Identify features of the organisation of Text B which make it more like written than spoken discourse.

### Lexical choice

Another micro-level feature of organisational coherence within texts is *lexical choice*. Ideas are interwoven and entwined with each other through the language user's choice of words: meanings and associations support and parallel each other, or they conflict with and oppose each other. Text B in Activity 30 on page 86 contains illustrations of this feature of discourse coherence.

## Activity 32

> ▶ Find examples in Text B in Activity 30 of words or phrases which help to establish *contrasts* of ideas.
> ▶ Find examples of words or phrases which help to establish *parallels* or *supports* among ideas.
> ▶ Assuming that the writer believes 'alienation' to be an undesirable state, find all the words or phrases that have *negative associations* and thus support the negative meaning.

[12] For sources of detailed discussion and analysis of discourse markers in spoken and written discourse see Brazil *et al.* 1980; Coulthard 1997, 1992; Hoey 1983; Coulthard and Montgomery 1981; Tannen 1984(a), 1984(b); Schiffrin 1987, 1994.

### Example 2.15

**Text A**

**Text B**

... what we're going to DO is to try and $^\downarrow$LOOK at $^\uparrow$++ what do we mean by this idea of myth$^\downarrow$OLogy what is myth$^\downarrow$OLogy ++ um is it any $^\downarrow$DIFferent + to + some of the things that we see going on in the media these $^\downarrow$DAYS or is it$^\uparrow$ in $^\downarrow$FACT + the very $^\downarrow$BASis on which + er the media $^\downarrow$WORKS ++ $^\uparrow$I'm going to $^\uparrow$START by looking at some kind of er theoRETical ideas a$^\downarrow$BOUT + myth$^\downarrow$OLogy + what do we actually $^\downarrow$MEAN by this $^\downarrow$TERM what $^\downarrow$COULD it mean + um $^\uparrow$+ IN this lecture I'm $^\downarrow$NOT trying to put across to you the ideas that you'll go a$^\downarrow$WAY from here and think to yourself well + I $^\downarrow$NOW know ex$^\downarrow$ACTly what mythology $^\downarrow$IS I know how it works in the MEDia$^\uparrow$ um + I have $^\downarrow$LEARNT all this + I'm not trying to $^\downarrow$DO that ++ $^\uparrow$what I'm trying to $^\downarrow$DO is to$^\uparrow$ sugGEST some i$^\downarrow$DEAS to you a$^\downarrow$BOUT how you might start to think $^\downarrow$DIFferently + about the $^\downarrow$MEDia + and the way that it interacts in $^\downarrow$YOUR $^\downarrow$LIFE + um because we're for all of us the media is an important + ASpect + um of our LIVES ++ OK $^\uparrow$so let's START with some of the more theor$^\downarrow$ETical stuff +++ um$^\uparrow$ the first thing about mythOlogy is is that is A $^\downarrow$STRUCTured $^\downarrow$SYSTem ++

*(From Example 1.6, Chapter 1)*

Today, I'd like to talk to you about group discussions, which, in an academic context, are usually known as 'seminars' and 'tutorials'. I want first of all to deal with the meaning of these terms; then I want to cover the aims of group discussions; next I'll go on to look at some problems that learners of English are likely to experience in work of this kind; and then finally I'd like to offer a few pieces of advice.

Firstly, then, let's look at the meaning of the terms 'seminar' and 'tutorial'. Nowadays it's becoming more and more difficult to draw a precise distinction between the meaning of the two words that all lecturers would be willing to accept. The traditional differences which are still accepted by many lecturers, are firstly the size of the group and secondly, and perhaps more importantly, their purpose. A tutorial was usually for a small number of students, say between two and five, whereas a seminar was attended by a larger group, say between ten and fifteen ...

*(James K., R. R. Jordan and A. J. Matthews. (1979).* Listening Comprehension and Note-Taking Course. *London: Collins, p. 119)*

## Some macro-level features

Moving on to macro-levels of text structure takes us into the realms of organisation of discourse at whole-text level. Here, we look briefly at the notions of *genre* and *text-type;* our expectations about 'language events', to use McCarthy's term (1991:137); and possible cultural differences in expectations of how discourse is organised.

### Genre and text-type

We saw in Chapter 1, 1.3.1 and 1.3.3 that the notions of genre and text-type are useful indicators of purposes and likely formats for specific instances of language-in-use. As an example of a relatively sophisticated genre we could take poetry. Our expectations of this type of discourse are that language users will consciously craft language structures and patterns into a coherent artefact with devices such as:

- clear divisions of the text into verses or stanzas, with plenty of 'white space' around them
- conscious choice of 'musical' elements like rhythm or beat, which rely on regular patterns of stress and emphasis
- conscious choice of sounds to form patterns or reflect meaning
- repetition of syntactic structures
- choice of words and images to reflect theme relations

This conscious manipulation of organisation is apparent even in the work of the relatively young writer responsible for the poem in Example 1.9 on page 34.

## Activity 33 ▷

> Look back at the poem in Chapter 1, Example 1.9 on page 34, and see if the writer has used any of the devices in the list above to make her text organisationally coherent.

### Expectations about 'language events'

As we said earlier, in 2.2, we acquire familiarity with the organisational frameworks of the genres and text-types which occur in speech and writing in our first language partly through formal education and partly by virtue of having been born into our particular set of socio-cultural circumstances. Thus, we have strong expectations, not only regarding assumptions we can make about shared knowledge, but also about what form 'language events' are likely to take. In spoken discourse we know about roles and relationships of participants in particular settings, and about how the discourse is likely to develop, for example; or, in written discourse, we are familiar with the stereotypical arrangements of information to be found in a CV, a business report, a set of instructions for operating a new gadget, or a Victorian novel, to name but a few types. There are strong links here with *schema theory*[13] which claims that our ability to predict on

---

[13] See Brown and Yule 1983, Chapter 7 for a full discussion of schema theory.

the basis of past experience enables us both to recognise these patterns and to make sense of them, even though we might not be consciously aware of them.

**Cross-cultural rhetoric and discourse organisation**

The implications of schema theory for teachers of language are considerable, because the extent to which discourse patterns – particularly at macro-levels of organisation – are similar or different across cultures will have some bearing on how effectively, and perhaps how quickly, language learners will be able to operate in the new language. The comparison of discourse patterns across cultures is sometimes referred to as *cross-cultural* (or *contrastive*) *rhetoric*, an often controversial field. There is considerable disagreement, for example, about the extent to which discourse organisation patterns differ from language to language, and if they do, the extent to which they either interfere with, or help with, learning a second language.[14]

Most language teachers will probably agree that there indeed can be problems of first language discourse interference, particularly when people create written texts in a second language. However, a conscious awareness of differences in organisational patterns could actually help learners to develop their L2 discourse competence and indeed, in EL2 contexts where students are learning the language as part of the process of assimilation into a second culture (in Australia or the United States, for instance) this kind of knowledge is seen as essential for full participation in and contribution to the new culture. (This issue of 'empowerment' through language is taken up in Chapter 6.)

Example 2.16 on page 91 shows us, on a very small scale, how awareness of conventions of L2 discourse organisation might help to make a message clearer. We have here the first and second draft versions of one paragraph of an EL2 learner's text about the dangers of *Pachinko,* the popular Japanese pin-ball machine game. In a writing tutorial with the learner after the first draft had been written, her tutor discovered that the point she wanted to stress was the potential danger of becoming addicted to the game.

## Activity 34 ▷

> ▶ Compare the two versions of the *Pachinko* text in Example 2.16 on page 91. In what ways has the information in the first draft been reorganised in the second draft?
> ▶ Can you identify any principles by which the information has been rearranged?
> ▶ Do you think the second draft puts across the point about addiction more clearly than the first? What 'clues' have helped you make the comparison?

---

[14] See Carter 1997; Connor 1995; Connor and Kaplan 1987; Grabe and Kaplan 1996, Chapter 7; Kaplan 1987, 1988; Kramsch 1993; Mercer and Swann 1996; Purves 1988; Smith 1987, for further extensive discussion of issues associated with contrastive rhetoric.

**Example 2.16**

**Draft 1**

As Pachinko becomes popular, it has caused various problems. In one case, while some parents were enthusiastic for playing Pachinko, their children were kidnapped in a Pachinko hall. In another case, while other parents were gone to Pachinko, their children died in a fire. These accidents should have been avoided if the parents had been more careful. To prevent these tragedies, some Pachinko halls have started setting up nurseries. Not a few Pachinko players are addicted to Pachinko, and they do not try to find a job apart from playing Pachinko. They are called Pachi-Pro which means a professional Pachinko player.

**Draft 2**

As Pachinko becomes popular, it has caused various problems. The most serious is that not a few players are addicted to Pachinko: they cannot stop playing till the hall is closed. They do it for a living, and do not find a job. They are not able to live without Pachinko. This has resulted in some tragedies. In one case, while some parents were enthusiastically playing Pachinko, their children were kidnapped in a Pachinko hall. In another case, while other parents were gone to Pachinko, their children died in a fire. These accidents might have been avoided if the parents had been more careful. To prevent these tragedies, some Pachinko halls have started setting up nurseries; however, these accidents have been coming to light only lately, so we do not know whether or not this attempt is useful to prevent these tragedies.

*(Authors' data)*

## 2.3.6 Purposes

The final aspect of discourse we want to focus on is the importance of people's purposes when they write or speak. We can understand neither the linguistic choices they make nor the force these choices have without being aware of the participants' reasons for taking part in the language event and what they hope to achieve.

### Different types of purpose

A distinction often made in discourse studies concerns two broad categories of purpose:

- *transactional language* – used to describe communication whose primary aim is to get something done in practical terms
- *interactional language* – used to describe communication whose primary aim is to look after social relationships

Though this distinction is useful in helping us to understand to some extent grammatical and lexical choices made by speakers and writers, it is probably rare to find any language event which does not contain a mix of both transactional and interactional language. Two examples here will illustrate how an abrupt transition from one type of purpose to another can sometimes throw people off balance. In Example 2.17, from McCarthy (1991:137), a university porter is registering some newly arrived foreign students at their campus accommodation.

### Example 2.17

     Porter:  So, Foti ... and Spampinato ...(*writes their names*) are you Italians? I'm studying Italian Art, only part time, of course, I love it, I love Italian Art.
     Student:  (*looking bewildered*) Excuse me?

It is the element of the unexpectedness of the interactional in what the students obviously expected to be a transactional encounter which perplexes them. Example 2.18 shows the opposite happening. Here, one of the authors (A) was attending a professional conference, and during a break between presentations was engaged in conversation by another delegate (B) who was totally unknown to A.

### Example 2.18

     B: Have you had a nice holiday?
     A: Yes, thanks, lovely – we went to Brittany.
     B: Do you think it is necessary to have lived abroad to be able to teach EAP[15] successfully?
     A: ... er ...

                                                            *(Authors' data)*

These two examples show how communication can break down when expectations about purposes are not fulfilled. In most cases, of course, transitions between transactional and interactional language are accomplished perfectly smoothly, and people understand exactly what is going on in terms of purpose, and how they should respond. However, in cases where real breakdowns do occur, we have a wide repertoire of strategies for repairing them – a facility termed *strategic competence* in the literature.[16]

It may be that what we sometimes perceive to be the artificiality of scripted dialogues in many language teaching materials (even up-to-date ones) can be explained by the fact that they do not contain a realistic mix of transactional and interactional language. Indeed, their purpose is often neither transactional nor interactional in the discourse sense, but rather pedagogic, in that they are created to introduce or practise a certain structure or function, or to provide exposure to

[15] EAP: English for Academic Purposes
[16] See Canale 1983:7 for discussion of breakdowns and repairs.

certain vocabulary, or to act as a stimulus for a classroom activity. One implication of discourse studies for language teachers, therefore, is whether teaching materials should, or indeed whether they can, actually be expected to reflect in any realistic way the natural mix of purpose found in real-world speech.

## Activity 35 ▶

> The two texts in Example 2.19 below are from two different beginner level coursebooks. Both are scripted dialogues, and both are based on the function of inviting someone out.
>
> ▶ Which would you say was more authentic in terms of the mix of interactional and transactional language?
> ▶ Looking at the two texts as teaching materials, how effective do you think they would be as a basis for introducing learners to the functions of giving, accepting and rejecting invitations?

## Example 2.19

### Text A (a telephone conversation)

Anna: Hello?

Tony: Hi, Anna! This is Tony.

A: Hi, Tony! How are you doing?

T: Good, thanks. Say, what are you doing Friday night? Would you like to go out?

A: Oh, sorry, I can't. I'm working late.

T: Well, how about Saturday night? Are you doing anything then?

A: No, I'm not.

T: Well, would you like to see a musical?

A: Sure, I'd love to! My treat this time.

T: All right! Thanks!

(Richards *et al.* (1990). *Interchange 1*, p. 96)

### Text B

A: **Are you free** tomorrow night?

B: **Yes, I think so.**

A: **Would you like** to go to the theatre with me?

B: **Yes, I'd love to. Thanks.**

*... If you are not free or you don't want to accept an invitation, this is what you can say:*

B: I'd like to invite you to a party on Saturday.

A: **That's very nice of you, but I'm afraid I can't go. ... I'm busy on Saturday.**

(*Shepherd and Cox (1991).* The Sourcebook (Pre-Intermediate), *p. 23*)

## 2.4   Discourse studies and their relevance to ELT

In this final section of the chapter, we highlight some issues which arise from the study of discourse and possible applications to teaching and learning a second language. Our focus has been on raising *awareness* of the importance of discourse competence, rather than making extensive practical suggestions for what teachers can do to help learners acquire it.[17]

Nevertheless, since helping learners achieve discourse competence can be considered as a goal for language teachers, we end this chapter by considering the relevance of discourse studies to teaching. We will be concerned with three areas:

- the use of authentic spoken interaction as teaching material
- teaching L2 conventions of spoken language
- 'relevance' in L2 teaching and learning contexts

First, though, an activity inviting you to brainstorm some general constraints on teaching discourse.

### Activity 36 ▷

Formulate some questions you might want to think about or discuss with others in relation to acquisition of discourse competence in a second or foreign language. Your questions could relate to the following general areas:

▶ the *point in a teaching programme* when you think it would be appropriate to consider discourse competence in learning a language

▶ the *ways* in which discourse competence is acquired in L1, and the implications of this for teaching L2

▶ the *constraints* imposed on teachers by materials and teaching contexts

**Follow-up:** Think of some *practical suggestions* for preparing learners to cope with real-world discourse.

### *Can authentic spoken interaction become teaching material?*

How can all the sophisticated mechanisms of spoken language be translated into language teaching *materials*? The answer is that it is very difficult, if not impossible, to do this. As we have seen, the discourse of spoken interactions in textbooks and coursebooks often bears little resemblance to that of real-world communication.

One reason – though of course not the only one – why language teaching materials rely to such a great extent on invented or simulated versions of 'the real thing' is that the real thing is impossible to reproduce in textbooks. Even when textbooks are accompanied by audio or video tapes, it is no easier to reproduce *exactly* how the language in question was used in the original context: the only foolproof way for anyone to know how it was used is to have been part of the context, because only then would one have the necessary knowledge of who the

---

[17] Detailed discussion of this can be found in both McCarthy 1991, and Cook 1989.

participants were, why they were taking part in the interaction, what the interpersonal relations were between the interactants, what came before and what would be likely to come after the interaction and so on.

In any case, materials writers and teachers may feel that completely authentic materials are not necessarily either the most effective or the most practical tools for language learning. One strong argument for constructed material is that such samples of language have a clear pedagogic value in helping learners to focus on particular items of form or lexis. They are not intended to be authentic, and their coherence has to be created artificially in the absence of a true context and purpose. However, we feel that to expose L2 learners *only* to the order and neatness of such contrived conversations is to do them a disservice when it comes to encounters with the real thing outside the classroom.

One possible avenue for opening up a larger window on how discourse really works is to use interactions which actually take place in the classroom – between learners themselves and between learners and teachers – as a basis for exploration. Part of learners' day-to-day work could be to tape or video-record such interactions, to examine the language and strategies they use to interact with each other, to listen to teacher feedback recorded on tape, and to pay attention to language and strategies used by the teacher. Such awareness-raising might go some way to providing an alternative type of 'immersion' in discourse.

## Why it is difficult to teach conventions of spoken interaction

Discourse studies show us that all languages have culture-specific conventions for turn-taking, interrupting, initiating and closing exchanges, and that these conventions contribute to the system and structure of conversation, even the most apparently casual. The question for teachers is whether these conventions can be taught. Some would argue that there are more important things to be dealt with, and that in any case a learner's L1 discourse competence is adequate enough to cope with L2 contexts.[18] But then, why is it that learners so often have the sensation of what Cook (1989:57) depicts as 'floundering in conversation' when they leave the classroom for the world outside?

One reason may be that teachers do not give learners adequate experience of, or exposure to, non-classroom interaction where the discourse skills we have been considering are required. Studies of the discourse of classroom interaction make us aware of a general bias towards teacher domination.[19] Sinclair and Coulthard's (1975) data suggest that teachers often set the agenda for the speech event of the lesson: it is usually they who organise and control the turn-taking; it is they who nominate participants, often by way of asking questions to which they (the teachers) obviously know the answers; it is often they who initiate exchanges; they frequently interrupt a turn to correct, or impose their own agenda on the development of the interaction; they often do most of the talking. To a certain extent it is natural that this should be the case: as other educational research has shown, such classroom discourse patterns may be essential in the

[18] See Swan's (1985a and b) arguments in his critique of 'communicative' approaches to language teaching.
[19] See Sinclair and Coulthard 1975; Sinclair and Brazil 1982; Flanders 1970; Chaudron 1988; Stubbs, 1983b.

construction of a 'common knowledge' as the basis of the shared understanding and 'mutuality of perspectives'[20] fundamental to the educational process.

However, in language classrooms the ostensible goal is to enable *learners* to use the language. This may be particularly difficult if teachers are operating within a cultural context where it is they who are *expected* to take the predominant speaking role in the classroom, and where they are assumed to be doing their job badly if they do not conform to the prototypical role described above. It can be argued, of course, that the language classroom has to be – or might have to be – a controlled and 'sheltered' environment. How else can the language be learned? How else can one 'deliver the goods' given the external constraints imposed by government-dictated syllabuses, examination criteria, or pressure from parents? Nevertheless, we still feel that one essential goal for teachers is to attempt to achieve the optimum balance in their particular circumstances between, on the one hand, teaching *about* the tools of language, and on the other, providing opportunities for learners to *use* their language tools in real-time, real-world communication.

## 'Relevance' in teaching and learning contexts

We discussed earlier (see 2.3.1) the centrality to discourse of the relevance maxim. Language teachers in their classrooms, like participants in any other type of discourse, are governed by relevance. Just as awareness of linguistic angles on politeness is needed (see 2.3.1), so sensitivity to differences in teaching and learning contexts is, we would argue, essential. Some learners may come from cultures where to challenge, contradict or argue with a teacher is the height of disrespect for face. They may be at a loss in class settings where learners are expected and encouraged to do precisely this – academic seminar settings in tertiary level educational institutions in the UK, Australia or the USA, for instance. Norms relating to terms of address between teacher and adult learners are another potential source of confusion: how easy is it for learners coming from contexts in which a teacher is always addressed by an honorific title to adjust to classrooms where teachers expect to be on familiar first-name terms with their learners? Even such simple things as the informality of a teacher sitting on the desk, or teachers being (as they assume) friendly by making jokes, or asking about learners' families and personal situations may be open to misinterpretation.[21]

Being 'alive' to the cultural dimensions of discourse could alert teachers to the possibility that the whole ethos of teaching methodologies based on encouraging learners to assert themselves, to interact with each other in tasks and problem-solving activities in the classroom, to ask questions, to make decisions for themselves, to develop independent learning strategies, and to challenge what people in authority say, may be alien and possibly inappropriate in certain EL2 teaching and learning contexts. Teachers for whom such notions are unexceptionable and largely taken for granted as the 'best' way to learn the language may need to develop a particular sensitivity to other-cultural or multi-cultural teaching contexts. They may even need to change their opinions as to the 'best' way to learn a language.

[20] See Mercer 1995 and Edwards and Mercer 1987.
[21] See Kramsch 1993, for further discussion here.

## A final activity

It is not part of our brief to advocate any particular methodological approach. However, we do strongly feel that a reasonable goal for any teacher is to acquire as broad a knowledge as possible of what it is they teach. Thus we would like to suggest that not the least relevant aspect of discourse studies for language teachers is that they might be encouraged to become expert eavesdroppers. Activity 37 might be a start in this direction.

### Activity 37

Record – or keep a record of – some conversational data or some discourse encounters of your own and analyse them for information about the aspects of discourse we have focused on in this chapter. You might find that your data is generally in line with the claims we have made here, or that there is room for disagreement. Areas you might like to focus on for analysis include:

▶ the *relevance* of people's language choices in light of the context of the discourse
▶ *conflicts* between *co-operative and politeness principles*
▶ *cultural constraints* on people's language interactions
▶ the extent to which *knowledge* is *shared* among interactants
▶ why people often do *not mean what they say*
▶ the relation between *form and function*
▶ structures, boundaries, signposts and markers in *discourse organisation*
▶ the relationship between *transactional* and *interactional purposes* in discourse

**Follow-up:** Consider whether your data would be at all useful in your classroom context, and if so, how you could exploit them for teaching purposes.

## Key references

Brown, G. and G. Yule (1983). *Discourse Analysis*. Cambridge: Cambridge University Press.

Carter, R. (1997). *Investigating English Discourse*. London: Routledge.

Cook, G. (1989). *Discourse*. Oxford: Oxford University Press.

McCarthy, M. (1991). *Discourse Analysis for Language Teachers*. Cambridge: Cambridge University Press.

McCarthy, M. and R. Carter (1994). *Language As Discourse*. London: Longman.

Smith, L. E (1987). *Discourse Across Cultures: Strategies in World Englishes*. New York: Prentice Hall.

Thomas, J. (1995). *Meaning in Interaction: An Introduction to Pragmatics*. Harlow: Addison Wesley Longman.

# 3    Grammar

## 3.1    Overview

In Chapter 1 (1.3.7) we saw how fundamental rules and patterns are to language. The present chapter looks in more detail at the notion of grammar as a basic organisational feature of language and at different approaches to using, interpreting and teaching it. We consider some key points relating to what is meant by *grammar* and how it can or should be taught, including:

- the difficulty of finding a satisfactory definition of English 'grammar'
- the variety of different views on grammar
- the different approaches to the teaching of grammar
- the need for (and possible dangers of) a 'reduced model' of grammar for ELT

We also consider an alternative approach to grammar which deals in broad categories such as relevance, flexibility, volume and range; we discuss some of the implications of this and the other points raised in the chapter for the teaching of grammar in ELT.

At different points in the chapter we refer to a number of sometimes overlapping categories of 'user'. These include the following:

- language specialists such as linguists and writers on grammar
- English language teachers
- children learning English as their first or mother language (EL1 learners)
- adult mother-tongue speakers of English (EL1 users)
- learners of English as a second or non-mother-tongue language (EL2 learners)
- writers and producers of language teaching materials

## 3.2    What is grammar?

### *Why is it difficult to define the word 'grammar'?*

Part of the answer to this question is that the word *grammar* seems to mean different things to different people. Linguists use the word in their study of language to describe how syntactic and structural systems operate, but the word is also used in numerous other contexts, both in a general and a specific sense.

For instance, *Collins COBUILD English Dictionary* and the *Cambridge International Dictionary of English* give definitions of *grammar* which include:

- the rules of a language (the system)
- the way an individual uses the rules (someone's personal 'grammar')
- a book containing the rules (a grammar book)
- the study of the rules (the subject called *grammar*)

## 3.2.1 Some different interpretations

If variety in the interpretation of the meaning of the word is a common feature, we would expect to find *grammar* used differently in differing contexts. Each of the ten sentences in Example 3.1 below includes the word *grammar* but the meaning is not the same in all of them. If we consider what the various speakers or writers had in mind when they used the term, we can see that, while rules are clearly part of what people have in mind when they think about grammar, trying to reach one absolute definition of the word *grammar* is almost impossible.

### Activity 38 ▷

> ▶ Look at the sentences in Example 3.1 below. What do you think the word *grammar* refers to in each of them? Is it the same thing in each case?
> ▶ What do you think the context or situation was for the different sentences? Who might have said each one? Where? To who(m)?

### Example 3.1

a) I don't mind so much about pronunciation, it's grammar that annoys me.
b) She's writing a grammar of Romanian.
c) English grammar is not very complicated.
d) Look it up in a grammar book.
e) A child's grammar develops from a very early age.
f) I don't teach grammar any more, I teach functions.
g) We studied grammar at school.
h) Such a grammar would attempt to account for all the possible utterances in a language.
i) There are rules to grammar as to any other subject.
j) I was taught French by the grammar-translation method.

*(Authors' data)*

### *Rules and more rules*

All the dictionary definitions above contain the word *rules*. If grammar is a basic part of any language system, then presumably there have to be rules which govern how language, or a language – in this case English – operates. But what are the rules and where do they come from? Are they rules that everybody knows about? How do people find out about the rules? Which ones should we teach?

Rules also take us into the difficult areas of acceptability and definitions (see Chapters 4 and 6 (4.3.3 and 6.3.3) for more on this and the debate on Standard

English). For some people grammar is an attempt to describe how a language is used, while for others it is a question of what is correct or perceived to be correct (sometimes called prescriptive grammar because it prescribes rules that people *believe* to be correct). Rules are not necessarily accepted by and acceptable to everyone, even assuming it is possible or practical to list them all. In Britain there is a history of popular debate over grammatical correctness, for example in letters that people write to newspapers and in discussions in the media about the use and abuse of language. There are regular newspaper columns on aspects of grammar and vocabulary. There are hundreds of books published on grammar (not just for EL2 learners) ranging from abstract theoretical models of language, designed to account for all possible utterances, to general everyday books which attempt to tell you the rules of writing clearly or how to avoid making mistakes in grammar. From this wide variety we can see that grammar might encompass all sorts of things including, for instance, stylistic constraints.

Chapter 2 was concerned with the desirability of broadening our view of language, going beyond the basic 'rules' of grammar to take into account discourse features such as context, choice and purpose. As teachers of language (and grammar) it is therefore useful for us to think about some *structural* differences in the way English behaves in various types of context – written or spoken, formal or informal – or the different ways the language can be organised at sentence-, paragraph- and discourse-level. We can do this by comparing different types of language examples and by thinking about how different forms of language may be used for different purposes and in different contexts.

## Rules or patterns?

Not everybody who studies grammar considers it to be just a set of rules. The functional grammar school, for instance,[1] sees the patterns of language as the main starting point for analysis and concentrates on looking at the way language is organised (including a sort of 'pre-rule' stage) rather than at the rules and terminology. The metalanguage[2] is sometimes complicated, and the basic concept differs in several ways from traditional grammar, with its view of language as a set of structured rules within which it is possible to distinguish between grammatical and ungrammatical sentences. Functional grammar, by contrast, examines the way language works across texts and situations and looks at how we do things with language. If we take verbs as an example, traditional grammar would look at the formation of tenses or regular and irregular forms, whereas functional grammar sees 'a distinction between *doing* (material processes), *being* (relational processes) and *saying, thinking* and *feeling* (projecting processes)' (Butt *et al.* 1995:29). Word functions are more important than word classes: 'the primary concern is with the *functions* of structures and their constituents and with their meanings in context' (Lock 1996:1). There are strong links between functional grammar and some of the points made earlier in the book about the importance of context.

[1] See Butt *et al.* 1995, for a general introduction and Lock 1996, for a more detailed analysis.
[2] i.e. the language – including concepts and terminology – used to talk about language

## 3.2.2 Some different viewpoints

### *Who are the real 'experts' on grammar?*

The views expressed on grammar are as wide-ranging as the definitions of the word itself. In this section we give some examples of views of language and grammar from differing perspectives, and consider whether it is possible to say who the real 'experts' are.

**A grammarian's view**

Those who study, teach and write about grammar are often concerned with particular details of grammatical systems. In Extract 1 however, the writer also sees a grammar as an attempt to describe a system of communication which is shared by the community. The emphasis here is very much on the need to *describe* (i.e. say what happens in language *use*) rather than *prescribe* (say what you think *should* happen). The writer is also looking at language and grammar from a wide, sociolinguistic perspective.

### Extract 1

In order to write a grammar for some language ... we must study the realities of people's language behaviour and give an account of it in terms of some agreed framework of description. This is a very different thing from attempting to influence people's language behaviour and make them do it 'better'. The grammar that we write will be an account of the structural and functional principles of the language itself. This is no trivial matter, since the language spoken by a community of speakers is one of the most essential factors in the life of that community. The community could not exist without this means of controlling almost every aspect of its life; and language is no less than that. A grammar, then, is an attempt to describe the system of communication which every normal member of the community 'possesses' and which is shared by the community at large. It has both a psychological existence within the individual and a social existence within the community.

*(Young 1984:11)*

**A language teaching viewpoint**

The definition above is probably far too wide to appeal to most teachers of English. A grammar 'shared by the community at large' is both too big and too vague. Certainly on a day-to-day basis teachers are more interested in what their learners need to know to communicate effectively, to master structures laid down in the syllabus or coursebook and to pass examinations. This need for clear basic advice helps to explain why ELT grammar is traditionally often limited to much narrower areas of usage and rules. Extract 2, from a teacher training series, exemplifies this approach:

### Extract 2

Grammar ... is the way in which words change themselves and group together to make sentences. The grammar of a language is what happens to words when they become plural or negative, or what word order is used when we make questions or join two clauses to make one sentence.

*(Harmer 1987:1)*

### A functional viewpoint

Functional grammarians, however, would disagree with Extract 2 for a variety of reasons, as illustrated in Extract 3:

### Extract 3

It is true that the word *grammar* can mean something like a grammar book or a set of grammatical rules, particularly rules that people will keep breaking unless they are firmly taught them. But there is another sense of the word which means something like *the way in which a language is organised*. In this second sense all of us have a command of grammar, even if we speak only one language and have never consciously learned any grammatical rules or terms.

*(Butt et al. 1995:26)*

### The 'declining standards' viewpoint

Personal and professional opinions on the way language is used are to be found everywhere. They are found not only in teaching or academic situations but in everyday life – in the press, on television, on radio. In 1990 the Prince of Wales, heir to the British throne, joined the wide-ranging political, public and educational debate over what should be taught in the new British national school curriculum for English. His impassioned plea, in Extract 4 below, is perhaps most notable for the wide range of general areas he manages to include in a few lines. He, too, mentions 'the rules of grammar' although he gives no examples of precisely what he means. The speech is concerned with what many would call a 'traditional view' of language and EL1 language teaching.

### Extract 4

In the last two decades we have witnessed a situation where our education has no longer been centred on the idea that the English language is an enormously precious legacy to be handed on carefully. We have seen the abandonment of learning the rules of grammar and the parts of speech as boring and irrelevant. Learning poetry by heart has been abandoned, together with the idea of English as something really to be *learnt* [his emphasis], by effort and application, by long and careful familiarity with those who had shown how to clothe their thought in the most precise, vivid and memorable language ... But there is now, I think, a growing consensus on what needs to be taught and it is heartening to witness the widespread recognition of this in the new national curriculum for English.

*(Guardian Weekly, 7 January 1990, cited in Hudson 1992:13)*

**The political viewpoint**

Grammar is, for many people, an emotional subject and people often have strong views on grammatical usage. In Chapter 5 we look at how differences in usage, such as 'standard' and 'non-standard' forms, are at times linked by some to social differences. The writer of Extract 5 below presents a detailed argument, based on the view that the study of Latin is crucial to the study, understanding and appreciation of English grammar in EL1 situations. It is not possible, however, given the political influences in the British education system, to address the influence of Latin on English grammar purely in linguistic terms. The writer is well aware of this.

**Extract 5**

The teaching of Latin in schools benefits the English both of those pupils who study it, and those who do not. Standard English has been formed through the centuries by its contact with Latin; and without some knowledge of Latin an Englishman [sic] will always remain, to an extent, a stranger to his own culture. But even those children not fortunate enough to be taught Latin gain by the fact that Latin is taught in schools; or – to put it in the form which present circum-stances make the more pertinent – will lose if Latin continues to vanish from the school syllabus. That Latin is taught, not just as a specialist discipline like Sanskrit or Japanese, but widely at school level, affirms that grammatical and lexical correctness are still valued; and, more practically, it ensures a supply of English teachers whose grasp of Latin will make their command of English and its grammar firmer and more explicit.

*(Marenbon 1987:38)*

**Activity 39** ▷

> ▶ Think about the viewpoints put forward by the different writers in Extracts 1–5 above. Try to pick out some of the keywords in the extracts. How would you then complete the phrase 'Grammar is ...' for each of the extracts?
> ▶ Which of the viewpoints do you feel most sympathetic towards and why?
> ▶ If you had to write a short paragraph on grammar teaching in your *own* situation, what important points or features of that situation would you highlight?
> ▶ Are you any nearer to being able to answer the question at the beginning of 3.2.2, i.e. who, in your view, are the 'real' experts on grammar?

## 3.3 Grammar in action

Having established that the notion of grammar can be interpreted in many different ways, we look briefly in this section at some samples of real language from various users of English:

- children who have English as their mother tongue
- adult mother-tongue (EL1) users
- EL2 learners

The main reason for examining these different usages is to identify some differences in how grammar operates in different contexts and with different types of speakers. The following general questions are ones you need to think about throughout this section:

- What sorts of grammars are we looking at? How can we describe them?
- Do grammars vary in terms of the language descriptions they offer?
- What characterises the grammar of learners of English?
- What elements of grammar are generally considered to be most important in studying EL2?

## 3.3.1  Children

### What sorts of difficulties do English-speaking children have with their mother tongue?

Children offer a fascinating view of how language is learned and acquired, whatever the language they are learning. The data contained in studies of *child language acquisition* are often revealing about the processes of learning the rules of language use. Example 3.2 shows how difficult it can be to actively teach children English grammar or syntactic rules.

**Example 3.2**

| | |
|---|---|
| Child: | Nobody don't like me. |
| Mother: | No, say "nobody likes me." |
| Child: | Nobody don't like me. |
| *[eight repetitions of this dialogue]* | |
| Mother: | No, now listen carefully: say "nobody likes me." |
| Child: | Oh! Nobody don't LIKES me. |

*(Clark and Clark 1977:366, quoting David MacNeill)*

The illustrations in Example 3.3 on page 105 come from David Crystal's book *Listen to Your Child*, a highly readable account of how English-speaking children acquire language. Crystal uses his own knowledge of language to encourage others to explore what happens as a child's grammar is developing, although this development is by no means uniform. His examples show some typical errors made by children aged two to four years; they also illustrate the fact that children do not all acquire the same language at the same rate and that their language use is often highly creative. Sorting out the rules and the systems takes some time.

## Activity 40 ▷

> Look at the eight instances in Example 3.3 of children (ages given in brackets in some cases) acquiring their language, and see if you can identify what has 'gone wrong'. Some areas to consider are:
>
> ▶ lexical and verb formation
> ▶ pronunciation
> ▶ deixis[3]
> ▶ plurality
> ▶ comparison

## Example 3.3

**a)**

| | |
|---|---|
| Mother: | You run on ahead and I'll catch up with you. |
| Jane (2.6): | Whose head, Mummy? |

**b)**

| | |
|---|---|
| Mother *(going through the alphabet)*: | Say T. |
| Mary (3.6): | T. |
| Mother: | U. |
| Mary: | U. |
| Mother: | V. |
| Mary: | V. |
| Mother: | W. |
| Mary: | Double me. |

**c)**

| | |
|---|---|
| Marcus (3.0) *(in train, approaching London)*: | Are we there yet? |
| Father: | No, we're still in the outskirts. |
| *(pause)* | |
| Marcus: | Have we reached the inskirts yet? |

**d)**

| | |
|---|---|
| Michael (4.0) *(in bedroom)*: | Don't shut my door, Mummy. |
| Mother: | Well I have to close it darling, because the light will keep you awake. |

---

[3] Features of language whose meaning relates directly to given contexts such as time and place: *now/then; here/there; this/that; I/you* are all examples of deictic features. Deixis also has a forward- and backward-pointing function in texts (see Extract 7 on page 127).

| Michael: | No, don't want you to. |
| Mother: | I'll leave it ajar, then. |
| Michael: | Can you leave it one and a half jars? |

**e)**

| Lucy: | Squeak, squeak – that's what mouses does. |
| Mother: | That's what mice do. |
| Lucy: | What do mices does? |

**f)**

You bettern't do that.

**g)**

It just got brokened.

**h)**

My hand's the biggest than Ben's.

*(Crystal 1986, pp.108–120)*

By the time children reach the age of five or six, most can manipulate a very large number of structural processes in their mother tongue(s), although many parts of the grammar systems will still need to develop further – complex tense systems and modality, for instance, where English-speaking children are concerned. Interestingly, they do not encounter difficulties with some of the English grammar which causes major problems for older EL2 learners, such as question tags (*it's hot, isn't it?; we've already seen it, haven't we?*) and articles (the use of *a* and *the* or *zero* article). One reason for this is that these are very high frequency items, especially in spoken English; children are therefore likely to have met them on a frequent and regular basis from a very early age.

We can thus already identify some differences in the sorts of problems that exist in learning a first language as a child and in later study of a foreign language. Examples 3.4 and 3.5 on pages 107 and 108 show EL1 children having problems with two aspects of language which are relatively late to be acquired: 'knowledge of the world' and conventions of written language. In such areas, it might well be the case that adult L2 learners have an advantage over L1 children, in that they have already acquired this kind of knowledge through their first language.

### Problems with 'knowledge of the world'
In Example 3.4 on page 107, Lucy has a high degree of functional fluency and she makes no errors of syntax. She and her father have no trouble communicating but she *does* have some difficulty with the double meaning of the expression *well-done*. As Crystal points out, Lucy has learned the literal meaning of the phrase *well-done*, but she has not yet discovered that it can be used in a special way as a term used in cooking.

**Example 3.4**

> Dad: What do you want to play, then?
> Lucy: I'll be the waitress and you have to eat in my shop. You come in, and
>        sit down, and I can come and see you.
>
> *(Dad acts his part obediently. Over walks Lucy, clutching an imaginary
> notebook and pencil.)*
>
> Lucy: Good afternoon.
> Dad: Good afternoon.
> Lucy: What do you want to eat?
> Dad: Ooh, I'd like some cornflakes, and some sausages, please.
> Lucy: We haven't got any sausages
> Dad: Oh dear, well let me see ... Have you got any steak?
>
> *(There is a silence, while Lucy considers this possibility with enormous
> gravity. Finally, she allows it.)*
>
> Lucy: Yes. We got steak.
> Dad: I'll have steak then.
> Lucy: OK. 'Bye.
>
> *(She turns to go, but Dad calls her back.)*
>
> Dad: Hey, hold on a minute. You can't rush off like that. If a customer asks
>        for steak, you have to ask him 'How would you like your steak?'
>        That's very important if you're going to be a waitress.
> Lucy: Oh. *(Pauses.)* How would you like your steak?
> Dad: I'll have mine well done.
> Lucy *(Trotting off to the kitchen)*: OK. We'll do the best we can!

*(Crystal 1986:30–31)*

The implications of the misunderstanding in the conversation in Example 3.4 are that full and competent language use is not just about having an accurate control over grammatical structures. Vocabulary and grammar are both important, of course, but so are other factors, such as the cultural and social knowledge relating to the type of food mentioned in the conversation, or the type of behaviour expected of waitresses. As we saw in Chapter 2, becoming a competent language user involves mastering a complex set of discourse features.

**Problems with learning to write**
Examples 3.2, 3.3 and 3.4 all come from spoken language. We can, however, also see a child's grammar emerging in their writing. Example 3.5 on page 108 shows part of a pattern of what is often called *emergent writing*, starting at about four or five years, and linked with, though usually somewhat behind, the process of learning to read. Emergent writing is characterised by a number of grammatical and orthographical features, two typical ones being a kind of 'running' sentence structure (lots of *ands)* and the actual formation of the words themselves (the handwriting).

**Example 3.5**

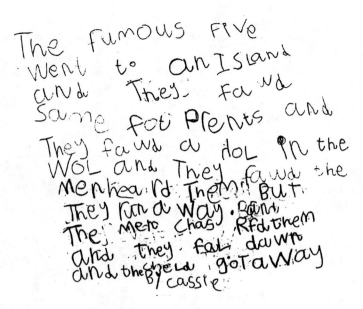

(The Famous Five went to an island and they found some footprints and they found a hole in the wall and they found the men heard them but they ran away. And the men chased after them and they fell down and the child got away – By Cassie)

*(Authors' data)*

**Activity 41**

> ► Look back over Examples 3.2–3.5 on pages 104–108 and identify some of the areas where the children exhibit difficulties.
> ► In your experience are these difficulties the same as those encountered by adult EL2 learners? If not, how are they different? Are there any examples of the children successfully using structures which often cause problems for older learners?

## 3.3.2  Adult EL1 users

As we have already seen, there are many factors that influence how mother-tongue speakers use their language (in both speaking and writing). Some typically important ones, explored in other chapters of the book, are variety, context, audience, register[4] and appropriacy. The next three examples (Examples 3.6, 3.7 and 3.8 on pages 109 and 110) show adult EL1 usage in various spoken and written contexts.

---

[4] Defined by Crystal (1980:301) as follows: 'a variety of language defined according to its use in social situations, e.g. a register of scientific, religious, formal English.' (See Chapter 4, 4.2 for further discussion of register.)

## Example 3.6: 'Standard' and 'non-standard' spoken varieties

| Non-standard dialect | Standard dialect |
|---|---|
| Being on me own had never gone through me head | Being on my own had never gone through my head |
| We was for ever having arguments | We were forever having arguments |
| Anyway they done it for me | Anyway they did it for me |
| I hadn't got nothing to fall back on | I had nothing to fall back on |
| Go to the pub is it? | Let's go to the pub, shall we? |
| Where's it by? | Where is it? |
| Over by here | Over here |

*(Montgomery 1986:73–74)*

## Example 3.7: Spoken language written down

*The speaker is telling a story in an unedited radio conversation programme. Just before the speaker tells the story, the subject of the conversation has been the inventing of stories and games by computer.*

I've just started WORKing on one which is + um + um + + where the ↑major obJECTive of the gaa it's called buREAUcracy the major obJECTive of the game is actually + to get your BANK to acknowledge a change of adDRESS card + um + (laughter) ↑ this will lead you from one + ↑ one + HUGE EPic adventure to anOTHer though in fa though the the the ONE thing that's imPELLing you is just TRYing to get your bank to DO this + ↑this actually CAME from something that occurred to me when I when I MOVED to my current FLAT I got a mortgage from the BANK + er + but nevertheless when I was sending OUT a change of address card I thought well I'd better send them one ANYway they SHOULD know I'm here because they're PAYing for it + um + + ↑ um + and the next statement I got was + sent to my old adDRESS so I sent them an ↑ OTHer change of address card and the next statement after THAT was sent to my old adDRESS ↑ so I WROTE them a letter saying look you ↑ MUST know I'm here because you're ↑ INto this flat for x numbers of thousands of pounds + + um + I've SENT you two changes of address cards + um + ↑ PLEASE will you sort of UPdate your records and make sure you send stuff to my new adDRESS + ↑ so they wrote me back a very + um + a ↑ POLoGETic letter saying we DO realise this is VERy silly I'm VEry sorry it won't happen again + + + ↓ GUESS where they sent the LETter + + (laughter)

*(Authors' data)*

## Example 3.8: Two examples of written language

### a) A note to a colleague

We need to order 12 copies of the exam books a.s.a.p. It's <u>urgent</u> but I can't find any account details at present. Could you phone and sort it out?

### b) Part of an academic article

> Historical accounts of language education in the U.S. show that monolingual approaches to the teaching of English have by no means always been the norm (Baron 1990; Daniels 1990); rather, there have been cyclical fluctuations in policy often determined by political rather than pedagogical factors. In the 19th century, for example, the decentralized and locally controlled nature of public schooling allowed for bilingual education in accordance with the political power of particular ethnic groups. It was the resurgence of nativism and antiforeign political sentiment in the late 19th century that signaled the decline of bilingual education ...

*(Auerbach, E.R. (1993). TESOL Quarterly, 27/1:12)*

These three examples serve to underline a number of points that we want to make about grammar:

- grammar, although systematic, is not constant or rigid; grammatical usage varies widely, particularly in spoken English (see Example 3.6)
- the differences between spoken and written English are crucial to an understanding of grammar (compare Examples 3.7 and 3.8)
- there is huge variety within large general categories, e.g. the category *written English* contains a multitude of different forms and genres (see Example 3.8)
- there are many other factors which affect the way language is used; grammar is not only the way words fit together to form utterances (see the effect of the different contexts in Examples 3.7 and 3.8)
- the purposes for which the language is used – i.e. the functions it fulfils – are important and affect the way people structure the language they use (again, see the effect of the different contexts in Examples 3.7 and 3.8)

A further general point we could make in relation to ELT is that the range of grammatical structures in EL1 use is much larger than that often seen in EL2 learning environments, or covered by ELT materials.

Examples 3.6–3.8 show that even the main categories of spoken and written language are really very vague. A note to a friend or colleague is nothing like an academic essay; a train departure announcement is very different from a politician's speech or from children talking in the playground. A considerable part of an L1 speaker's competence is being able to handle such variety, usually without being aware of it. While it would be absurd to suggest that ELT grammar reference materials should attempt to include descriptions of features of all possible varieties, there is sometimes a worrying mismatch or even contradiction between what such grammar reference materials tell us (or don't tell us) and what actually happens when people use the language (see the discussion on range in 3.6).

## Activity 42 ▷

> ▶ What – for teaching purposes – do you think are the most important differences between spoken and written English? (You might like to refer back to Chapter 1, 1.3.3.)
> ▶ Do *you* have any personal or professional concerns about the 'contradiction' mentioned in the paragraph above? What could be included in language teaching to help students towards a better understanding of, for example, features of spoken language?

### 3.3.3  Learner (EL2) English

*What kinds of 'typical' grammar problems do EL2 learners have?*

There are a number of important factors that may influence the problems that learners have with English grammar. These include:

- *structural difficulties*, e.g. differences between the learner's first or other languages and possible interference from these
- *cultural adjustments*, e.g. in the required genres, styles and settings of the target language (learning English for Academic Purposes in an English-speaking educational environment, for instance)
- *educational factors*, e.g. the perceived role and importance of grammar learning and teaching
- *pedagogic questions*, e.g. the role of the teacher and teaching materials as a source of advice on correct or appropriate grammar
- *functional differences*, e.g. different languages may do things in different ways

Example 3.9 on page 112 shows us some problem areas for EL2 learners in the written forms of English, whilst Example 3.10 illustrates various difficulties with spoken forms. From a grammatical viewpoint, it is possible to analyse the particular problems and also to speculate on why and how they originate. Even if we do not have direct knowledge of learners' first languages we are often aware that certain parts of the English system will cause problems. Sometimes we may be aware of a general grammar fact – that the way English verbs operate in relation to time is complex, for instance – or more specific ones – that Japanese students of English often have difficulties with passive constructions or that German and Arabic speakers often find the word order in the sentence structure of written English problematic.

## Example 3.9: Written EL2 language

Extract from an essay on the possible effects of TV on children

Violence nowadays one of the serious problem facing a lot of governments in the world. Druges and murders are the main problemes in the society and thay were affected by youth mostly. In my opinion I can say that T.V and vedio are the most ones seductive by childern and young people, Because those two are watching violence films in T.V, for example people killing each other using druges and committing thift crime So the childern and the young people try to do same, without thinking or using their mind to seperate what thay have seen in T.V and doing it in the real life Therefore, parents shouldn't let their childern watch these sort of films and trying their best by keeping them away or make them busy by learning the very good manners of behavioures towards their friends and their socity as well as let them busy in home by doing their homeworks and reading books to be in future a very successful man in your life.

*(Authors' data)*

## Example 3.10: Spoken EL2 language

a)  I don't want to think twice to answer that question.
b)  They can't use the knowledge that they had in school outside with the normal living life.
c)  They became hating everything about education.
d)  I stopped being a child when I started having a drink.
e)  If any adult man he spend more than 4 or 5 years in his work, I think it's very hard to him to change his routine to be as a student.
f)  Everything I have to do it I have to put my plan before I done it.
g)  I don't agree with those ways of thinking who want to use with the help of science to prolong our lives.
h)  Five years ago the government allowed to advertise by the TV.

*(Authors' data)*

**Activity 43**

> ► Identify instances of grammatical usage in Examples 3.9 and 3.10 on page 112 that, as a teacher, you would wish to correct.
> ► Can you generalise from these examples and say what areas of grammar are causing problems for the students?
> ► How typical are these areas of the difficulties that *your* learners have with English grammar?
> ► To what extent do you think it is necessary to correct grammatical 'errors' in learners' spoken and written language?

## 3.4 Factors in teaching grammar

Here we look first at how teachers are often required to make decisions about grammar usage; then we consider how important it is to be able to use grammatical terminology if we want to talk about grammar.

### 3.4.1 Decisions and judgements

#### *The role of the teacher in grammar teaching*

Where grammar is concerned, the teacher may have a number of different roles depending on the teaching situation. In general, teachers are often required to make qualitative decisions and judgements, as to whether for example a certain grammar usage is right or wrong, or how they would assess a learner's level of English after marking an essay, or checking an exercise. Part of being a language teacher, therefore, is having both a reasonable understanding of different parts of the system and how they work in conjunction with each other, and an ability to explain what is wrong or inappropriate and how it might be corrected or improved. In the majority of teaching environments, learners certainly expect their teachers to know more about grammar than they, the learners, do. The teacher's role(s)[5] as far as grammar is concerned could thus be some (or all) of the following, depending perhaps on what grammar materials are available:

*guide*
*mentor*
*corrector*
*critic*
*supporter*
*adviser*
*examiner*
*marker*

---

[5] Note that fulfilling these roles may not always be easy, and sometimes they may be imposed by syllabus or examination or institutional requirements.

Whatever role we may have (and this includes the role of simply being a speaker or writer of English), there are a number of ways in which we categorise language and grammatical usage. Chapter 4 will describe in more detail how people talk about language and how we often use generalisations when we make a professional or personal judgement on a particular example. Meanwhile, Activity 44 below contains a list of some words teachers use when they categorise language. Some are directly linked to teaching, others are more general. Although the categories are listed in pairs, several of them represent a continuum rather than an either/or choice. The activity is designed to clarify what we actually mean when we use such terms.

## Activity 44

▶ Look at the list of 'categorising' terms below:

| | |
|---|---|
| right/wrong | acceptable/unacceptable |
| spoken/written | easy/difficult |
| formal/informal | standard/non-standard |
| appropriate/inappropriate | L1 speaker/L2 speaker |

▶ Think about how you might define the terms in the above pairs in relation to your views on grammar. One possible approach is to find a brief, acceptable definition for each of the terms, using the format: 'If something is ..., then this means that ...'. You could discuss your definitions with a colleague or use a dictionary to help.

▶ Now, look at the ten examples below from authentic language use, containing grammatical inconsistencies (or are they 'mistakes'?):

a) People happy are.
b) She brang the book downstairs.
c) The shirt ironed.
d) He said her some terrible things.
e) They must to go.
f) I seen them yesterday.
g) There are less apples on the trees this year.
h) We were checked and stuff.
i) He don't know nothing.
j) There was this frog sitting on the pond, a sort of china frog.

▶ Can you identify any grammar in a–j above which you would want to comment on or perhaps correct (e.g. the forms or combinations of words or the word order)? Try using some of the terms from the 'categorising' list above.

▶ What additional terms, such as the names of tenses or types of words, might you need to describe the grammar in each of the examples? (You also need to think about who might have said or written the utterances, and in what context.)

▶ Is there ever an overlap between the two elements of each pair of categorising terms? For instance, in a grammatical sense is it possible for something to be both acceptable and unacceptable? Which pairs of words cause the most problems or are most difficult to define?

## 3.4.2 Explanations and terminology

### Talking about grammatical categories

Language is made up of a number of different constituent parts. What we call these parts may vary according to whether we are describing spoken or written language, but a general list of describing words would include for instance: sounds, letters, words, syllables, phrases, sentences, paragraphs, texts, discourses. In general terms, many people are familiar with some of the basic terminology of language and it occurs fairly regularly in everyday usage. However, as teachers, we are usually expected to be familiar with a wider range of grammatical terms; in fact terminology is one of the shortcuts in talking about grammar and the shared use of concepts like *noun, verb, adjective, past tense* can help with classroom explanations. Teaching materials also often make use of such terms.

In grammar, as with other areas of language, there are different ways of describing how component parts of the system work. *Morphology*[6], for instance, refers particularly to how words are made up. You do not, however, need to be a morphologist to know that there are categories in English grammar such as plurals *(book/books)*, compounds *(hair-dryer, motorway)* and comparatives *(bigger, easier)* or that English verbs may have several different forms (the irregular verb *to know* has five: *know, knows, knowing, knew, known* whilst other verbs – regular ones – have fewer: *walk, walks, walking, walked)*[7].

In other ways of categorising language, patterns and combinations of clauses are important. This approach is particularly useful if we are interested in how people *do* things with language. Halliday (1994) describes language in terms of a 'rank scale', with a hierarchy of components building upon each other, as illustrated in Figure 4.

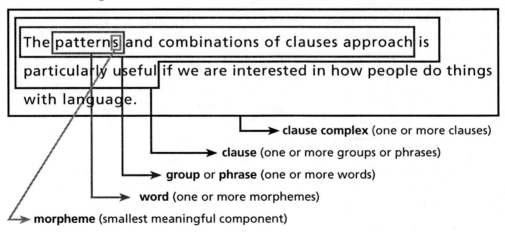

*Figure 4*

[6] Morphologists are interested in looking at the smallest meaningful part or parts – morphemes – of a word: *talking*, for example has two morphemes – *talk* and *ing*; *teacher* also has two – *teach* and *er*.
[7] It is not unusual to hear people claim that English grammar is relatively simple or uncomplicated by comparison with other languages, such as Russian or Polish, which are morphologically much more complex. However, this is not a helpful comment, as *every* language has complicated aspects to its grammar system: it is simply that the complicated aspects may not be the same in every language.

Activities 45 and 46 look at different ways of talking about how language is structured; Activity 45 uses the traditional terminology of parts of speech while Activity 46 looks at a short text from a functional grammar perspective. Grammatical terminology, without necessarily being over-complicated, can be a very useful tool for learners and teachers. It is a convenient pedagogic reference point for talking *about* language, though you do not actually need the terminology to be able to *use* the language: some categories of learners (children for instance) learn language without necessarily being aware of what the words and structures that they use are called.

## Activity 45

► Look at the 12 sentences below. They all have a gap – or gaps in the case of (l) – which can be filled with one word, but notice how in some of the sentences a much wider range of words is possible than in others.

a) She arrived ..........
b) There's .......... pen on the table.
c) The train now .......... at Platform 7 is for London Paddington only.
d) For her birthday they gave her a ..........
e) Where did you .......... her?
f) .......... did you meet?
g) What time .......... you leave?
h) For his birthday they gave him a ..........
i) A .......... cat was sitting outside the door.
j) He .......... hanging out the washing.
k) They were .......... the garden when we arrived.
l) If anyone rings, tell .......... I'll call .......... back.

► Fill each of the gaps with a suitable word.
► For each sentence, say what grammatical category (or part of speech) the word you've chosen belongs to. Is the word part of a big group (or *open set*, in linguistic terminology – nouns, for instance) or part of a small group (or *closed set* – pronouns, for instance)?

## Activity 46

► Look at the following extract from a children's book:

Once on a rainy day there were four small bears in bed: they were called William, Charles, John and Andrew. Robert had already got up to bring the others a cup of tea. Under the bed was a dog, whose name was Fred.
Soon all the bears were in the bathroom. William gave his teeth a specially hard brush: he brushed his bottom teeth up and his top teeth down, and sideways to the left, and sideways to the right. "I'm hungry," thought William, "it must be time for breakfast."

William ate grapefruit, bacon, scrambled eggs, butter, toast and marmalade for breakfast. Charles ate hardly anything at all, for he was reading the cereal packet. On the packet was a picture of a space suit. "How I would love to have a space suit!" he said; "Wouldn't you, Andrew?" "Yes," said Andrew, "there's only one thing to do. We shall have to make some space suits."

*(Gretz 1986)*

► Answer the questions below with information from the text:

Who did something to someone else?
How did someone do something?
Who had something done to them?
Where did something happen?

► The questions above are generated by an approach to grammar which is very different from that in Activity 45. Can you say in what way, or ways, it is different?

## 3.5   Pedagogic approaches to grammar

In this section we review some ways in which grammar has been approached in the classroom, starting with traditional approaches in language teaching, then looking at changes in emphasis in EL2 teaching, and finally considering some questions arising from the 'reduced' model of grammar which often forms the basis of ELT materials.

### 3.5.1 Traditional grammar

Traditionally, an important source of language learning material was the grammar book. Such books divided grammar into various sections, often according to verb tenses or word classes and used a terminology to match: the present continuous, the present perfect, adjectives, prepositions, adverbial clauses and so on. Much traditional grammar teaching for EL1 learners was based on a Latin model; exercises involved *parsing* (the dividing up of sentences into constituent parts), and this approach also influenced the way grammar was presented in L2 learning situations, for example in the teaching of French and other modern foreign languages in Britain. Reference materials would usually contain advice for teachers and learners as to the correct usage of particular forms. Sometimes grammar books contained exercises to practise particular structures. Rules were usually prescriptive and the examples and exercises were, on the whole, thought up in order to illustrate the particular structure in question. Extract 6 probably illustrates the establishment view in Britain of what, once upon a time, grammar was all about.

Extract 6

CHAPTER V.—VERBS.

SECTION 1.—The Kinds of Verbs.

134. **Verb defined.**—A Verb is a word used for *saying* something about some person or thing[1] (§ 13).

The most important item in this definition is *"saying."* "Verb" is the English rendering of Lat. *verbum*, which signifies merely "word." "Verb" has thus acquired the dignity of being pre-eminently *the word*. Why is this? Because of all Parts of Speech it holds the highest rank, higher even than a noun. It is the *saying* something about something else which makes a *sentence*, and this cannot be done without a verb.

135. **The Kinds of Verbs.**—Verbs are subdivided into three main classes :—

I. Verbs used Transitively.  II. Verbs used Intransitively.

III. Auxiliary.

*Note* 1.—Verbs which are not used in all the moods and tenses are called "Defective." But the student must not suppose from this that "Defective" constitutes a separate or fourth class of verb. This is not all the case. *Quoth*, for example, is a Defective verb, but also Intransitive. Again "wit" is a Defective verb, but also Transitive. Again, "may" is a Defective verb, but also Auxiliary.

*Note* 2.—Verbs are distinguished into Strong and Weak according to *conjugation* ; see below, §210.

*(from Nesfield, (1944). English Grammar: Past and Present,*
*originally published in 1898)*

## 3.5.2 ELT approaches

In ELT materials of the 1950s and 1960s there was evidence of some of these traditional influences. The *structural* approach, as it is known and as was current at that time, was influenced partly by contemporary interests in linguistics[8]. Teaching materials were concerned with sentence-based grammar; different units or sections of a book dealt with separate identifiable grammatical forms such as *affirmative sentences* or *the present continuous* or *comparisons*; and the grammar which was presented was based largely on written forms. Example 3.11 on page 119 illustrates this approach and, as can be seen from the contents pages of many recent EFL grammar books and coursebooks, there is evidence that this approach is still widely used today. Examples 3.12 and 3.13 on pages 120 and 121 also show these influences: notice how the particular structure to be taught in Examples 3.12 and 3.13 is highly prominent in the texts and how there is little or no attempt to make the language in any way realistic. The forms of the language are much more important than the functions.

---

[8] Bloomfield's *Language*, for instance, first published in 1935, was very influential.

## Example 3.11

39.2 (Elementary and) Intermediate 'SUBJECT' OF THE GERUND

Since the GERUND is a noun, it is logical to find it preceded by a POSSESSIVE PRONOUN or a NOUN IN THE POSSESSIVE FORM.

    Do you object to a cigarette?
    Do you object to our cigarettes?
    Do you object to smoking?
    Do you object to our smoking?
    Do you object to our smoking cigarettes?

In practice this pattern is restricted almost entirely to pronouns and proper names. Non-personal nouns do not normally have a possessive form, nor can we easily make a possessive form with more complicated subjects. So we also have a parallel pattern using the objective (common) case.

    There was no sign of *the dinner* appearing before I left. We insisted on *rich and poor* being treated alike. Will you approve of *me and my friend* attending the class as visitors?

Examples of this pattern are very common. They are not participle constructions but true gerunds, since the 'object' in each case is not merely the portion in italics, but the whole phrase to the end of the sentence. Therefore it is not surprising to find the same pattern used when a pronoun or proper noun is in SUBJECT relation to the gerund.

Do you mind *their/them* coming too?
I don't like *your/you* coming late every time.
I'm not very keen on *Mary's/Mary* living there alone.

In general the POSSESSIVE form is considered to be more literary and elegant; the OBJECTIVE form is found mainly in the spoken language, where it is probably just as common as the possessive form.

The following short passage from Dickens's *David Copperfield* is of interest:

    (A dream) of *the pair of hired post-horses* being ready; and of *Dora's* going away to change her dress: of *my aunt and Miss Clarissa* remaining with us; and *our* walking in the garden; and *my aunt* ... being mightily amused with herself ...

    (The whole of this long description of David's wedding in Chapter 43 is written in gerunds, and is well worth reading carefully.)

● Read the following, replacing the (pro)nouns **in bold type** by possessives:

1  Our teacher won't like **us** coming late to school.
2  I don't mind **you** talking to Cyril, but I always remember **him** complaining of you staying too long.
3  Please excuse **us** calling you by your first name.
4  I wonder why Maisie hates **me** wearing this pink shirt and green tie?
5  It's no use **you** asking him to lend you any money.
6  I'm afraid of **John** losing the way.
7  They insisted on **me** going again next week.

*(Stannard Allen 1974:178–179)*

**Example 3.12**

MRS HARRISON:  Are you in the bathroom now, Arthur?
ARTHUR:  No, I'm not. I'm here.
MRS HARRISON:  Ah, good evening, Arthur.
ARTHUR:  Good evening, Mrs Harrison.
MRS HARRISON:  What's that?
ARTHUR:  This here?
MRS HARRISON:  Yes.
ARTHUR:  It's a bottle.

MRS HARRISON:  Yes, it's a bottle. But what's in the bottle?
ARTHUR:  Orange squash. Are you thirsty, Mrs Harrison?
MRS HARRISON:  Yes, I am. Thank you, Arthur. The glasses are on the shelf.
ARTHUR:  Which glasses? These glasses here or those glasses?
MRS HARRISON:  Those in front of you.
ARTHUR:  These blue glasses?
MRS HARRISON:  No, not those. They're too small.
ARTHUR:  These? The green glasses?
MRS HARRISON:  Yes, those. That's right. Arthur! Be careful!

*(Coles and Lord 1974:12)*

**Example 3.13**

Martin is putting a five pence piece in the tea machine. Now, he is pushing the button and a plastic cup is coming out. Now the machine is filling the cup. Martin is opening the little window and getting his cup of tea. Now he is putting his tea on the table.

Jillian is very angry. Her five pence piece is in a machine but the coffee is not coming out. Now she is pushing the machine but the coffee is not coming out.

MARTIN: What are you doing, Jill?

JILLIAN: I'm pushing this coffee machine. My five pence piece is in it, but there isn't a cup and there isn't any coffee.

MARTIN: Perhaps it's a bad five pence piece.

JILLIAN: No, it isn't, I'm sure.

MARTIN: Have you any more five pence pieces, Jill?

JILLIAN: Yes, I have two. They are here.

Now Martin is teaching Jillian. She is looking at the machine. He is putting her five pence piece in it. Now he is pushing a button. A plastic cup is coming out and the machine is filling it. But the machine is putting milk in the cup.

JILLIAN: Oh, Martin. That's milk, it isn't coffee. That's the milk machine. Milk is horrible. Oh, Martin, you are silly. Now I have only one five pence piece. And I still haven't any coffee. I'm putting this five pence piece in the coffee machine.

MARTIN: Jill!

JILLIAN: I'm not listening. Look, I'm pushing the button.

*(Broughton 1968:68)*

As more *communicative* English language teaching approaches emerged in the 1970s and '80s, the emphasis shifted away from written language and more towards the teaching of spoken language. As a result there was an increased need for communicative fluency as well as grammatical accuracy. Grammar as a subject in its own right, however, was still considered to be important and many syllabuses, and examinations such as Cambridge *First Certificate* and *Proficiency*, continued to teach and test it. Whether in coursebooks, supplementary materials or specific skills practice books, a large amount of space and time continued to be devoted to providing opportunities for the learning of grammar items based on written, sentence-level forms. Traditional grammatical components remained in syllabuses and many learners, whether they liked it or not, spent (and still spend) a great deal of time in and out of class studying the grammar of English.

**Activity 47** ▷

> ► What particular grammar areas do you think Examples 3.12 and 3.13 on pages 120 and 121 are designed to practise?
> ► How useful would such texts be for *your* learners?
> ► Can you think of any disadvantages of this approach to teaching grammar?

Alongside the continued perceived need for the teaching of grammar there have been, since the advent of the materials illustrated in Examples 3.12 and 3.13 above, several identifiable changes in emphasis:

- the amount and variety of grammar *practice material* has actually increased
- a more *learner-centred* approach has become popular and many more publications for *independent study* have appeared (with exercises and answer keys, for example)
- there has been a trend for publishers to *sub-divide materials by both skills and levels* to produce books aimed at practising discrete areas of grammar such as modals and phrasal verbs
- grammars have appeared with their own *workbooks*
- more *grammar awareness*-type activities have appeared

However, much of the traditional way in which exercises were constructed has continued to be used and the approach of dividing up grammar into recognisable discrete parts (verbs and tenses, nouns, adverbs and so on) has remained largely the same. Some typical exercise types were (and still are):

| Type | Example |
|------|---------|
| *gap-filling and blanks* | She .............. waiting since 2 o'clock. |
| *transformation* (i.e. changing the structure of a sentence while retaining its meaning) | He managed to persuade them, but it was difficult.<br>Only with ................................................ |
| *correcting the mistake* | I had the breakfast at 8 o'clock this morning. |
| completing a sentence *using prompts* | I hope ....... (see) ........ you soon. |

At the same time, the rapid development of, and improvements in technology in recent years now provide many more computer-based tools which can help with the study and learning of grammar. These include:

- increasingly standard features of word-processing packages such as spelling and grammar checkers, and revision and editing tools
- more sophisticated and accessible Computer Assisted Language Learning (CALL) materials

- considerable 'on-line' reference and practice facilities (e.g. dictionaries)
- the use of the Internet both to access and to produce teaching and learning materials

Linked to these are the relatively recent developments in grammar teaching which have resulted from work on database and corpus materials. Traditionally, as we have seen, structural points such as the past simple tense or indirect speech were exemplified in sentences that were specially compiled, that is, the grammar point was decided on and then examples were invented to show how this particular point worked. Corpus materials, by contrast, offer a different approach: large quantities of authentic data are collected and sorted and then patterns of usage can be identified and analysed. Projects such as *COBUILD (Collins)* and the *Longman Corpus Network*[9] make it possible to see real examples instead of invented ones and provide a level of accurate detail that was not previously possible. *Concordances* (the sorting of database information) also offer new insights into actual language use: they show us which words and structures are most commonly used, for instance[10].

Example 3.14 below shows how precise information can be provided on specific and contextualised categories of vocabulary. Example 3.15 on page 124 explains *delexical verbs*, a very common occurrence in spoken English, but a pattern which is not usually found in teaching grammars or coursebooks.

## Example 3.14

1.82 A small number of '-ing' nouns, most of which refer to sporting or leisure activities, are much more common than their related verbs. In some cases there is at the moment no verb, although it is always possible to invent one. For example, you are more likely to say 'We went caravanning round France' than 'We caravanned round France'.

Here is a list of the commonest of these nouns:

| | | | |
|---|---|---|---|
| angling | caravanning | paragliding | surfing |
| blackberrying | electioneering | shoplifting | weightlifting |
| boating | hang-gliding | sightseeing | window-shopping |
| bowling | heliskiing | skateboarding | windsurfing |
| canoeing | mountaineering | snorkelling | yachting |

Although these words are not always associated with a verb, most of them can be used as present participles.

*He fell fully-clothed into the lake while <u>boating</u> with a girlfriend.*
*I spent the afternoon <u>window-shopping</u> with Grandma.*

(*Collins* Cobuild English Grammar *1995:24*)

---

[9] Details of these projects can be found on websites at http://titania.cobuild.collins.co.uk and http://www.awl-elt.com/dictionaries.
[10] According to *CANCODE*, (the Cambridge and Nottingham Corpus of Discourse in English) the three most commonly occurring words in spoken English are *the*, *I* and *you*, and in written English *the*, *to* and *of*.

## Example 3.15

**verbs which are often delexical**

3.34 In this section we focus on the very common verbs which are used in this transitive structure. They are called *delexical verbs*, and the structure which consists of a delexical verb followed by a noun group is called a *delexical structure*.

Here is a list of verbs which are used as delexical verbs. The first four are very commonly used in this way.

| | |
|---|---|
| give | do |
| have | hold |
| make | keep |
| take | set |

Note that 'have got' is not used instead of 'have' in delexical structures.

Delexical structures are very common in current English. Although the total number of delexical verbs is small, they include some of the very commonest words in the language. Delexical structures contribute to the impression of fluency in English given by a foreign user.

3.35 In many cases, there is a verb which has a similar meaning to the meaning of the delexical structure. For example, the verb 'look' means almost the same as 'have a look'. When the word is a verb, as in 'I looked round the room', you are focusing on the action of looking. When you use the word as a noun in a delexical structure, you are naming an event, something which is complete. This structure often seems to be preferred to a structure in which the verb has greater prominence. Note that the verb which corresponds to the delexical structure is often intransitive.

She _made a signal_.
She _signalled_ for a taxi.
A couple _were having a drink_ at a table by the window.
A few students _were drinking_ at the bar.
She _gave an amused laugh_.
They both _laughed_.
He _gave a vague reply_.
They _replied_ to his letter.

There are also some verbs which are transitive.

I _had a glimpse_ of the speedometer.
I _glimpsed_ a bright flash of gold on the left.
He _gave a little sniff_.
I _sniffed_ the room.
Comis _took a photograph_ of her.
They _photographed_ the pigeons in Trafalgar Square.

*(Collins Cobuild English Grammar 1995:147)*

**Activity 48** ▷

> ▶ Can you think of any reasons why *delexical* verbs (Example 3.15 on page 124) are not usually included in ELT teaching materials?
> ▶ How useful would such grammar/lexical forms be for your learners?
> ▶ Can you think of any disadvantages of the material in Example 3.14 on page 123 for teachers and/or learners?

### 3.5.3 A 'reduced model' of grammar

It seems axiomatic that language has to be 'reduced' in some form or other for learners. This generally accepted need to present the language – especially for learners at lower levels – in identifiable, discrete chunks means that many ELT grammar teaching materials have adopted an approach based predominantly on decontextualised written forms at sentence level. Coursebooks, and teachers, tend to concentrate on recognisable areas such as the role and use of verb tenses in English and treat them as separate 'bits' of language to be learned, rather than as parts of the whole system. In relation to the teaching of grammar, we could usefully consider the following issues, even if the answers may not be immediate or obvious.

- who decides which forms are to be taught and in which order?
- what principles underlie the hierarchy of difficulty? (Is the past tense more 'difficult' than the present tense for instance, and if so, why?)
- is it possible to avoid over-simplification?
- why are some language areas largely ignored (for instance, features of spoken language such as overlaps, repetitions, redundancies, false starts, incomplete structures, miscues and so on)?
- what effect does a reduced model have on learners at a later stage?
- how difficult would it be to introduce some features of language use such as those highlighted by functional grammar (see 3.2.2 and 3.4.2)?
- what effect does the lack of meaningful contexts have on learners' views of language?
- how much control do teachers have (or wish to have) over what kind of grammar they are required to teach?

## 3.6 Some alternative approaches

In this final section of the chapter we look at some alternative ways of thinking about grammar, which derive from the way language is used, rather than how it is often divided up in teaching materials. We look at four general concepts, each with a representative language example to illustrate it:

- relevance
- flexibility

- volume
- range

The aim of this section, in keeping with the overall 'broadening' aim of the book, is to suggest, not that there is one undisputed 'best' way of teaching grammar, but that it may be rewarding to investigate a number of different ways of approaching grammar and grammar pedagogy.

We have already established that grammar itself is a difficult term to define and that there is a multiplicity of views on grammar. Some teachers may already have a clear view of how they see grammar; others, particularly at the start of a career, may find the terminology confusing and the potential complexity daunting. On a day-to-day basis the needs of most language teachers are clear: they have to be able to understand grammar points; they also need to be able to explain things clearly and simply – a skill which takes some time to acquire. To summarise some basic pedagogic points relating to the teaching and learning of grammar, we could say that the constraints of a 'typical' teaching context will require teachers to:

- be aware of the grammatical requirements of their learner
- have a basic understanding of these grammatical requirements
- understand the grammar of the teaching books they use
- be able to give clear and informed judgements on what is and is not correct
- be aware that learners expect teachers to know about grammar and to correct their mistakes

Thus, particularly in the light of the 'traditional' approach underlying much of the published language practice material available, the classroom grammar skills that most teachers require are often those which will enable them to answer questions such as:

- Why is the past perfect tense used in sentences such as *By that time she had already decided to go*?
- Why is it wrong to use *the* in this sentence: *I usually have the breakfast at 7.30 every morning*?
- What is the difference between: *she used to go there* and *she is used to going there*?

We think now about how the four concepts mentioned above – and we stress that they are only examples – might contribute to giving useful answers to such questions.

### Relevance

The 'reduced model' of grammar discussed above in 3.5.3 has some difficulty with the concept of relevance. It is very difficult to say that one component of sentence-based grammar is more relevant than another: is the present tense, for example, more relevant than the past tense, and if so why, and on what grounds? How is it possible to decide which of the conditional structures in English is most relevant for learners?

What is clear from looking at 'high frequency' items – i.e. language items that occur very often – is that some structural aspects of the language system *are* highly relevant in that we use them all the time in communication. *Deixis* is an example of a highly relevant language feature which is normally divided up into separate components (pronouns or adverbs of place, for instance) and then included among the 'items' taught in sentence-based grammar. In Extract 7 Carter and McCarthy (1997) explain the relevance of deixis.

### Extract 7

This term describes what may be termed the orientational features of language as deixis involves words which point backwards and forwards in a text as well as outside the text to a wider extra-textual context. For example, words like *these/that/this/those* locate an utterance in relation to space and to the speaker's sense of closeness or involvement with something, words like *now* and *then* relate to the current moment of utterance and words like *we/you/they/him/I* relate to who is speaking, who is present, included, excluded, etc. Thus, 'I'd like to pop in to that little shop over there before we leave' contains deictics which orientate a listener interpersonally, temporally and spatially in relation to the proposition of the sentence. Certain contexts of language, such as language used to do things like packing, cooking, moving furniture, etc. involve a lot of deictics because the objects and other phenomena being dealt with are normally immediately visible to all speakers and thus forms of language such as 'Could we just move that into this corner here?' are relatively commonplace.

*(Carter and McCarthy 1997:13)*

### Flexibility

As we have seen in Chapters 1 and 2, and as we will see in Chapter 5, language is a flexible instrument: 'rules' are not carved in stone, but can change and appear in various guises depending on the context in which the language is used. This may be potentially confusing for learners, but they need to know, nonetheless, that it happens. All language has flexibility, not least because we have to use it for a very wide range of purposes. Thus, in grammar terms, a useful notion for learners to be aware of might be that language items do not necessarily pack away neatly into one category and one category only. *Transitivity* is a good example here: whether a verb can take an object or not is a basic concept in the grammar of English but one that also includes some flexibility: the verb *to progress*, for instance, is not invariably intransitive (witness the utterance *we are progressing our enquiries* in a police context). Where verbs are concerned, coursebooks have traditionally concentrated on the structure of tense patterns and used these patterns as the basis for a considerable proportion of grammar work. But much more could be made of how verbs operate semantically, by emphasising what verbs *do* in the language and how different categories of verbs behave.

Another example of flexibility is the concept of *nominalisation*, as seen for instance in the use of nouns as adjectives in noun combinations such as *world bank* or *school dinner;* the flexibility here arises from the fact that the same item (e.g. *bank*) can have more than one meaning (what is called *polysemy)* and can also be in more than one grammatical category (another basic feature of English words connected with nominalisation). Both these aspects of flexibility are illustrated in the list of examples below where pairs of nouns come together to form compounds:

*book token*
*driving licence*
*power cut*
*can opener*
*mineral water*
*fire brigade*
*blood pressure*

### Volume

In 3.3.2 above we saw that there are some areas of English grammar that EL1 speakers have little difficulty with, largely because they meet them very regularly and frequently. If we identify all the different kinds of article usage in the 'four small bears' text from the children's book which appeared previously in Activity 46 on page 116, we can appreciate how complicated the system is: even though the text is written for younger learners, the usage of articles is actually quite complex. One of the clues is to do with frequency: both *the* and *a* appear in the list of the top five most frequently used words in English. Article usage, however, remains a baffling concept for many EL2 learners and is a particularly difficult one for many to acquire, given many learners' typical learning patterns of two or three 50-minute classes a week in a 'foreign language' classroom situation.

The teaching implications are that learners will often fail to master the system of article usage in English. This is not because they are poor learners or are taught ineffectively but because they are measured against an ideal which is actually only achievable by constant and lengthy exposure to an L1 environment. Thus, as far as articles are concerned, it could be argued that learners might be profitably encouraged to spend more time on reading to gain more exposure to usage and less time on gap-fill exercises where they practise decontextualised 'rule' application.

### Range

The concept of range relates to the circumstances in which a grammatical item may appear. Adverbs, for instance, are not only the most flexible word class in English in terms of where they can go in a sentence, but they also have a wide range of uses: to describe, to qualify or to add precision. Traditional grammar often classifies them in terms of manner, place or time and many current teaching books still adopt this basic approach, although it is quite clear that they can be used for a much wider range of functions. In everyday speech for instance, adverbs can quite often function as answers to questions:

Q: *Are you interested?*   A: *Quite/Not really/Definitely*

Compare this with traditional grammar teaching which tends to concentrate on short form responses:

Q: *Are you interested?*   A: *Yes, I am/No, I'm not.*

These short forms are, of course, used widely but they are not the only way of replying to a question. They also tend to convey a very definite positive or negative meaning whereas, as well as being somewhat simpler in form, adverbs can add different shades of meaning, as the following examples show:

Q: *Is it important?*            A: *Maybe*
Q: *Are you interested?*         A: *Very*
Q: *Are you ready?*              A: *Not quite*
Q: *Is she sick?*               A: *Not really*
Q: *Do you want to go?*          A: *Sure*
Q: *Does he want the job?*       A: *Definitely*
Q: *Were they drunk?*            A: *Hopelessly*
Q: *Have you done it?*           A: *Of course*
Q: *Are you certain?*            A: *Absolutely*
Q: *Is the answer that easy?*    A: *Possibly*
Q: *So, it's broken?*            A: *In effect*

## Using new information to broaden our teaching base

The above four 'productive' grammar features – relevance, flexibility, volume and range – bring us to the final implication of what we have been discussing in this chapter. It is the case, with grammar as with other subjects, that the teacher's level of knowledge and understanding is usually ahead of that of the learners they teach. However, knowledge is constantly being added to, revised and re-shaped. Over the last few years there has been a huge increase in the amount of grammar teaching resources available, and there is now a wide range of ELT grammar reference materials at all levels from 'beginners' to 'advanced'.[11] Many of these are influenced by the new kinds of information at our disposal about how language is actually used and they capitalise on this awareness to help explain grammatical problems to learners and teachers. At the same time, ELT dictionaries increasingly contain much more information on grammatical structures and patterns, such as how a particular word is used in phrasal verbs or how its meaning might change in a range of formal/informal settings. This kind of 'cross fertilisation' between grammatical and lexical awareness adds a new dimension to the knowledge language teachers need.

Nevertheless, despite this increasing volume of language data and evidence, a great deal of grammar teaching and learning clings stubbornly to the traditional model, with many ELT coursebooks and grammars still dealing with what is in effect written English at sentence level. Also, it is still often not made clear that the forms being dealt with in the grammar books relate to written English, and without adequate contexts it is often uncertain to what extent the explanation in question is appropriate to the particular grammatical point under consideration. Language teaching materials may be designed to help the process of explanation, but unfortunately they do not always reflect the way language is used.

With this in mind, then, we might expand the list of pedagogic points at the beginning of this section with the following:

• knowing as much as possible about how English works in as many different contexts as possible is a useful pedagogic aim (for teachers and learners)

[11] See Thornbury 1997; Bolitho and Tomlinson 1995; Wright 1994; Van Lier 1995.

- understanding the limitations of classroom grammar is advantageous
- an understanding of language factors such as change, function and informality is a useful addition to more traditional modes of approaching grammar

We could also suggest that the prospect of teaching and learning English via an approach which does not always neatly divide the language into small separate compartments might be an interesting and motivating one for some of the following reasons:

- such an approach helps and encourages meaningful comparisons between EL1 and EL2 usage
- it might also prepare learners better for encounters with 'real' language, for example through the media or travel or contact with other speakers
- traditional pattern practice is not always particularly successful (e.g. in helping speakers of languages without articles to master the English article system)
- teachers and learners might gain more insight into how the language actually works in use

## Key references

*Collins COBUILD English Grammar.* (1990). London: Collins ELT.

Crystal, D. (1995). *Cambridge Encyclopedia of the English Language.* Cambridge: Cambridge University Press.

Hawkins, E. (1987). *Awareness of Language.* Cambridge: Cambridge University Press.

Hudson, R. (1992). *Teaching Grammar: A Guide for the National Curriculum.* Oxford: Blackwell.

Thornbury, S. (1997). *About Language.* Cambridge: Cambridge University Press.

Van Lier, L. (1995). *Introducing Language Awareness.* London: Penguin.

Wright, T. (1994). *Investigating English.* London: Edward Arnold.

# 4 Variety

## 4.1 Overview

This chapter is concerned with the notion of variety in the use of language. In particular, we consider varieties of English and attitudes towards them as well as looking at the notion of appropriacy of language use as it applies to the teaching and learning of English.

Section 4.2 presents some of the key terms used in the description of varieties of language and attempts to clarify some of the confusion that surrounds the use of these terms. The description of EL1 varieties of English has been the subject of study for a long time, but the attitudes people have towards these varieties is a relatively recent area of study. These attitudes are the concern of Section 4.3 along with issues concerning the status of and attitudes towards the varieties of English used in countries where it is not the mother tongue of the majority of the population (often referred to as 'new' Englishes). Section 4.4 looks at the relationship between appropriate use of language and the situations in which it is used and the challenges this aspect of language use raises for teachers and learners of EL2.

## 4.2 Terminology

The following terms are frequently used to refer to varieties of language:

| | |
|---|---|
| *accent* | *register* |
| *dialect* | *jargon* |
| *style* | *idiolect* |

While these terms are useful, there is some confusion surrounding their definitions and, consequently, how they are used. There are some differences between what they mean in general use and how they are used by linguists. Even among linguists there is lack of agreement over the meanings of *style* and *register*, and *jargon* is used with various meanings depending on one's attitude to the particular instance of language use referred to. In the following section we attempt to clarify some of these areas of confusion.

## 4.2.1  Some common confusions over definitions

### Accent and dialect

Concerning *accent* and *dialect*, the following definitions are taken from the *Cambridge Encyclopedia of the English Language*:

**accent**   features of pronunciation that signal regional or social identity (*p. 448*)
**dialect**   a language variety in which use of grammar and vocabulary identifies the regional or social background of the user (*p. 451*)

From these definitions we can see that *accent* and *dialect* are not freely interchangeable, although people do sometimes use them as if they were synonyms. Also significant in the definitions of these two terms is the reference to the social background of the user. Less useful definitions refer only to the geographical, or regional, origins of users. If we accepted these less useful definitions we would find it difficult to place the most prestigious *accent* of British English: *Received Pronunciation*, commonly referred to as *RP* (in linguistic and ELT contexts), which, although it has its origins in a particular region, is now more associated with social class, education and, possibly, occupation. The most prestigious *dialect* of British English, usually referred to as *Standard English,* is similarly more closely associated with the social background of its users than their geographical origins. Figure 5 (from Trudgill 1983:41) represents the relationship between social class membership and the use of Standard English.

The relationship between social class membership and the use of standard English (from Trudgill 1974:41)

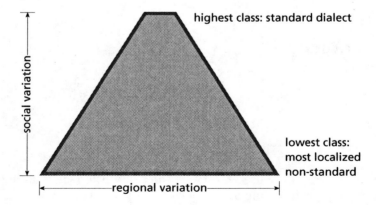

*Figure 5*

Trudgill's 'pyramid' indicates that among 'higher' social classes there is little variation from Standard English, while a wide variety of local non-standard dialects are used at the 'lower' end of the social scale. Trudgill also describes a similar relationship between the use of RP and the social background of its users in that RP is associated with 'higher' social groups.

## Style and register

Crystal (1997a:66) refers to *style* as one of the 'thorniest concepts' to be dealt with in talking about language. He identifies two broad senses of style, the *evaluative* and the *descriptive,* as follows:

> Under the first heading, style is thought of in a critical way: the features that make someone or something stand out from an 'undistinguished' background ... the second sense lacks these value judgements and simply describes the set of distinctive characteristics that identify objects, persons, periods or places.
>
> *(Crystal 1997a:66)*

As far as *register* is concerned, the following set of quotations serves to illustrate the confusion likely to beset those searching for a precise definition:

> Registers are usually characterised solely by vocabulary differences: either by the use of particular words, or by the use of words in a particular sense.
>
> *(Trudgill 1983:101)*

> Registers are sets of vocabulary items associated with discrete occupational or social groups. Surgeons, airline pilots, bank managers, sales clerks, jazz fans and pimps use different vocabularies. Of course, one person may control a variety of registers: you can be a stockbroker and an archeologist, or a mountain climber and an economist.
>
> *(Wardhaugh 1992:49)*

> **register:** In stylistics, a socially defined variety of language, such as scientific or legal English.
>
> *(Cambridge Encyclopedia of English Language 1995:457)*

> [Register refers to] variations caused by the use to which the individual is putting the language in the particular situation being investigated, rather than those caused by the relatively permanent characteristics of the user such as age, education, social class membership and so forth.
>
> *(Bell, 1976:27)*

As with the definitions of *accent* and *dialect*, there is some potentially confusing overlap between the use of the terms *register* and *style.* According to Hudson (1996:23), these two terms mean much the same thing:

> ... registers (a term meaning roughly 'style'...)

But *register* often refers specifically to varieties of language associated with occupations, and we turn our attention to this usage in the next activity which is based on the doctor–patient dialogue which appeared in Chapter 1 as Example

1.2 on page 24. This dialogue is an example of what we might call the 'medical' register of English. It provides an opportunity to apply the definitions given above to one sample of language-in-use.

## Activity 49 ▷

Look at the doctor–patient exchange in Chapter 1, Example 1.2, on page 24.

▶ Which of the definitions of register given above seem most relevant in describing the doctor's use of language?
▶ Find some examples of vocabulary and grammar used by the doctor which indicate his language belongs to a 'medical' register of English.
▶ What do you consider to be the doctor's various purposes in using the language as he does?

## *Jargon*

Concerning the term *jargon* The *Oxford Companion to the English Language* (1992:543) tells us that the word derives from late Middle English forms meaning 'the twittering and chattering of birds, meaningless talk, gibberish'. This derivation of the term relates to one way in which it is currently used, i.e. as a means of dismissing what we read or hear as meaningless. When we refer to a piece of language as 'just jargon' we are conveying a clearly negative attitude towards it. However, the term is also used, in a non-pejorative sense, to refer to the specialised language of particular professional or occupational groups. Example 4.1 below is taken from the notes written by the doctor in Example 1.2 for the benefit of his colleagues in the hospital who would be involved in the care of the patient.

## Example 4.1

Dyspnoea – moderate; occasional after exertion; at night.
Orthopnoea?
△ Hypertension.
Tests: blood

*(Authors' data)*

Here the doctor is using technical terms, particular forms of punctuation and a symbol, which are presumably not only understandable to professional colleagues but also effective in communicating the relevant information to them. It is obviously cost-effective in terms of time and effort for hospital staff to make use of this specialised variety of the language, and the same could be said of other occupational groups. Sometimes, however, it is suggested that the use of specialised or technical language by members of such a group in the presence of non-members is a convenient way of preventing the latter from understanding what is going on. Allegations of this kind of exclusive use of language have been levelled at doctors, lawyers and criminals, to name but a few.

## *Idiolect*

Finally, *idiolect* is a term that can be used to include all the features of language use typical of an individual, whether these are traces of regional accent or dialect or idiosyncratic vocabulary or any non-standard items. The *Cambridge Encyclopedia of the English Language* defines it as follows:

> **idiolect:** the linguistic system of an individual speaker (*p. 453*)

Thus, idiolect distinguishes individual use of language from an identifiable group use, or dialect, since there is huge variation between individual users even when there are factors which tend to encourage relative uniformity such as social class and identity. But, like many areas of language use, an idiolect is not static: the way a person uses language changes both over a period of time as they develop and grow older and also on a day-to-day basis depending on who they are communicating with and for what purpose. So, for instance, people may adapt their pronunciation according to who they are talking to.

### Activity 50

Think about your own personal use of English – i.e. your *idiolect*. What are important priorities for you, either as an EL1 or EL2 user, in the way you use English? (e.g. do you consciously try to use 'correct' language? do you consciously adjust your 'code' according to the context? do you try to be clever, witty, impressive, etc.? do you try to use fashionable expressions or 'in-words'?)

The terms used to refer to varieties of language that we have considered above are sometimes sorted into two broad categories: those referring to *user* characteristics and those referring to *use* characteristics. *User* terms refer to more or less 'permanent' characteristics of a person's use of language, while *use* terms are more to do with the way people use language for particular purposes in various contexts.

### Activity 51 ▷

Look again at the six terms which refer to varieties of language: *accent, dialect, style, register, jargon* and *idiolect*. Which of them refer to the *user* of language and which to the *use* to which language is put?

## 4.2.2 Code-switching

A distinction was made in Activity 51 between varieties to do with *user* and *use*. The commentary on this activity (see page 259) indicates that accent and dialect are more to do with the *user* and register and style with *use*. However, just as people make stylistic choices or adjustments in order to achieve particular effects, it is not uncommon for people sometimes to vary their accent or dialect for the same purpose, so the *user/use* distinction becomes a little blurred. This variation of style and accent and dialect is often referred to as 'code-switching'.[1]

Sometimes it seems that the desired effect of 'code-switching' (using an expression which might seem at odds with the context in which it is used) may not be what is actually achieved. Consider the following example and try the activity which follows it.

## Example 4.2

> *(A priest is addressing a large congregation of women, men and children in a church in a working class district of London.)*
>
> Of course, God knows that you're all good chaps, really ...
>
> (Authors' data)

## Activity 52 ▷

> ▶ Does anything strike you as odd or unexpected about the language used by the priest in Example 4.2?
> ▶ What do you think was the speaker's intended purpose in choosing the language he uses?

# 4.3  Attitudes towards varieties of English

People constantly make judgements, spoken or unspoken, about the way other people use language. This is as true of English as it is of other languages. We now consider the opinions of professional linguists concerning varieties of English as well as some of the attitudes frequently expressed by British people who are not linguists.

## 4.3.1  Evaluating varieties

A question which relates to many of the social, educational and political issues touching people's lives[2] is the following: *Is one variety of the language better than others?*

### *Views of linguists*

We approach this question first of all by considering the views of two linguists regarding varieties of British English. The first of these, Peter Trudgill, provides a summary of what we might call the 'egalitarian' position:

---

[1] For a detailed discussion of this term, see Wardhaugh 1992:103–116.
[2] For a detailed analysis of how language varieties are intertwined with people's destinies in a bilingual American context, see Zentella 1997.

> Standard English is only one variety among many, although a peculiarly impor-
> tant one. Linguistically speaking, it cannot even legitimately be considered
> *better* than other varieties. The scientific study of language has convinced most
> scholars that *all* languages, and correspondingly *all* dialects, are equally 'good'
> as linguistic systems.
>
> *(Trudgill 1983:20)*

At the same time as asserting the equality of varieties of English, Trudgill also
discusses the way that certain English accents and dialects are nevertheless
perceived, quite generally in British society, as more prestigious than others.

In contrast to Trudgill's view is the 'non-egalitarian' position. In his book,
*Language is Power*, the linguist John Honey takes the view that:

> ... standard English is not merely one variety among many, but instead is a
> specially important and valuable variety which derives its value from a set of
> qualities which are not shared by other, non-standard dialects.
>
> *(Honey 1997:5)*

It is outside the scope of this book to examine the issues which underlie the
opposing positions apparent in these extracts. The opinions expressed are linked
to educational, social and political issues in British society. Teachers of EL2 might
question the relevance of the discussion to their professional concerns. However,
we feel that for mother-tongue teachers of EL2 it is no bad thing to be reminded
that the role of Standard English and RP in Britain is subject to lively and
sometimes vituperative debate. For non-mother-tongue teachers, awareness of
the debate provides an insight into one aspect of the cultural context in which
English is used as a mother tongue.

In Section 4.3.3 below, we will look into a wider, but related matter: the
position of Standard English and RP in relation to the so-called 'New Englishes'.
Now, though, we move from the opinions articulated by language 'professionals'
to a review of what the 'people' say.

## Views of lay-people

When people talk about accents and dialects and the quality of a person's use of
language, certain value-laden words and phrases frequently occur. Here, for
instance, are some expressions you might hear about certain regional varieties of
English:

- *broad* Yorkshire
- *thick* Liverpool
- *lilting* Irish
- *flat* Northern
- *whining* Birmingham
- West Country *burr*

Expressions sometimes used to describe RP include the following:

- *posh*
- *lah-dee-dah*
- *far back*

And it is not only features of accent or dialect which attract comment. There are facets of language use which contribute to what we might call the quality of a person's speech or writing. A list of words commonly used to describe this aspect of the use of English appeared in Chapter 1 (page 41). The point about such expressions and those given above is that they all, in one way or another, convey commonly-held attitudes people have towards the way their language is used by others.

## Activity 53

Here are the words given in Chapter 1 as examples of evaluations of people's use of English: *articulate, eloquent, fluent, fractured, lazy, posh, slovenly, sloppy, uneducated.*

▶ Say which words indicate a positive attitude and which a negative one, using a dictionary to help, if necessary.
▶ Choose one positive word and one negative word. What features of language use (spoken or written) might be described by each of the words you have chosen? ('Features' here might include pronunciation, grammar or choice of vocabulary.)

## 4.3.2 Evaluating quality of language use

When we begin to analyse the easy and rather unthinking way in which we pass judgement on other people's use of language, certain questions arise. In particular, we may question the actual meaning of some of the expressions commonly used. Do the terms mean the same to different people? Is it possible to measure the 'quality' referred to in the expressions? Can one person's speech be more 'sloppy' than another person's, for example? The context in which language is used is also a factor to be considered: what may be regarded as 'lazy' in one situation might well be thought of as 'casual' or even 'friendly' in another.

The ways in which regional varieties of British and American English (particularly accents) are judged and evaluated by mother-tongue speakers of the language have been the subject of much research[3]. An early investigation into how accents of British English are evaluated was conducted by Howard Giles in 1970. Part of his study required a group of people listening to the same message spoken in several different accents on an audio tape to evaluate each accent in terms of how pleasant or unpleasant it sounded. The results showed that RP was considered the most pleasant, compared with a variety of British regional accents, and that accents associated with large industrial cities were considered the least pleasant.

The research also shows that, as well as favouring certain varieties over others for their 'aesthetic' qualities (as in Giles' work), British people tend to evaluate the personalities and characters of others on the basis of their speech. To some extent, this is not all that surprising since, when we meet someone for the first time, it is natural to assess that person in various ways, if only to work out how

[3] For a summary of this research see Hudson 1996:203–220.

we should behave towards them. Their use of language is one means we have of assessing people.

However, the research shows that, in Britain, people also tend to associate certain stereotyped behaviour and personality traits, as well as certain occupations, with particular varieties of speech. In one experiment reported by Hudson (1996:213)[4], secondary school pupils in an area of east London were asked to evaluate voices speaking with their own local 'Cockney' accent. They gave negative evaluations on such personal traits as friendliness, honesty, intelligence, cleanliness and good looks, compared with how they evaluated voices with more standard accents. Other investigations reviewed by Hudson show some alarming tendencies for students to evaluate negatively teachers with non-standard accents and, perhaps more alarmingly, for teachers to do likewise with regard to students.

Whether this phenomenon makes Britain a linguistically-prejudiced society or simply an accent-conscious one is a matter of some debate. However, there is some evidence that Britain has become more tolerant of regional accents. It is not so long since we would not have heard serious news items being presented on the British broadcast media in anything but RP. In fact, it is not all that long ago that we would have heard only male voices reading the news.

## Activity 54 ▷

Various factors influence the way we react to accents and dialects of our own language including the age, appearance and occupation (if we know it) of the person we are listening to.

▶ Can you think of other factors ?
▶ Which factors do you think are the most influential?
▶ Have you ever experienced a negative reaction to your use of your own (L1) language? If so, what sort of negative reaction was it and what was it about your use of language that caused it?

We end this section with a quotation from David Crystal, which presents a realistic and positive view of the linked phenomena of linguistic variety and social division. His encouragement of his readers to 'learn about it' neatly locates this aspect of language within the scope of language awareness:

> There will always be social division, and so there will always be linguistic variety. We can't remove this variety, but we can learn about it, and try to understand the way it shapes our attitudes and outlook. At the very least, it's a pleasant enough way to pass the time. At best, some good might come out of the enterprise, in the form of greater linguistic – and therefore social – tolerance. It's no coincidence that 'communication' and 'community' are closely related words.
>
> *(Crystal 1984:11)*

[4] This experiment was conducted by G. Smith in 1979.

### 4.3.3 'New' Englishes

We turn now to considering some of the implications of the spread of English as a widely spoken international language, and the resultant emergence of varieties known as 'new' Englishes.

#### *Some examples of 'new' Englishes*

By way of an introduction to this topic, we have selected two examples of spoken English and two of written English produced by EL2 users. We have provided the source of each of the examples and, with the help of these, it is certainly possible to understand the general intended meaning in each case. However, it is clear that these examples of English in use do not conform to all the 'rules' and conventions of standard EL1 English. The activity which follows the examples invites you to consider what it is about each one that marks it as non-standard in this sense.

#### Example 4.3

*From the 'Regulations for Guests' leaflet in a Tokyo hotel*

Not to give annoyance to others by making a loud noise or disgusting behaviour
Not to bring the following articles into the room or hall-way
   A Animals, birds etc.
   B Things with loathsome smell
Not to gamble or behave in a demoralizing manner in this hotel

#### Example 4.4

*From the publicity leaflet of an Istanbul restaurant*
Those days the sea was not far away from Kumkapi. After the sea was filled even Kumkapi like other coasts retired from the sea. Those days our nearly beside the sea being restaurant has been renovated according to its historical architecture.

#### Example 4.5

*A Kenyan policeman speaking to a motorist who had parked his car in a restricted area*
This a great unlawf.

#### Example 4.6

*A Kenyan school student to her teacher*
Sorry for late. I had to foot all the way.

*(Authors' data)*

## Activity 55 ▷

> ▶ Find instances of non-standard usage in Examples 4.3–4.6.
> ▶ Do you agree with the claim (made earlier) that it is possible to understand the general intended meaning of each example?
> ▶ Are any of the examples more difficult to understand than others? If so, can you say why?

## *Attitudes towards 'new' Englishes*

Discussion of the concept of 'new' Englishes requires us to examine our attitude towards the kind of non-standard use of English illustrated in Examples 4.3–4.6 above. If 'non-standard' refers to deviations from an EL1 model, is it valid to apply the term to the use of English by EL2 users? Answers to this question will vary according to the particular concerns of those who address it.

It is probably true to say that in most countries teachers and learners of English in formal school systems are still faced with the situation in which the performance of the learners is assessed according to EL1 criteria. The examinations in English by which learners and, indirectly, their teachers are judged require candidates to produce English which approximates as closely as possible to EL1 usage. The closer the approximation, the greater the reward in terms of higher grades. Since so much may depend on examination results in terms of career opportunities, as long as these formal examination criteria remain in force, it is unlikely that many teachers, learners, parents or employers would advocate the adoption of a local, or 'new' model of English as the target of achievement for learners. According to this approach, 'non-standard' usage means 'non-EL1' usage and its occurrence is seen as evidence of incomplete learning or inefficient teaching.

An opposing view to that summarised above denies the necessity to label non-EL1 varieties of English as non-standard. Wong (1982:263) refers to Third World Englishes as being 'different in various ways from native-speaker English and justifiably and understandably so'. She relates the development of what she calls 'nonnative' varieties of English to the acquisition of political independence by former colonies and the accompanying feelings of national pride:

> … each country has gone ahead to forge for itself not only its own national language but also its own distinctive variety of English. The newly acquired dignity of these nonnative varieties of English arises from the realization that there ought to be no inherent reason why native-speaker standards for English should be imposed upon nonnative contexts.
>
> *(Wong 1982:263)*

Wong clearly feels that EL1 varieties have no intrinsic superiority over EL2 varieties. She is one writer among many to promulgate this view, and issues related to the status of and attitudes towards 'new' Englishes[5] are the subject of

---

[5] Crystal (1997b:130–140) presents a summary of the history of the concept of 'new' Englishes.

much discussion in the pages of the journal *World Englishes*.

We may well agree with the claim that 'new' Englishes or 'nonnative varieties' are not inherently inferior to EL1 varieties, but this does not invalidate the more pragmatic and utilitarian concerns of those with a personal or professional involvement in EL2 teaching and learning which were expressed above. Teachers' attitudes towards the variety of English that their learners learn and use will continue to be strongly influenced by the needs of their learners. These needs will be largely determined by the particular cultural, educational, political and economic forces at work in their society and they will change as these forces change. On the other hand, even in situations where an EL1 model is the preferred learning target there is a danger that teachers can be over-ambitious on behalf of their learners and insist too strongly on standard EL1 pronunciation, for example. Sometimes this over-ambition may result from the teacher's own strong attachment to and aesthetic appreciation of English – feelings that are not necessarily shared by their learners.

### Are attitudes likely to change?

Attitudes towards the relative positions of EL1 and EL2 varieties as desired learning models will obviously vary from country to country. But it is unlikely that these attitudes will remain unaltered over time. It will be as well for all of us to be aware of changing attitudes and to be prepared to adapt the expectations we have of our learners. Brown (1995) in an article concerning the reasons why, up to the time of her article, language teaching and teacher training programmes had lacked a World English perspective, argues that this will not necessarily be the case in the future:

> Three primary areas in language teaching will be affected by research in world Englishes: language education policies with respect to choice of pedagogical models, examination standards and standardized testing, and materials development in listening and reading.
>
> *(Brown 1995:239)*

The issues discussed so far in this chapter – varieties and standards of English and attitudes towards them – cannot be divorced from questions to do with the ownership and control of the language. We look at these questions in the general context of power and language in Chapter 6.

## 4.4   The notion of appropriacy

Most people have experienced occasions where they have wished that they had put something differently and other occasions where they have not liked the way other people have expressed themselves. All language users have some feel for appropriate and inappropriate ways of expressing meanings. In some languages there are quite prescriptive 'social' rules concerning certain areas of language use where failure to observe the rules may result in offence being taken. Such rules may be related to the age or gender or perceived status of people or simply how long they have known each other. Other languages may not be so prescriptive in this way, but users are nevertheless expected to observe certain conventions of use. One area of language use where we can observe these 'social' rules or conventions in action concerns the way in which people address each other: when to use a person's given or family name, or both, with or without a title and so on.

Rules or conventions of use may also be concerned with the expression of meanings which require the use of more complex structures than those used for addressing people. Activity 56 invites you to consider a range of expressions, all of which could be used to express gratitude.

## Activity 56

> ▶ Look at the expressions below as exponents for indicating gratitude:
>
> | | |
> |---|---|
> | a) Thanks. | f) I'm very grateful to you. |
> | b) Cheers. | g) Thanks a lot. |
> | c) Thank you very much. | h) I can't thank you enough. |
> | d) That's very kind of you. | i) What can I say? |
> | e) I'll never be able to repay you. | j) Ta. |
>
> ▶ These expressions would not be used in free variation, i.e not all of them would be equally appropriate in every situation. Think of a very *formal* situation in which you wish to express gratitude to someone and then decide which of these expressions you would *not* use and why they would **not** be appropriate.

Activity 56 is intended to demonstrate how various aspects of situations influence the language choices we make in those situations. In Chapter 2 (2.3.1) we saw the importance of *context* and *relevance* in understanding how discourse works. The principles identified in Chapter 2 have equal bearing on our awareness of the appropriacy of the language we use and experience. In particular, appropriacy is associated with the assumptions interactants make about the following:

• the relationships existing between them
• their respective roles in the interaction
• the purpose of the interaction
• the topic of the interaction
• the place and time of the interaction

The degree to which the factors mentioned above influence language choices varies from one situation to another, and from one culture to another. There is another important element to be considered, however, and that is the *extent* to which an individual is influenced by any or all of the factors. This, of course, relates to the individual's perception of the situation as well as their mood at the time. We should not forget, either, that an individual's own personality also determines, to some extent, how much they will be influenced by situational factors. The point is that no two people are likely to be influenced equally by these factors; language would be a particularly sterile and uninteresting area of study if they were.

**Activity 57** ▷

> ▶ Think of two different situations in which you have expressed strong disagreement with the opinions of others (e.g. at home, at work or with friends).
> ▶ What situational features do you think influenced your choice of expression?

## 4.4.1  Appropriacy in ELT materials

For some considerable time now there has been an emphasis in foreign and second language teaching on developing the communicative skills of learners. Part of effective communication in a language has to do with the user's awareness of what is appropriate to say or write in particular situations. The following examples illustrate how some EL2 coursebooks deal with this aspect of the use of English.

In Examples 4.7, 4.8 and 4.9 on pages 144 and 145 learners are provided with information on stylistic aspects of certain expressions used for giving advice in English. Example 4.10 on page 146 deals with certain conventions of written academic English. Read through these four examples and then consider Activity 58.

### Example 4.7

> There are many ways of trying to get people to do things for their own good. The expressions you use depend on:
> a)  how difficult or unpleasant the course of action you suggest is.
> b)  who you are and who you are talking to – the roles you are playing and your relationship.
>
> In this list the expressions are in order of tentativeness:
>
> TENTATIVE  *I was wondering if you'd ever thought of ...*
> *Might it be an idea to ...*
> *Have you ever thought of ...*
> *Don't you think it might be an idea to ...*
> *You could always ...*
> *If I were you I'd ...*
> *Why don't you ...*
> DIRECT  *You'd better ...*

*(Jones 1981:59)*

**Example 4.8**

| Giving advice |
|---|
| **General**<br>I (don't) think you *should/ought to* …<br>If I were you, *I'd/I wouldn't* …<br>*I'd/I wouldn't* …, if I were you. |
| **Informal**<br>You'd better (not) …<br>Take my advice and …<br>The way I see it, you *should/shouldn't* … |
| **Formal**<br>My advice would be to …<br>If I were in your position, I *would/wouldn't* …<br>I *would/wouldn't advise/recommend* …<br>My reaction would be … |

*(Hinton and Marsden 1985:108)*

**Example 4.9**

7  Other ways of giving advice

a) Informal

*It's time you went to class.* (+ past form of the verb)
*You'd better (not) run.* (+ base form without *to*)
*Try sending it by fax.* (+ -*ing*, or *to* + base form if it means 'make an effort')
*Take my advice and give it back to her.*
*If I were you, I'd get a taxi.*

b) More formal

*I would advise you to look for a new job.*
*I would recommend that you change your doctor.*
*I would appreciate some advice on the car to buy.*

*(Bell and Gower 1992:46)*

**Example 4.10**

> 1  Written academic English will *not* normally contain the following:
> a  **Contractions** (i.e. 'it did not' would be used instead of *it didn't*; 'they have' would be used and not *they've*.)
> b  **Hesitation Fillers** (i.e. *er, um, well, you know* ... which might be common in the spoken language are omitted.)
> c  **Familiar Language** that would not be appropriate in the academic context. For example:
>    1  A number of phrasal or prepositional verbs are more suitable or appropriate in an informal style, i.e.
>
>       | FORMAL | INFORMAL |
>       |---|---|
>       | conduct | carry out |
>       | discover | find out |
>       | investigate | look into |
>
>    2  Personal pronouns, *I, you, we* tend not to be used in more formal writing (except in letters etc.). Instead the style may be more *impersonal*. An introductory *it* or *there* may begin sentences or even the impersonal pronoun *one*; passive tenses may also be used.

*(Jordan 1992:101)*

**Activity 58**

> ▶ In Examples 4.7–4.10 on pages 144–146, how useful do you find the stylistic labels (i.e. 'Tentative', 'Direct', 'General', 'Informal', 'Formal', 'More formal') given for the various expressions?
> ▶ Do the labels cause any confusion?

Example 4.11 on page 147 takes the form of an exercise in which learners are asked to apply their awareness of appropriate use of English to two examples of invitations which are presented along with possible situations where they might be used.

**Activity 59**

> Do the descriptions of the situations in Example 4.11 on page 147 provide enough information to help learners complete the exercise? (You might like to refer to the earlier discussion in Section 4.4. in considering your response to this activity.)

Example 4.12(a) on page 148 offers learners another exercise in making appropriate choices of expression, this time in written English, with a focus on phrasal verbs. The answers proposed by the authors of the exercise are in Example 4.12(b) on page 148. Activity 60 invites you to express your opinion on these answers.

## Example 4.11

c) Look at these examples of invitations. When could you use them?

1 Fancy a quick cup of coffee, then?

2 Do you like Mozart? I've got tickets for a concert next week and I was wondering whether you might be interested in coming with me?

Now tick invitation 1 or invitation 2 for each situation.

| Situation | 1 | 2 |
|---|---|---|
| A   You know the person quite well or very well. | | |
| B   You don't know the person well. | | |
| C   You feel very nervous. | | |
| D   It is important to you that the person accepts your invitation. | | |
| E   The invitation isn't particularly important to you. | | |
| F   You feel sure the person will accept your invitation. | | |
| G   You think the other person might not be interested in your invitation. | | |

*(Sinclair 1995:44)*

## Example 4.12(a)

Although phrasal verbs may sometimes be used in formal writing, they are much more common in informal texts. Look at these sentences. Decide which of the words or phrases in *italics* best complete each sentence.

1 Expenditure on recruitment has *gone up / increased* substantially since 1994.

2 I'm really exhausted – think I'll *turn in / retire* for the night.

3 Can you try to *find out / ascertain* what's the matter with Anna?

4 Our company would be pleased to *fix up / arrange* accommodation for you.

5 Please take a seat and *hang on / wait* until the doctor is ready to examine you.

6 Dave never stops eating – he had a huge breakfast and now he's *polished off / consumed* my last packet of biscuits.

7 The aim of this report is to *pin down / specify* five areas where improvements could be made.

8 Julie's visit will have to be *put off / deferred* until the house is ready.

9 The Managing Director will be *dropping in on / visiting* these offices on the 16th of March.

10 Adam was *told off / reprimanded* by his mum for coming home late.

11 I'm really sorry to *let you down / disappoint* you over our hols, but I can't make those dates now.

12 The Principal had no more appointments so couldn't *get out of / avoid* attending the meeting.

*(Aspinall and Capel 1996(a):16)*

## Example 4.12(b)

Answers

| | | | | | |
|---|---|---|---|---|---|
| 1 | increased | 5 | wait | 9 | visiting |
| 2 | turn in | 6 | polished off | 10 | told off |
| 3 | find out | 7 | specify | 11 | let you down |
| 4 | arrange | 8 | put off | 12 | avoid |

*(Aspinall and Capel 1996(b):16)*

## Activity 60 ▷

> ▶ Do you agree with the answers given in Example 4.12(b) on page 148?
> ▶ Can you think of situations where the apparently 'wrong' answer might actually occur?

## 4.4.2 Teaching appropriacy

### *Two views on the value of appropriacy in ELT*

The two extracts which follow represent rather different perspectives on the notion of appropriacy. The first writer is sceptical about its value for language learners, especially as it seems to decrease the importance of accuracy:

> English in the corner shop is different from English in science lessons. With this view of language, accuracy is far less important: fluency and appropriacy are the main criteria for successful language use ... The words 'appropriate', 'appropriately', appropriateness', 'appropriacy' are alarmingly frequent in language syllabuses, assessment schemes and language awareness materials in current use. 'Appropriacy' sounds more liberal and flexible than 'accuracy', but I believe it is just as much of a straitjacket for the bilingual trying to add English to her repertoire.
>
> *(Ivanic 1990:124)*

The second writer, on the other hand, claims that appropriacy of use does not exclude matters of form.

> Sociolinguistic competence ... addresses the extent to which utterances are produced and understood *appropriately* in different sociolinguistic contexts depending on contextual factors such as status of participants, purposes of the interaction and norms or conventions of interaction. Appropriateness of utterances refers to both appropriateness of meaning and appropriateness of form.
>
> *(Canale 1983:7)*

## Activity 61 ▷

> ▶ Which of the views expressed above is closer to your opinion on the place of appropriacy in second language teaching and learning?
> ▶ Do you think it is possible to teach appropriacy?

## *Some professional challenges associated with teaching appropriacy*

Teachers and learners may experience some degree of insecurity when exploring matters of appropriacy. Some may understandably feel far more secure when dealing with matters of formal accuracy than with the seemingly unstable features of appropriacy. On the other hand, it is worth remembering that language-in-use *is* subject to a huge range of variable factors and that it is unrealistic to attempt to confine this unpredictable, shifting human phenomenon within any set of 'rules of accuracy'. Teachers and learners need only reflect briefly on the complexities of their own languages to become aware of both the importance of appropriacy and the difficulties that exist in trying to pin it down.

Non-mother-tongue teachers of foreign languages often complain of their particular difficulties in arbitrating on matters of appropriacy. There is no denying these difficulties, but it is also true to say that mother-tongue teachers are not always better off in this respect. Uninformed mother-tongue judgements may be of much less worth to a learner than the judgements of non-mother-tongue teachers who have given the matter some thought and have attempted to maintain their awareness of this aspect of the language.

A potential danger of attempting to teach appropriacy in EL2 contexts is that of the values of EL1 cultures being imposed on learners. Since so much of appropriacy in language use is associated with the culture in which the language is used, there must be some risk of EL2 learners being subjected to a kind of 'cultural imperialism' under which they are required to behave, linguistically, in ways that do not accord with their own culture. Liu (1998) writes about what he calls the 'ethnocentrism' of training programmes in North America, Britain and Australia for students preparing to become teachers of EL2. He argues that the special needs of international students preparing to become teachers of English in their own countries are often neglected on these programmes. One such need he identifies is for international students to study the culture of English-speaking countries since cultural understanding is 'an indispensable part of second or foreign language acquisition' (1998:8). However, he goes on to warn that:

> studying another culture does not mean embracing it or following its socio-cultural customs, nor does it mean losing one's own culture ... cultural study in ESOL is meant to empower the students to become competent English users in their own context and on their terms so they can express themselves in whichever way they choose without giving rise to the unintentional conflicts or misunderstanding frequently caused by lack of intercultural competence.
>
> *(Liu 1998:8)*

Whether to attempt to teach learners to use the target language appropriately as well as accurately – and if so, how to do it – is a professional challenge and a matter for continuing debate. To take up the challenge and contribute to and benefit from the debate we need at least to be aware of the parameters of the issue. As a final thought on this subject, the words of Hymes (1972) are as good a way as any of summing up the major pedagogical implication of our discussion relating to appropriacy of language use:

> There are rules of use without which the rules of grammar would be useless.
> *(Hymes 1972:278)*

## Key references

Crystal, D. (1995). *Cambridge Encyclopedia of the English Language.* Cambridge: Cambridge University Press.
Hudson, R. (1996). *Sociolinguistics.* Cambridge: Cambridge University Press.
*World Englishes* (quarterly journal, published by Blackwell)

# 5 Change

## 5.1 Overview

The main purpose of this chapter is to raise awareness of some aspects and implications of language change. We look at some of the main features of language change (with particular reference to English) and consider some historical, linguistic and social factors which bring it about. We consider how language change is reflected in teaching approaches and materials. We encourage teachers to learn more about changes in English; to look at how technology and other influences may affect future developments; and to consider the possible impact of this on language teaching. Key areas include:

- the historical development of English
- the ability of English to change and adapt
- mechanisms of change
- the effect of change on the core language systems of vocabulary, structure (grammar) and pronunciation
- social factors bearing upon language change
- attitudes to language change

## 5.2 Some background to language change

From a teaching point of view, there are a number of questions associated with language change, illustrated here with particular reference to English:

- How can language teaching keep pace with the propensity for English to change?
- Which model(s) should be used for teaching?
- What are the implications of the large increase in exposure to language use which is available via technology?
- What use should be made of authentic materials and corpus data?
- What help with sensible and accurate advice on language change should we expect from modern reference grammars and dictionaries?
- What will the future be like for English language teachers?

## Everything changes, including language

A basic but important point to make is that it would be surprising if language did *not* change. There is an inevitability about change in many aspects of society in general – political, economic and technological change – and, as we have seen, language is intrinsically bound up with these and other socio-cultural factors. Change is a feature of *all* languages, not just English, and it is likely that most EL2 teachers and learners are aware of some of the many elements that contribute to language change. Aitchison (1991:4) points out that even though some people may object to change, changes, including those in language, are all around us:

> Language ... like everything else, gradually transforms itself over the centuries. There is nothing surprising in this. In a world where humans grow old, tadpoles change into frogs and milk turns into cheese, it would be strange if language alone remained unaltered. As the famous Swiss linguist Ferdinand de Saussure noted: 'Time changes all things; there is no reason why language should escape this universal law'.

Beyond beginner level, most learners will at some stage encounter aspects of change, in the same way that they are likely to meet different varieties of English. Reference and teaching books reflect change to varying degrees; many, particularly some dictionaries and grammars (*Longman Dictionary of Contemporary English* and the *COBUILD Grammar*, for example) try to incorporate examples of new or productive language items and to give advice on how learners should approach changes in the language. There are, therefore, some avenues through which teachers and learners can gain access to information on current changes in English grammar and vocabulary.

However, the question of how and to what extent teachers of English *need* to keep abreast of language change is not easily answered. How, for example, are teachers who are not in direct contact with EL1 environments able to keep up-to-date with new changes in the language they may have been teaching for years, and does it matter if they are not? Who decides which 'model' of English should be taught and how can teachers and learners keep pace, assuming they want to, with the ability of English to accept new linguistic forms? Discussions over what exactly are the 'correct' forms of the language are relevant here as well.

## Diachronic and synchronic change

The dynamism of any language comes from its ability to change and adapt. English happens to be a very good example of this phenomenon. It is possible to look at change both from a historical or chronological perspective – known as *diachronic* change – and to use a theoretical or actual point in time as the basis for analysis – known as *synchronic* change. While both perspectives are useful, in reality there is a considerable overlap between the two and it is probably equally productive to consider language change from a combination of both. Thus we can view change diachronically as part of a historical process (e.g. the differences in the way standard British English is pronounced now compared with fifty years ago); but at the same time, looking at change from a synchronic perspective, we

153

can appreciate how particular influences (opinions on language, or technology, for example) have affected the language in a number of different ways at a given time, for instance at the end of the twentieth century.

Changes in the English language are apparent in both a historical and a contemporary sense in all the major parts of the system (traditionally classified as structure, vocabulary and pronunciation) and these changes have some clear implications for teaching and learning.[1] As teachers we are aware that for most English language learners, current, contemporary language is understandably more motivating than, say, the language of Shakespeare. However, as we shall see, the pace and variety of change make it difficult to single out a definitive version of what we could call 'pedagogic' English at any particular historical point.

## 5.3  Reasons for change

One major reason why English has changed and continues to change relates to the historical development of the language itself and the influences that other languages such as Latin, Greek, French and German have had on English. It is also clear that some parts of the structure of modern English are flexible and allow movement and changes, across word categories for instance, or in pronunciation. Then there is the current role of English as an international and global means of communication which has led not only to a considerable increase in the sheer amount of English which is now used, but also to a constantly expanding range of influences upon it[2]. Huge and rapid advances in communications technology during the twentieth century have also contributed to this spread of the language and the consequent likelihood that it will change as it spreads.

If change is so common and so continuous, we might well ask why the language hasn't simply fallen apart. Some people think that this is precisely what *is* happening,[3] reflecting a general fear of change, perhaps, or a reluctance to come to terms with language change. However, the basic framework of the English language – the main grammar of the language – remains intact despite the fact that history and the spread of English have brought about a large number of changes in the forms and uses of the language. The major components of the systems which make up the language – grammar, vocabulary and pronunciation – all show signs of diachronic or synchronic change but the 'core' grammar of the language remains largely unchanged. The systems are robust enough to allow adaptability without permitting total deterioration or disintegration of the language as a whole.

[1] A related debate over the role of spoken corpus materials and their relevance to ELT can be found in the correspondence section of *English Language Teaching Journal*, Vol 50 (1) and (4).
[2] Crystal (1997b:10) suggests a 'middle-of-the-road' estimate of 1,200–1,500 million English users who possess 'reasonable competence'.
[3] See the comments of Prince Charles, for instance, in 3.2.2 and 6.3.2.

We look now in more detail at some of the major influences on language change in English: history, borrowings, creativity, the media and technology.

## 5.3.1 History

### *From Old to Modern English*

It is quite clear that the English that is written and spoken today is very different from that of five hundred or a thousand years ago. History also brings a number of uncertainties: we cannot be absolutely sure how English sounded in the Middle Ages, for example. Examples 5.1 and 5.2 demonstrate the point that specialised study is involved in order to understand written forms of Old English (roughly the period between c.450–1100 – see Example 5.1 below); even by the Middle English period (c.1100–1450 – see Chaucer's writing in Example 5.2 on page 156) some effort and specialist knowledge is required to make sense of what is written. When we get to the nineteenth century (Example 5.3 on page 156 is from the writings of Charles Dickens) there are still some differences, but by that time Modern English has become very similar to the language used today.

### Activity 62 ▷

> ► Can you find any words in Examples 5.1 and 5.2 below and on page 156 which exist in modern English?
> ► In Example 5.3 on page 156, how have the current meanings of the words *nearly* (7) and *station* (18) changed from the meaning that Dickens intended?

### Example 5.1: Old English

**THE BATTLE OF MALDON**

| | |
|---|---|
| Byrhtƿold maþelode, bord hafenode— | Byrhtwold spoke; he grasped his shield— |
| se þæs eald ȝeneat—æsc acƿehte; | he was an old follower—he shook the ash spear; |
| he ful baldlice beornas lærde: | very boldly he exhorted the warriors: |
| 'Hiȝe sceal þe heardra, heorte þe cenre, | 'Courage shall be the fiercer, heart the bolder, |
| 5  mod sceal þe mare, þe ure mæȝen lytlað. | spirit the greater, as our strength lessens. |
| Her lið ure ealdor eall forheapen, | Here lies our chief all hewn down, |
| ȝod on ȝreote. A mæȝ ȝnornian | a noble man in the dust. He has cause ever to mourn |
| se ðe nu fram þis ƿiȝpleȝan þendan þenceð. | who intends now to turn from this war-play. |
| Ic eom frod feores. Fram ic ne ƿille, | I am advanced in years. I will not hence, |
| 10 ac ic me be healfe minum hlaforde, | but I by the side of my lord, |
| be sƿa leofan men licȝan þence.' | by so dear a man, intend to lie.' |
| Sƿa hi Æþelȝares bearn ealle bylde | Likewise, Godric, the son of Æthelgar, exhorted them all |
| Ȝodric to ȝuþe. Oft he ȝar forlet, | to the battle. Often he let the spear fly, |
| pælspere ƿindan on þa ƿicinȝas; | the deadly spear sped away among the Vikings; |
| 15 sƿa he on þam folce fyrmest eode, | as he went out in the forefront of the army, |
| heoƿ 7 hynde, oð þæt he on hilde ȝecranc. | he hewed and struck, until he perished in the battle. |

*(cited in Crystal 1995: 12)*

## Example 5.2: Middle English

From Chaucer's *Canterbury Tales*. The first line of each set of three is written Middle English, the second the Modern English 'translation' and the third a phonetic transcription of what the language probably sounded like.

> Whan that Aprille with hise shoures soote
> When April with its sweet showers
> 'hwan əat 'aːprıl, wıə hıs 'ʃuːrəs 'soːtə
>
> 5   The droghte of March hath perced to the roote
> has pierced the drought of March to the root
> əə 'druxt ɔf 'martʃ haə 'pɛrsəd ˌtoː ðə 'roːtə
>
> And bathed every veyne in swich licour
> and bathed every vein in such liquid
> and 'baːðəd 'ɛːvrı 'væin ın 'swıtʃ lı'kuːr
>
> 10  Of which vertu engendred is the flour
> from which strength the flower is engendered;
> ɔf 'hwıtʃ vɛr'tiu ɛn'dʒɛndrɛd ıs əə 'fluːr

*(cited in Crystal 1995: 38)*

## Example 5.3: Modern English

He had risen, as his father had before him, in the course of life and death, from Son to Dombey, and for nearly twenty years had been the sole representative of the firm. Of those years he had been married, ten – married, as some said, to a lady with no heart to give him; whose happiness
5  was in the past, and who was content to bind her broken spirit to the dutiful and meek endurance of the present. Such idle talk was little likely to reach the ears of Mr Dombey, whom it nearly concerned; and probably no one in the world would have received it with such utter incredulity as he, if it had reached him. Dombey and Son had often dealt in hides, but never in
10  hearts. They left that fancy ware to boys and girls, and boarding-schools and books. Mr Dombey would have reasoned: That a matrimonial alliance with himself *must*, in the nature of things, be gratifying and honourable to any woman of common sense. That the hope of giving birth to a new partner in such a house could not fail to awaken a glorious and stirring
15  ambition in the breast of the least ambitious of her sex. That Mrs Dombey had entered on that social contract of matrimony: almost necessarily part of a genteel and wealthy station, even without reference to the perpetuation of family firms: with her eyes fully open to these advantages. That Mrs Dombey had had daily practical knowledge of his position in society. That
20  Mrs Dombey had always sat at the head of his table, and done the honours of his house in a remarkably lady-like and becoming manner. That Mrs Dombey must have been happy. That she couldn't help it.

*(Charles Dickens,* Dombey and Son *1848/1995)*

## Colonial impositions

The imposition of Latin as the colonial language, consequent upon the invasion and settlement of Britain by the Romans between c.55BC and c.449AD, the influence of Germanic dialects from Europe brought by Anglo-Saxon invaders from c.449AD onwards, and the influence of the French language after the Norman conquest of Britain in 1066 are all examples of how English has been heavily influenced in the past by other languages. Thus we find in English many examples of vocabulary from Latin (*school, circle, paper*) and from French (*castle, beef, courage*). Cultural influences are also important, shown for example in the many words of Greek origin *(philosophy, geology, criterion)* stemming from the 'classical' education dominant in the Middle Ages and Renaissance.

A general awareness of historical influence can be an advantage in some areas of language study, for instance in understanding why English spelling behaves as it does. It does not necessarily help learners to master spelling patterns, but at least it shows that many apparently illogical written forms are not just random chance but are the result of historical pronunciation changes (e.g. *break, knife* and *would*). However, while some would argue that it is useful for learning purposes (e.g. the understanding of vocabulary items) to know about these historical influences in detail, such knowledge is not actually necessary in order to be able to use contemporary English. An overview of the main points is probably sufficient for most teachers.

## Geographical factors

Language spread and geographical factors are also important: just as some parts of the language may remain the same while others may change, we find that changes may occur in one geographical region without necessarily spreading to all the other areas where the language is spoken. An example here would be the retention of the past participle form *gotten* in standard contemporary American English – a form which has died out in most parts of the British Isles (where it originally came from). Given the number of regional and national varieties of English, one would expect there to be considerable differences in the rate and forms of change.

## Evolution of meanings

Meanings are not necessarily constant and it is not at all unusual for words to change their meaning over time. The word *notorious*, for example, once meant 'widely-known' but now has a pejorative addition of 'unfavourably known'. In Example 5.2 on page 156, the word *vertu* (line 10) has changed its spelling and almost completely lost its original meaning of 'strength', being used in modern English to convey the more general meaning of 'a commendable trait or quality'. Nor is it especially unusual for semantic change to take place in the opposite direction, historically speaking: some language items may change back to take on a previously-held meaning. The word *disinterested*, for example, seems to be losing its mid-twentieth-century meaning of 'impartial' and has to some extent returned to its former, eighteenth-century, meaning of 'not at all interested'.

The study of the origins and history of word forms and meanings – *etymology* – raises the question of where the true or real meaning of a word lies. For some people the true meaning of a word is to be found in its historical origins; however, as we have seen, this may not always be an accurate guide to modern usage, even if acceptance of this fact proves painful (many people feel that something is 'lost' when a word changes it meaning). Dictionary compilers and lexicographers usually try to give definitions of the contemporary meaning of a word as well as its historical origins. This process involves having to make some difficult decisions as to the 'real' meaning of a word and it is therefore not surprising that dictionaries need to be updated on a regular basis. Modern technology can also help learners find their way through meaning problems, with, for instance, tools such as *COBUILD Wordwatch*.[4]

Even over a relatively short historical period the effects of language change can be clearly seen and this in turn has an effect on the type and style of language teaching materials, a point which is taken up in more detail in Section 5.6 below. Meanwhile, Example 5.4 below provides several instances of identifiable areas of change. It contains a model of how to write a formal letter, taken from a 1960 edition of an English language textbook for EL1 speakers in Australia.

## Example 5.4

> Universal Supply Co. Ltd.,
> 108–117 George St.,
> Sydney.
> 25th June, 1946.
>
> Mr. A. J. Smithson,
> 158 Sefton St.,
> Belgrave.
> Dear Sir,
>   I have received your letter dated 23rd June 1946. There are several vacancies for apprentice electrical fitters at our works, and we shall be pleased to consider your son for one of them.
>
>   Could you call on me any afternoon this week, between 2 p.m. and 4 p.m.? It would be as well for your son to accompany you, bringing with him his Intermediate Certificate and two character references, including one from the Headmaster of his school.
>             Yours faithfully,
>             R. K. Stephenson.
>             Staff Officer.

*(McGregor, H. E. (1960). English For the Upper School, p. 78)*

[4] *COBUILD Wordwatch* provides the chance to receive free by e-mail a weekly explanation of a particular vocabulary point based on the *COBUILD* corpus database. For more information, visit the *COBUILD* website at: www.cobuild.collins.co.uk/wordwatch.html.

**Activity 63** ▷

---

The letter in Example 5.4 on page 158 illustrates several areas of change: vocabulary, forms of address, style, formality, layout, typeface and even content.

▶ Can you suggest how a modern letter might differ in terms of any (or all) of these? Try rewriting the letter and see what it looks like.

▶ What reasons can you think of for these differences?

**Follow-up:** Find an equivalent model of formal letter writing in a current coursebook, and compare it with Example 5.4.

---

## 5.3.2 Borrowings

### *What happens to borrowed words?*

Historical influences both in Britain and from other countries where English has been extensively used (former British colonies, for example) have played a major role in shaping and extending the vocabulary of English. The process of importing words from a different historical or contemporary language is a common one and in Britain, unlike in some other countries such as France or Sweden, there is no official body which monitors and controls the introduction of new words into the English language. In theory, therefore, there is no limit to the number of words that can enter the English language, although, as we will see below, not all new arrivals remain forever.

One feature of new words is that they may need to change or adapt from their original forms in order to become recognisably English. This process of adaptation may involve the regularisation of pronunciation and pluralisation to fit common English patterns. Slavonic languages such as Russian or Polish have a much more complex inflection system than English (the supermarket name *Tesco* declines in Slovak: 'to the supermarket' is *v Tescu*), but borrowings of words originally from Russian (e.g. *sputnik, glasnost, vodka*) no longer need – in English – to have several different endings as they do in Russian to reflect the various forms that the Russian grammatical and morphological systems demand. As part of the borrowing process they take on the limited English noun morphology of two forms only (singular and plural). Similarly it doesn't matter that *spaghetti* is plural in Italian. The word is now also an accepted (uncountable) English noun and apart from the fact that it is relatively unusual for an English word to end with the letter *i* it conforms to the patterns of English. The following list of words in Activity 64 illustrates some borrowings into English from other languages:

**Activity 64**

| | | | |
|---|---|---|---|
| 1. *kayak* | 2. *spaghetti* | 3. *algebra* | 4. *juggernaut* |
| 5. *kebab* | 6. *hamburger* | 7. *glasnost* | 8. *robot* |
| 9. *corgi* | 10. *kung fu* | 11. *karate* | 12. *crocodile* |
| 13. *sombrero* | 14. *chipmunk* | 15. *bossa nova* | 16. *kangaroo* |

▶ Can you match each of the words in the list above with the language (in the list below) it originally came from? What helps you match them?

(a) Russian   (b) Japanese   (c) Spanish   (d) Italian   (e) German
(f) Hindi   (g) Portuguese   (h) French   (i) Inuit   (j) Welsh   (k) Aborigine
(l) Chinese   (m) Arabic   (n) Czech   (o) Turkish   (p) American Indian

## 5.3.3 Creativity

### New creations

As we shall see later in this chapter (5.4.1), English has several devices for creating new words or forms of words, known as *neologisms*. Along with borrowings, neologisms are responsible for a constantly-changing vocabulary. New words are coined to handle new cultural and social phenomena or, as Carter (1997:5/6) puts it: 'to fill particular semantic spaces which had not previously been occupied or for which previously there had been no semantic need'. In one sense such linguistic innovations are necessary to help express changes in society itself.

It is difficult to say exactly *who* it is that creates these new words, although some general responsibility for the popularity of words and expressions can readily be attributed to the media. Unlike sources of borrowings, where the origin of the word is often relatively easy to trace, precise sources of neologisms can be difficult to identify, even though the linguistic mechanisms for creating words are well-documented (e.g. the ability of English nouns to become verbs or adjectives – see 1.3.8).

Another feature of innovation is that it is impossible to predict which words will appear, and likewise which will disappear. There is also an ephemeral nature to the creation of new words: it is equally hard to predict which words will remain in the language and which will fall out of usage. Example 5.5 on page 161 lists some of the words from the 1990 edition of the *Longman Register of New Words* (new words entering the language in 1989/90).

Even a few years later some of these are already dated or have disappeared while others, *karaoke* and *all-seater*[5] for instance, seem to have successfully entered the language. It is unlikely that most people would know the meaning of all the words in the list, or would even want to. The lack of context makes a number of them impossible to guess. Following on from this some generalisations may be possible:

[5] A sports stadium where everyone is seated

- that the number of words entering the language is very large
- that there is an ephemeral nature to some types of words, slang in particular
- that where the words are linked to a particular phenomenon which itself comes to an end then the chances of it disappearing seem to be greater (*Gorbymania* for instance)
- that learners need to be aware of the existence of new words but only need to know a small proportion
- that it is not necessary for anyone, apart perhaps from lexicographers, to know what all neologisms mean

We have to accept that the creation of neologisms is inconsistent, and that prediction and identification are not precise arts. This should, at least in theory, be an encouragement to learners. A number of modern vocabulary books point learners towards strategies for identifying the words they need to know and advise them to concentrate on mastering linguistic patterns such as suffixes and prefixes which affect the forms of English nouns. The logical additional advice is that it is not worth worrying too much about learning individual neologisms that may never be needed.

## Activity 65

> ▶ Choose six words from the list in Example 5.5 below and look them up in two or three different dictionaries.
> ▶ Note whether they appear in the dictionaries you referred to; if they do, what sort of information about their origin is given?

## Example 5.5

| | | | |
|---|---|---|---|
| agg | callanetics | fattist | mad cow disease |
| all-seater | cardboard city | fatwah | motormouth |
| Balearic | charge capping | geeky | noodle western |
| basho | daytimer | Gorbymania | rai |
| B-boy/B-girl | Deep House | jheri curl | scrum pox |
| bimboy | diffuser | karaoke | sicko |
| blag | dreads | lager lout | skippy |
| blush (as in *Janet* | dweeb | Lambada | skorts |
| *blushed herself*) | eco-friendly | libero | zero option |
| bum bag | | | zouk |

*(Trask 1994: 4)*

While the potential of some words to outlive their original connections is generally accepted (words which come from the names of people, for instance, such as *sandwich*, or *wellington*), nobody really knows which words will survive. Tracing the origin and lifespan of words is a speculative and sometimes subjective business. At one time perhaps people thought that words such as *telephone* or *computer* might not – or should not – make it into common usage. *Private Eye*, a satirical magazine published in Britain, ran a regular column in the 1970s called *On-going Situations* which was designed to lampoon the use of words like *situation*; twenty years later, *on-going* and *situation* are no longer the source of ironic laughter they once were. Language change has a habit of overtaking opinion as to what should and shouldn't happen, although this in no way negates the pleasure people find in ridiculing new items. As we shall see in Chapter 6, on a more serious note, sometimes it pays to question aspects of language usage.

### Activity 66

In British English the semantic area of *food* is a productive one to look at in terms of innovation (new words and expressions). Some typical new words which came into common usage in the 1990s are: *balti, penne, stir-fry* and *pitta*.

▶ Why do you think the topic of *food* is such a productive area (in Britain) for new words?
▶ Can you list some more words that are relatively recent additions to the food vocabulary of British English? Where do these new words come from and how have they found their way into English?

## 5.3.4  The media

The sheer scale and extent of the English language media, which now includes a large electronic component, contributes greatly to introducing and sustaining language change in modern societies, as does the keenness of the press in general to invent and to talk about new additions to the English language. The spread of English as an internationally used language in business and technology, and the widespread availability of English (via satellite TV and the World Wide Web for instance) contribute to the overall pattern. The mechanisms for language change that are described in this chapter are therefore constantly in the public eye. Example 5.6 on page 163 shows how even a very specific situation is able to produce new forms – which may or may not survive to become part of general usage. The context of this example is the interest shown by *The Times* newspaper in the creative linguistic abilities of political parties during the 1997 UK General Election campaign.

**Example 5.6**

# Spin nurses keep media on message in the holding pen

### James Landale and Polly Newton on the language of Labour's battle bus

THE strange enclosed world of the election battle-bus, where spin doctors, party leaders and journalists shuttle up and down the country for up to 18 hours a day, has begun to spawn a language of its own.

The Labour camp is the most creative but all parties, after three weeks on the road, are developing a jargon impenetrable to outsiders. The *Times* correspondents on the buses translate:

*Holding pen.* Area cordoned off for the media during Labour's stage-managed walkabouts to prevent easy access to Tony Blair. Example: "Get back into the holding pen now!" John Major calls them *cordons sanitaires.*

*Slightly corralled.* Labour spin-doctor description of what happens to the media in holding pens. Example: "Of course you will be able to talk to Mr Blair. You will only be slightly corralled."

*Spin nurses.* Junior Labour press officers, often women who get frustrated when the media refuse to obey them. Example: "The spin nurses are getting their knickers in a twist again."

*On message.* Spin doctor-speak for stories written by reporters which faithfully follow the party's agenda and report everything their leader has said, however uninteresting. Example: "Stay on message and I'll treat you right."

*Off message.* Opposite of the above, usually occurs when reporters actually manage to speak to ordinary members of the public who have not all been personally vetted by a press officer. Example: "Stay off message and I'll never give you a story again."

*Tight schedule.* Spin doctor-speak for the apparently urgent need for the media to get back on the battle bus to avoid being late for the next stop. In reality, a device to prevent reporters talking to people who might be off message. Example: "We are on a tight schedule, please get back on the bus now!"

*Muffins.* Name given by Tory men to the hordes of young blonde women who answer the phone in the press office at Conservative Central Office. Example: "Don't worry, one of the muffins will make the tea."

*Mother.* Tory-speak for Baroness Thatcher. Example: "Mother is returning to the fold."

*A briefette.* A briefing done by Paddy Ashdown from the front of the top deck of his battle bus.

*A photo opportunity.* Liberal Democrat-speak for anything that involves their techno-fiend leader looking at computers.

*Paddy's rally speech (Take 1).* The text of Mr Ashdown's evening speech, issued to journalists under embargo in mid-afternoon. *Paddy's rally speech (Take 2).* The speech Paddy actually makes.

*TB.* Labour acronym for Tony Blair. Example: "TB's on the BB, the press on PB 1 and 2. ETD to ICA ASAP. Return ETA at MBT at 14.30 hours." Translation: "Tony Blair is on the battle bus, the media are on the press buses One and Two. Estimated time of departure for the Institute of Chartered Accountants is as soon as possible. Estimated time of arrival back at Millbank Tower (Labour's London HQ) 2.30pm.

*(The Times)*

## Activity 67 ▷

In Example 5.6 on page 163 a *spin doctor* is someone who gives out or makes statements on behalf of a political party.

► Can you work out what the following expressions mean and how they have come into existence?
► What processes have the expressions undergone in order to take on their new form or meaning? (Refer to the list of lexical structures in 5.4.1 for help, if you like.)

| | |
|---|---|
| *spin nurses* (l. 32) | *Mother* (l. 75) |
| *off message* (l. 47) | *briefette* (l. 79) |
| *corralled* (l. 25) | *muffins* (l. 67) |

Example 5.7 on page 165 contains another instance of media interest in language change, and the difficulties facing compilers of dictionaries in this respect. Text A reports the controversy surrounding a current coinage, *McJob;* Text B is a letter from the editors of the *Oxford English Dictionary* illuminating some of the complexities of dealing with such a coinage.

## Activity 68 ▷

► Besides its use in the coinage *McJob*, what other examples of the use of the prefix *Mc* to coin new words can be found in the two texts in Example 5.7 on page 165?
► Have you come across any other instances of this kind of language innovation based on names?

## 5.3.5 Technology

Language change, as we have said, is a continuing and constant linguistic process. It therefore follows that, as more language becomes more accessible, the more likely it is that aspects of change will be noticeable. The use of modern electronic technology by individuals, organisations, companies and the media has created a sort of 'super-library' of information. One outcome of this is that the potential for increase in the range and volume of English on the Internet and via other technologies such as satellite television is enormous, with an already vast current quantity of resources obtainable through these media. Typically, estimates suggest that around 80 per cent of current communication on the Internet is via English (Crystal 1997b:11).

There is also a growing interest in possible methodologies for exploring the available information for the purposes of language study. In the future greater use will doubtless be made of technology as both a provider of examples of language and language use, and as a support for language learning (through grammar reference packages, or grammar, style and spelling checkers). E-mail and discussion groups provide a means of communication which has great potential for teaching and learning, via the sharing of materials and through distance learning.

**Example 5.7**

**Text A**

# OED chickens out over 'McJob'

IN WHAT might be described as a case of McCensorship, the *Oxford English Dictionary* has been advised by lawyers not to include the word "McJob" in its next edition, **writes Mark Rowe**.

The libel victory last week by hamburger giant McDonald's, over two penniless environmental campaigners who attacked its reputation in a leaflet, has made the *OED* wary that the multi-national may seek to flex its muscles in other areas.

"McJob", to the great displeasure of the fast food chain, is widely used as a euphemism for any form of dead-end, low-paid employment. The *OED* believes the word is in common enough usage to be included within its esteemed covers.

The *OED* says it has yet to make a decision on "McJob", but lawyers have suggested it drop the word on legal grounds.

*OED* Chief Editor John Simpson said he intended to use the word in future, but it would not appear in the next 3,000-word supplementary edition, due out at the end of the summer. "We have taken legal advice, since we

> **Mc Job**/mək'dʒɒb / *n*. colloq. (freq. derog) [the name of the McDonalds chain of fast-food restaurants, regarded as a typical source of such employment + JOB *n*. Prob. not a direct reference to the programme mentioned in quot. 1985, but rather based on McDonalds' general practice of using Mc- as preformative element in a range of proprietary product names.] A poorly-paid job with few prospects, esp. one taken by an overqualified worker because of a shortage of other opportunities or lack of ambition.

**The definition in question**

are aware that companies may be unhappy and object to the tone of such words," he said. "To withdraw any word is against our policy. We have not yet made a decision."

In the McLibel case, McDonald's was awarded £60,000. The judge ruled that the company had been libelled by most of the allegations in a leaflet, *What's Wrong With McDonald's?* But he found it was justified in accusing McDonald's of paying low wages to its workers and being responsible for cruelty to some animals used in its products.

*(Independent on Sunday 22.6.97)*

**Text B**

# No McChicken

THE *Oxford English Dictionary* has not chickened out of using the word "McJob". Words are added on the basis of current usage, and there is no doubt that on this basis "McJob" deserves an entry.

I'm grateful to Douglas Coupland (Letters, 6 July) for drawing attention to the Random House dictionary's entry for "McJob" (published in 1995 and citing Mr Coupland's 1991 novel *Generation X* as the coinage), though it is noteworthy that the entry doesn't mention McDonald's. Our own search for McNuggets of truth shows that "McJob" originated in the mid-1980s. It was originally used by McDonald's in the context of an affirmative-action programme to assist people with disabilities in obtaining employment with the corporation. Examples of the current use can be found in publications from the mid to late 1980s. Tricky business, this lexicography!

**John Simpson**
OED, Oxford

*(Independent on Sunday 13.7.97)*

From a learner's point of view, new technology on the whole offers a positive and motivating new dimension. It is, however, still the case that *finding* particular and useful examples from a constantly expanding supply is not yet a straightforward task. In addition, access to the Internet is limited by the availability of appropriate technology, and also by cost in some instances (the majority of information is still aimed predominantly at the relatively wealthy US market). Teachers may feel threatened by these developments, but it is unlikely that technology will replace other social and cultural forces which have an effect on language and language learning. Graddol (1997a:61) points out that although the Internet will remain a major source of English language material this is partly because currently 90 per cent of the world's computers connected to the Internet are based in English-speaking countries. He suggests that new technology can also actively encourage the use of other minor and major languages, adding to the argument put forward by Maley (1992:18) that the future of language learning and teaching may need to be much more pluralistic than the present domination of English would indicate:

> Native speakers of English are in danger of losing respect for other languages and of failing to learn them ... Our aim should surely be for multi-lingual and multi-cultural awareness (and competence!), if we are not to be confined within the walls of our own language.

Example 5.8 below contains a list of just a few of the English language resources that are now (2000) available on the Internet but by the time you read this, it will almost certainly look out-of-date: the constantly changing and expanding world of technology moves fast.

### Example 5.8

*Encyclopaedia Britannica*

National Park Foundation (information on every National Park in the USA)

*New York Times*

Central Intelligence Agency

British university prospectuses

International Cannes Film Festival

UK Acts of Parliament (full text)

NASA's National Space Science Data Centre

Toyota

Nobel Prize Archive

Child Quest International (an inventory of missing children)

*Friends*, the US sitcom (complete scripts)

### Activity 69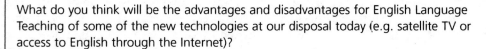

What do you think will be the advantages and disadvantages for English Language Teaching of some of the new technologies at our disposal today (e.g. satellite TV or access to English through the Internet)?

Example 5.9 below shows how well one particular area – the language currently (i.e. 2000) used to talk about the World Wide Web and its facilities – demonstrates the capacity for change and innovation. Again, we can note how quickly some new 'technology' words are able to make their way into the language: words such as *hacker* or *mouse*, for instance. And, again, by the time you read this some items will no longer be current.

## Example 5.9

| | | |
|---|---|---|
| *webcrawler* | *cybercafé* | *hacker* |
| *browser* | *online banking* | *mouse* |
| *white pages* | *high res digital images* | *URL* |
| *surfing* | *homepage* | *Netcast* |

## Activity 70

Look at the words or expressions in Example 5.9 above.

▶ Are they all new, or have some, or some parts of them, come from other domains of use?
▶ Think about the progress they are making into common usage in English. For example, how familiar are you with them, personally?
▶ If you don't know what the words mean, can you work out what they refer to?
▶ Try looking some of them up in a dictionary.

## 5.4  Language systems and examples of change

As we have suggested elsewhere in the book, it is something of an oversimplification to think about language only in terms of traditional categories such as vocabulary, grammar and pronunciation. However, for the sake of brevity, in this section we will look at some examples which can readily fit into these three large categories, remembering not only that the overlap between the categories is considerable but that if we were to examine all the potential elements of language change we would also need to think about other linguistic dimensions such as discourse and genre. Perhaps this is a good point at which to re-emphasise the fact that it is not the *systems* of the language as such that are changing (chaos would presumably ensue if this were the case) but rather *examples of language within the categories*. The big organising systems remain, no matter how much the language itself changes. And, as we will see below, the systems which allow and encourage change are themselves highly structured and very far from random, although the average speaker of English, faced with the potential for English to change and adapt, could be forgiven for thinking that this was not always the case.

## 5.4.1 Vocabulary

### When is a word not a word?

It is not easy to say how many words there are in the English language. A standard medium-sized monolingual dictionary might contain around 100,000 entries but if further, more specialised categories were included, for example technical terms and words from different varieties of English, the figure would rise to well over a million. An additional difficulty is that the linguistic diversity of English vocabulary can be measured not just by how many words there might be in the language – even assuming it was possible at any one time to count them all – but also by some of the different categories within what is sometimes called the *lexicon*. Linguists use this term to refer to the collection of all the meaningful units in a language and it therefore includes items beyond the traditional definition of a 'word'. Prefixes, abbreviations, acronyms and idioms, for instance, would all appear in a lexicon. Influences at word or item level include hyphens (*home-stay* or *homestay*?), capital letters and proper names, while wider concepts such as slang, jargon and humour also play an important role. The term *lexeme* has been adopted by linguists to refer to any unit of lexical meaning: thus *educationalists, fighting tooth and nail, put up with, BA, crucial, blotto, OK, bread and butter* are all lexemes. The usefulness of this term can be demonstrated if we want to talk about new combinations of words in English. The following are all in the dictionary as single words: *seriously, broken, rich, well,* but the new(ish) combinations of *seriously rich* (meaning very rich) and *well-broken* (meaning broken to a considerable extent) represent patterns of use that are not immediately identifiable by looking only at the individual words.

In English lexical structure there are a number of important elements, including two basic features:

- **polysemy:** a general characteristic of some languages including English where one form or word can have several different meanings, for example *chip, table, bank*
- **homonymy:** forms which look or sound the same, and which can be divided into:
  - **homophones:** words which have the same pronunciation but a different spelling: *fair/fare, bear/bare*
  - **homographs:** words which have the same spelling but a different pronunciation: *wind* or *read*

Lexical structures are a basic source of language change, which occurs in a variety of forms and processes:

- **affixation:** these forms give us prefixes (*telescope, semicircle, transplant*) and suffixes (*happiness, neighbourhood, fifteenth*) as well as highly informal infixes such as *absobloodylutely*
- **conversion:** this reflects the fact that English allows the same word to be in different word classes or grammatical categories: *bear, paper, bank* are all examples of words which can be both nouns and verbs
- **compounds:** *wallpaper, technophobia, scarecrow:* these turn more than one item into a single unit each with its own separate meaning

- **backformations:** new lexemes are formed by adding a prefix or suffix to an existing one: *unreliable* from *reliable* or the verbs *to televise* (from *television)* and *to longlist* (from *to shortlist*) and *to rule something in* (from *to rule something out)*
- **blends:** two elements are combined: *Oxbridge, breathalyser, edutainment*
- **clippings:** these are a form of abbreviation: *ad* from *advertisement* and *phone* from *telephone*
- **reduplicatives:** items where part or all of one element is repeated: *fuddy-duddy, goody-goody, walkie-talkie*

In addition informal, media and literary usages produce an enormous variety of different word forms: *fatso, footbrawl, webzine, brillig.*

The potential for change at lexeme level is huge, although the methods by which such items are formed are, in fact, quite limited. Once again, what might appear to be a random process is actually, in linguistic terms, part of a well-defined system. If we are particularly interested in language change, then examples which come out of these processes may well catch our attention. For some people they are a source of irritation or concern, for others part of an interesting generative process.

### Activity 71

> ▶ Choose three of the categories of lexical structuring which are highlighted in 5.4.1 above.
> ▶ Find some more examples of lexemes in the categories you have chosen. You could consult some of the following: dictionaries, books on slang and idioms, electronic, corpora, newspapers, vocabulary learning books.

## 5.4.2 Grammar

Grammatical change usually takes place more slowly and on a much smaller scale than changes in vocabulary. Also, there is often a difference between language variety and language change. If only a few people use a particular structure, it may well remain limited to a regional or local variety or to a particular set of circumstances. In addition, as we saw in Chapter 1, there will nearly always be differences between spoken and written language. And, because written forms tend to be associated more frequently with 'standard' forms, in order for any grammatical change to become an established part of standard language use, it will have to make its way into the written language. To do this it will probably start off as part of spoken language and will then need to go through several stages and processes until it is recognised as a standard form and as such, perhaps taught or accepted within education. As with innovation and change in vocabulary, it will probably meet considerable opposition on the way. An example of one type of grammatical[6] change is the appearance of a new form of

---

[6] This change is grammatical in that the form *Ms* has become part of a very limited or 'closed' grammatical 'set', i.e. gender-marked title forms (see Chapter 3 (3.4.2), Activity 45).

address – *Ms* – in standard English. *Ms* has performed a difficult feat in managing to make its way into a small, very 'closed' structural group of titles. *Ms* is now a standard category on official forms in the UK and for most people it is now generally accepted and acceptable.

## Some modern changes

As we saw in 3.4.1, there are several elements of grammatical change in standard British English which have appeared in recent years. Again, there is a tendency for these to appear in spoken forms before they are accepted in writing and some are still stigmatised, particularly in certain varieties of formal written English. The influence of real data from spoken language via corpus collections has been useful in highlighting these changes. From an ELT viewpoint, the resultant appearance of advice on these points in modern dictionaries and grammars is also a positive feature for learners and teachers. Examples 5.10–5.12 below show three common instances of these grammatical changes, but only those in Examples 5.10 and 5.11 have made their way into the written language.

### Example 5.10

| Version I | Version II |
|---|---|
| a) There were fewer apples on the trees this year. | There were less apples on the trees this year. |
| b) The one with the fewest errors is the winner. | The one with the least errors is the winner. |

### Example 5.11

| Version I | Version II |
|---|---|
| a) If someone phones, tell him I'll call him back. | If someone phones, tell them I'll call them back. |
| b) The policy helps any child to develop his potential. | The policy helps any child to develop their potential. |

### Example 5.12

| Version I | Version II |
|---|---|
| a) There are lots of people who believe that. | There's lots of people who believe that. |
| b) There are researchers working on it. | There's researchers working on it. |

**Activity 72** ▷

> ▶ Can you identify and describe the language changes illustrated in the pairs of sentences in Examples 5.10, 5.11 and 5.12 on page 170?
> ▶ What reasons do you think there might there be for such structural changes?
>
> **Follow-up:** Try collecting some spoken data yourself and see if any of these forms or other examples of structural change appear in your data.

Other areas of language use provide different examples of grammatical change. Perhaps not surprisingly, the increased social awareness of gender issues has resulted in certain forms of what is known as 'gender neutralisation'. Corpus analyses have identified some contemporary changes in grammar in American English, for instance: the extension of expressions like *she's a bitch* to *he's a bitch,* and the use of *you guys* to refer to women (Waksler 1995). The latter is already acceptable for some people in informal spoken British English.

Another example from a different corpus analysis is provided by Bauer (1994) who suggests that in both British and American English there is a shift away from the *happier/happiest* form of comparatives and superlatives towards the *more/most happy* form, even when the adjective is a single-syllable one. This area of grammar already has some flexibility built into the system when two-syllable words are involved (should it be *more easy* or *easier*?) and the evidence, although not yet conclusive, suggests that the usage may be reasonably well-established for some users of English.[7]

## Historical changes in grammar

If we examine them across a relatively substantial period of time, changes in English grammar are obvious, as in a comparison between the grammar of *contemporary English* and that of the *Old English* period. But the process of structural change is, of course, a very gradual one: if we compare structures of *Middle English* with those from a range of periods within *Modern English* we can see, for instance, how double negatives – used in Middle English to indicate a straightforward negative, whereas Modern English would use just one – gradually disappear, or the priority of word order over inflectional endings starts to become more established.

Examples 5.13, 5.14 and 5.15 on pages 172 and 173 compare three different eras of *Modern English*. The first two show how Shakespeare (early Modern, writing in the sixteenth century) and Jane Austen (writing at the end of the eighteenth century) still used grammatical constructions that would look odd to us today. Example 5.15 is from a contemporary British novel by the Scottish writer Iain Banks.

---

[7] A useful source of information on grammatical change is the definitive *A Comprehensive Grammar of English* (Quirk *et al.* 1985).

### Example 5.13

Will you sit?

What disease hast thou?

What wouldst thou think of me if I should weep?

I would think thee a most princely hypocrite.

Do you use me thus?

No word to your master that I am yet come to town.

Comes the King back from Wales, my noble lord?

*(Shakespeare, 1597, extracts from* Henry IV Part 2*)*

### Example 5.14

ABOUT thirty years ago, Miss Maria Ward of Huntingdon, with only seven thousand pounds, had the good luck to captivate Sir Thomas Bertram, of Mansfield Park, in the county of Northampton, and to be thereby raised to the rank of a baronet's lady, with
5   all the comforts and consequences of an handsome house and large income. All Huntingdon exclaimed on the greatness of the match, and her uncle, the lawyer, himself, allowed her to be at least three thousand pounds short of any equitable claim to it. She had two sisters to be benefited by her elevation; and such of their
10   acquaintance as thought Miss Ward and Miss Frances quite as handsome as Miss Maria, did not scruple to predict their marrying with almost equal advantage. But there certainly are not so many men of large fortune in the world, as there are pretty women to deserve them. Miss Ward, at the end of half a dozen years, found
15   herself obliged to be attached to the Rev. Mr Norris, a friend of her brother-in-law, with scarcely any private fortune, and Miss Frances fared yet worse. Miss Ward's match, indeed, when it came to the point, was not contemptible, Sir Thomas being happily able to give his friend an income in the living of Mansfield, and Mr and
20   Mrs Norris began their career of conjugal felicity with very little less than a thousand a year. But Miss Frances married, in the common phrase, to disoblige her family, and by fixing on a Lieutenant of Marines, without education, fortune, or connections, did it very thoroughly.

*(Jane Austen 1814/1966* Mansfield Park*)*

**Example 5.15**

Yolanda's good mood evaporated rapidly when we got to Edinburgh Airport and she couldn't remember where she'd left her hire car.

'Thought it'd be quicker just leaving it here instead of 5  turning it in and having to hire another one,' she said, stamping down another row of cars.

I followed, pushing a trolley. 'What sort of car was it?' I asked. Not that it would make much difference to me; cars are cars.

10  'Don't know,' Yolanda said. 'Small. Well, smallish.'

'Doesn't the car key tell you something?'

'I left the keys inside the exhaust pipe,' she said, with a hint of embarrassment. 'Saves carrying zillions of keys around.'

I'd noticed that some cars had stickers in the back window 15  identifying hire companies.

'Can you remember what company it belonged to?'

'No.'

'They've got these letters on posts all over the car park; was it near—?'

20  'Can't remember. I was in a hurry.'

'What colour was the car?'

'Red. No; blue. ... Shit.' Yolanda looked frustrated.

'Can you remember what cars it was parked between?'

'Get real, Isis.'

25  'Oh. Yes, I suppose they might have moved. But maybe they're still here!'

'Range Rover. One was a Range Rover. One of those tall things.'

We checked all the Range Rovers in the car park before 30  Yolanda thought to check her credit card slips. There was no sign of a car hire from Glasgow Airport.

'Probably left in the car,' she admitted. '... Oh, the hell with this. Let's hire another one.'

'What about the one that's here?'

35  'Fuck it. They'll find it eventually.'

'Won't you get charged?'

'Let them sue. That's what lawyers are for.'

*(Iain Banks, 1995,* Whit*)*

## Activity 73 ▷

> ▶ Identify some examples of language from Examples 5.13 and 5.14 on page 172 which are no longer found in contemporary English.
> ▶ Can you identify any features of Example 5.15 on page 173 which make it typical of contemporary English?

## 5.4.3 Pronunciation

Historically speaking, the changes in the pronunciation of English have been considerable, but they are harder to monitor than those that occur in written language because for the most part they are not recorded in any permanent form (though poetry can sometimes provide some clues). The examples in this section are limited to British English but there are innumerable instances of change identifiable in other varieties where English is a first language for many speakers, as well as in 'new' Englishes[8] contexts and those where pidgins and creoles are used. As with changes in the lexicon, the processes of change in pronunciation are many and varied. Nonetheless the basic elements of the system remain and are clearly identifiable.

Crystal (1997a:330) gives some examples of types of sound change. They include:

- **assimilation,** where one sound is influenced by the pronunciation of a neighbouring one (the Latin word for 'night', *noctem,* became *notte* in Italian, the /k/ being assimilated to the following /t/; this also happens in various forms in modern spoken English – try saying *ten bottles* quickly and see what happens to the final *n* of *ten*)
- **merger,** where two sounds become one as in Old English /eː/ and /æː/ which became Modern English /iː/
- **split,** which is the opposite of merger where one sound becomes two (in modern English /z/ and /s/ are two different forms, whereas Old English had only one form, /s/)
- **loss,** where a sound may disappear: for instance Old English had a velar fricative /x/, a variant of /h/, pronounced probably with a sound not unlike that preserved in the modern Scottish word *loch*

In Old English *h* was a common consonant and could occur in various positions in a word: *hit* (it), *niht* (night) and *ruh* (rough) would all have had the *h* pronounced. The phenomenon of *h-dropping* (the loss of the pronunciation of *h* in some words, despite its retention in the written form) has been a gradual process over a number of centuries. It tends to be stigmatised in England, particularly amongst standard English users who might disapprove of *'e* for *he* in initial position in a sentence, or *'at* for *hat*. Conversely, *h-accentuation* can still be found in some hyper-correct forms, though the number of speakers who still pronounce the *h* in words such as *where* and *what* is declining, and in rapid informal speech the initial *h* of structure words such as *his* and *her* is lost for the

---

[8] See Chapter 4, 4.3.3

majority of speakers. A (or should it be *An?* – cf. Jane Austen's *an handsome house* in l. 5 of Example 5.14) historical perspective is useful in that it shows how change spreads gradually across language items and speaker communities and how the many varieties of English reveal considerable differences in the way change has spread. It also demonstrates the point that trying to prevent change is a futile effort. No teacher would presumably spend their time trying to restore the lost *h* consonant in *light* or *it*.

The process of *r-dropping* is more recent, but equally noticeable, so that for many speakers of English in England the pronunciation of *farther* is identical to *father*. While r-dropping was once condemned as 'ignorant' the retention of *r* in words like *farmer* is now perceived by many British speakers to be part of a typical 'quaint' West country accent. It is, however, also used without any stigma or element of 'quaintness' by large numbers of speakers in Scotland and the USA.

It is not only at the level of individual sounds that change can be perceived. Other aspects of the English phonological system also show elements of change. There has, for instance, been a definite change in the intonation patterns of declarative statements (as opposed to questions), particularly among young people. A rising intonation at the end of a statement is now commonly heard, although the origins of this usage are perhaps harder to identify. One explanation that has been offered is the popularity of Australian soap operas on British TV, the rising intonation pattern being well established in Australian English. The illustrations in Example 5.16 below come from episodes of *Home and Away* and *Neighbours*[9]. The first set contains four questions, where you might expect to have a high rise at the end; the second set contains four statements, where the same pattern occurs (the one you can now often hear in UK English)[10].

## Example 5.16

Set A:

- Do you know who I just saw outside?
- Have you brought your books and everything?
- Did you see any sharks?
- Let's just drop it, OK?

Set B:

- He was pretty desperate by all accounts.
- I don't know about that.
- We came to a sort of arrangement.
- I'm sure you'll work it out in the end.

(Home and Away *and* Neighbours *23.2.98*)

[9] Two popular TV soap operas, originating in Australia.
[10] The two sets of examples are not connected – i.e. the statements in B are not answers to questions in A.

There are other contemporary examples of pronunciation change in Britain. Varieties can both evolve or disappear. Trudgill and others (e.g. Trudgill 1983) have suggested that the creation of a new town, such as Milton Keynes in Britain, can lead to the emergence of a new accent based in that specific socio-geographic area. In modern spoken English the pronunciation of *Tuesday* has become *chooseday*, the word *sure* now sounds identical to *shore* and *prince* sounds like *prints*. Similar examples can be seen in the rise of what has generally become known as *Estuary English*. Coined in the 1980s, the term is generally used to describe 'a mixture of non-regional and local south-eastern English pronunciation and intonation' (Rosewarne 1994:3). It is characterised by various features including glottal stops in words like *bottle* and *hospital*, the use of /w/ where RP would have /l/ (in *tall* and *ballpoint*), and a different realisation of /r/ in words such as *Sarah* and *record*. Structural words, prepositions, auxiliaries and *that-*clauses are all given a prominence in speech that they do not normally have in RP varieties.

For Rosewarne, one of the functions of Estuary English is that it 'disguises origins' and its spread is seen as a result of factors such as media usage and the increased influence of London-based culture. As well as being the subject of serious linguistic analysis, the phenomenon has produced a number of popular books and press articles. A book by Paul Coggle (1993) which mixes linguistic description with humorous social comments describes Estuary English as 'the new Standard English' and puts forward the theory that as a new form of spoken English it represents a fashionable and up-to-date model, particularly for young speakers. It also seems likely that much of the social distribution of the new variety is linked to its use by media personalities, whom it could be argued represent an attractive sociolinguistic model for young people.

An example of a variety losing its vigour is the change in the dominance, influence and extent of the use of RP, along perhaps with an increased awareness that phrases such as 'the Queen's English' or 'BBC English' no longer equate with RP pronunciation in the same way that they might have done thirty years ago. In Britain, Queen Elizabeth speaks a form of RP (sometimes known as 'advanced' RP) which is spoken by only a very small proportion of the population of the country and by almost nobody anywhere else, outside expatriate British communities.

English still has an enormous number of different spoken varieties but it seems probable that many of these will disappear, if only because of media influence and the effects of mass communication. Certainly the days when someone could live all their life in a rural area and perhaps never hear another variety of spoken English are all but gone[11].

---

[11] However, it is not so long ago that this *was* the case and it was not necessarily restricted to rural regions. John Peel, the British disc jockey and broadcaster from Merseyside in the north-west of England, when he was interviewed on television in a programme about National Service in Britain, recalled how he initially thought that some of his fellow conscripts were from Hungary (this was post-1956). They actually came from Newcastle in the north-east of England.

### Activity 74

The question of which model of pronunciation should be used for teaching is a difficult one.

▶ In your own teaching environment what forms of pronunciation of English are learners likely to encounter?
▶ Can you list some possible advantages and disadvantages of using any one particular form of pronunciation, for instance RP or a local variety, as a model for teaching?

### Activity 75

Think about your own personal use of English – i.e. your *idiolect*. (See 4.2.1.)

▶ Can you think of any examples of how your use of English has changed or developed during your life, e.g. in grammar, vocabulary or pronunciation? Can you think of examples of how it changes on a day-to-day basis?
▶ How important is it for your learners and you, either as an EL1 or EL2 user, that you are aware of changes in your use of language?

## 5.5   Socio-cultural influences on language change

So far, we have considered some general factors which influence or bring about language change, including the natural propensity of language itself to change (for example the process by which new pronunciations that are 'easier' in terms of articulation become accepted). In this section we look specifically at some social and sociolinguistic features of language which can lead to change.[12]

Modern linguistics might accept without any difficulty that change is present and observable, but measuring language change, particularly aspects of contemporary or synchronic change, is not easy. There are a number of tempting generalisations, for instance that English is becoming more informal, but proving that such assumptions are true is not easy. For quite a long time it was considered that language change was very difficult to observe in practice but more recent work in the area has been concerned with just that: the observable features of change. Aitchison (1991:38–40) gives the example here of Labov's[13] experiments in New York department stores, where he set out to determine in a natural context the pronunciation or non-pronunciation of *r*, and the social implications of this.

---

[12] See Hudson 1996, for a general introduction to sociolinguistics and sociolinguistic perspectives on language and language change.
[13] The American sociolinguist (see Labov 1972:43).

People might argue that studying such sociolinguistic factors might not necessarily help the task of teaching in any directly applicable way, but some of these factors are nonetheless basic to the study of language. We look now at four aspects of language use where sociolinguistic factors have a clear role to play in language change, and which learners of English might profit from knowing about (if they do not already do so): gender, taboo language, politically correct language and acceptability.

## 5.5.1 Gender

### Evidence of social pressure on language

Some useful evidence for examining language change comes from issues relating to *gender*. We might consider, for instance, the impact of 'gender-neutral' vocabulary such as *fire fighter, police officer, flight attendant, headteacher* as recommended lexical items for journalists and the media in general. We noted the ability of English to admit a new form of address – *Ms* – for women (see 5.4.2 above). Changes such as these are linked both to the grammar of the language but also to much wider questions relating to language and the power of social groups to bring about change. Increased awareness of social change and resulting pressure from interested parties to make language reflect the changes are powerful agents for innovation. Language teaching materials are increasingly likely to include examples of such changes and although learners may not necessarily need to understand how they came into being, it is useful to be aware of them.

Gender also reveals the emotive power of language use, particularly in the context of change. To demonstrate this we need only to look at the amount of time and effort devoted to discussions on the various perceived merits and demerits of expressions relating to what you call someone who runs a meeting: *chairman, chairwoman, chairperson, chair, madam chair*?

One final example related to the power of social pressure to bring about language change is the increasingly frequent use of the word *partner* (noted in Chapter 1 on page 21) to refer to the person with whom one has a close personal relationship (a kind of life partner, perhaps, rather than a business partner[14]). It implies an equality of status between married and unmarried relationships and, because it is not gender-specific, it bestows similar equality on same-sex and mixed-sex relationships. The use of this word with this meaning certainly reflects attitude changes in some societies towards gender relations. But we need also to consider whether these changes have occurred in all the cultures where English is taught as a foreign or second language. How appropriate would it be to teach this instance of contemporary English to learners in cultures where such changes in attitude are not valued?

[14] See Harvey 1997 for a discussion of the way people use terms like *partner*.

**Activity 76** ▷

> ▶ Look at the following expressions and decide whether they have a more 'gender-neutral' form. If so, what are these forms?
> *headmistress    actress    weather man    usherette    single mother*
> ▶ Which versions of the above expressions do you use?
> ▶ How do you feel about using them?
> ▶ Which forms of the above expressions do you find in other areas of everyday usage, for instance in the press, or on TV?

## 5.5.2 Taboo language

### *Is English becoming more tolerant?*

There is some evidence, for example from English-language TV programmes and feature films, to suggest that we are seeing an increased quantity (and therefore presumably by inference an increased tolerance) of *taboo* terms, perhaps as part of a general tendency for English to be becoming less formal. A 1997 survey on TV programmes by the Broadcasting Standards Commission in the UK found that while people objected to words with sexual or physical connotations, 70 per cent of the sample did not object to religious swear words (the word *hell* for example did not even appear on the four-point severity rating). The BBC's list of words which are not allowed to be used on broadcasts (or perhaps only allowed to be used after a certain time – usually 9 pm) has changed, and now admits words (*bugger* for example) which were unacceptable even ten or fifteen years ago. It is a reasonable conclusion that the measurable level – the quantity – of words which fit in general terms into the taboo category has increased in contemporary media contexts.

Despite such surveys, it is, nevertheless, very hard to define precisely what is and is not taboo. This is partly because it is extremely difficult to track the way in which such language is actually used and by whom, and therefore to generalise from such usage (this would require detailed analysis of language use by subgroups within society). Although we can find instances of apparently increased tolerance of taboo items – for example on TV or in contemporary novels and films – for many people taboo usages remain unacceptable. It seems likely that for most people the tolerance of words which have a religious or sexual connotation still does not extend to public speech. We do not, for example, expect judges or politicians or teachers to swear, at least not in public. Taboo usage is also closely linked to concepts of acceptability, which in turn are connected to culture-bound social groupings and social environments. Even the metalanguage itself can cause problems, as can be seen if we look at the following questions, to which there are no straightforward answers:

- What are the differences between taboo language, abusive language, swearing and obscenity?
- If our attitudes to taboo language *are* changing, is it possible to measure this accurately?
- Is it possible even to discuss the question of taboo usage openly?

You might have noticed that we have not included in the main text here the 'worst' words from the survey list above. Talking about taboo language is, almost by definition, going to be outside the limits of acceptability for many people. Even dictionaries have great difficulty with taboo terms; some choose not to list them at all. Only one EFL guide (Swan 1995) takes any time to address the question of taboo language items for learners of English. The author uses a star system to indicate the 'strength' of such items or how 'shocking' a word might be, but admits that 'individual reactions to particular words (and to swearing in general) vary enormously, and that attitudes are changing rapidly; so people are likely to disagree a good deal about the strength of the words listed' (Swan 1995:574).

## 5.5.3  Politically correct language

### PC or not PC?

The ability of language use to produce controversy is neatly demonstrated by debates over *politically correct language*. Such controversy stems largely from the fact that much of the language we use to talk about issues such as gender, race, sex and personal development is of a loaded and often emotive nature. Add to this the various views – radical, intellectual, political – on how elements of these issues should or should not be described, and the potential for language conflict is clear.

Many of the arguments related to political correctness (PC) are about culture and inequality in one form or another. It is therefore extremely hard to separate the language itself from society and social viewpoints. We can easily list some examples of new language items engendered by politically correct language: *African-American* instead of *black*; *senior citizen* for *pensioner*; *personnel* for *manpower*. We can also identify new lexemes, for instance *sexism*, *ageism*, *heightism*, which in a sense are attributable to PC attitudes. What is much more difficult, however, is to gauge the response to these: this includes the satire and irony with which many terms are greeted and the emotion with which the attempted introduction of such terms may be received.

For many people, political correctness is a pejorative term for some kind of imposed 'hard-line linguistic orthodoxy' (Crystal 1995:177). For people who hold such a view, the condemnation of politically 'incorrect' language has overtones of authoritarianism and censorship. For others, the use of politically 'correct' language is justifiable on various grounds. The feminist writer Deborah Cameron, for instance, presents a very different viewpoint from that of Crystal:

> Changing language is a form of cultural intervention, and experience shows it is just as provocative as any other form. One can only agree with Barbara Ehrenreich that the politics of the provocative gesture alone will not bring about lasting social change, but people who believe cultural politics to be inherently 'trivial' have not come to terms with the nature of the societies activists across the political spectrum are working to change at the end of the twentieth century ...

Yet even if we assume that language has no significant effect on perception, that does not license us to dismiss it as a wholly trivial concern; for speech and writing are not just about representing private mental states: they are also forms of public action, symbolic affirmations of an individual's or a society's values. As Stanley Fish says in his essay 'There's no such thing as freedom of speech and it's a good thing too' (1992: 241), 'words do work in the world of a kind that cannot be confined to a purely cognitive realm of "mere" ideas'.

*(Cameron 1995:142)*

Trying to analyse 'politically correct' language without appreciating the socio-cultural implications would be rash and nonsensical, although this does not stop people having strong feelings about it. Points which often arise from this debate include the following:

- Is PC merely an attempt to manipulate language in order to make a political or social point?
- Is political correctness necessarily a left-wing phenomenon?
- Does the introduction of PC terms actually work linguistically?

### Activity 77

▶ What views do you have on the merits or demerits of politically correct language?
▶ Do you think it is possible to define the term accurately?
▶ Have you come across any other examples of new politically correct language, in addition to those mentioned above?
▶ Check one or two current newspapers and see if you can find any examples of politically correct language.

## 5.5.4 Attitudes and acceptability

### *Whose view is right?*

As we saw in Chapter 4, *acceptability* is an important factor in the sociolinguistic investigation of language, and for many people the whole question of what is an acceptable level of language change is an emotionally charged one. On the one hand, most of the complaints about language that the BBC receives, for example, relate to relatively minor aspects of language change such as the pronunciation of words like *controversy*, or the perceived problem of split infinitives[15] (plus a large number about the use of bad language). On the other hand, and more seriously, establishment figures in the UK are occasionally heard to link the decay of language change with potential social decay. Norman Tebbitt, former Conservative Party Chairman, quoted in Cameron (1995:94), proposes a close link between morals and language, forecasting potential social disorder as a direct result of a lack of knowledge of grammar:

---

[15] Is it CONtroversy or conTROVersy? Is it acceptable to say: 'to boldly go'?

If you allow standards to slip to the stage where good English is no better than bad English, where people turn up filthy at school ... all these things tend to cause people to have no standards at all, and once you lose standards then there's no imperative to stay out of crime.

*(Norman Tebbitt MP, Radio 4, 1985)*

In terms of language change, we have already touched on a number of areas where acceptability is crucial. Aspects of language change related to gender, taboo and political correctness all involve a large element of personal and social acceptability: individual language users have different feelings and responses to language across a broad spectrum of grammar, vocabulary and pronunciation. The attitude of Bolinger and other linguists (e.g. Carter 1997) is that we need to *know* more about how our language systems work before we start to make any far-reaching conclusions about the extent of linguistic or social decay. From a language awareness point of view that seems like a sensible way forward. While such awareness will not necessarily solve the socio-cultural questions which are posed, making an informed judgement is greatly facilitated by a knowledge of how and why something happens.

## Activity 78

Can you think of any examples of language change which are 'emotionally charged' for you? Think about some of the areas we have covered in this chapter in relation to your own attitudes to language change.

| | |
|---|---|
| grammar | new vocabulary forms (e.g. verbs formed from nouns) |
| pronunciation | borrowed words |
| politically correct language | changes in meaning |

# Key references

Aitchison, J. (1991). *Language Change: Progress or Decay?* Cambridge: Cambridge University Press, (2nd edition).
Bauer, L. (1994). *Watching English Change*. Harlow: Longman.
Trask, R.L. (1994). *Language Change*. London: Routledge.

# 6    Power

## 6.1    Overview

The notion of language as a *dynamic* and *powerful* tool for human communication has been at the core of this book. Here, in the final chapter, we look at some areas illustrating different aspects of the relation between language and power:

- the diversity of approaches to the language/power connection
- four specific issues concerning:
  - how language can be manipulated to control thought
  - why knowledge about language is important
  - the power of standard varieties and notions of grammatical correctness
  - whether English is a 'sexist' language

- 'asymmetrical' discourses in contexts and settings involving:
  - 'laypersons'/'experts'
  - L1/L2 speakers
  - cross-cultural communication
  - female/male speakers
  - teachers/learners, particularly in 'communicative' methodology

- the current status of English as a global and international means of communication

We think of the implications of what we teach and why and how we teach it, bringing us back full circle to our starting point: the power of language as a communication tool, and our responsibility as teachers to 'empower' our learners.

## 6.2    Approaches to language and power

### A diversity of approaches

As has been the case with other areas we have addressed in the book, the wide range of approaches to language and power makes it difficult to find a comprehensive definition of the word *power* in this context. Some facets of its meaning are reflected in the following sets of questions, the first of which relates to language and powerful societal bodies:

- To what extent is power *institutionalised* in the language use of bodies such as governments or the legal profession?
- How, and in what contexts, is language used to *manipulate* what we think?
- What part does language play in the *hold* that advertising conglomerates and multinational companies have over us as consumers?

Another set of questions relates to expertise in, and control of knowledge about language:

- Whose 'expert' view of language should we most readily accept?
- Why is the word *standard* important in talking about language and power?

Yet another set of questions involves the teaching and learning of English:

- What implications for teachers and learners does the spread of *English as an International Language* (EIL) have?
- Should we think of our ultimate aim as teachers of English to be to 'empower' learners – to enable them to operate as effectively as possible in the language for their particular purposes?
- If this is our aim, how might we best achieve it?

In fact, the relationship between language and power is such a fundamental and all-pervasive aspect of human societies that it is not at all surprising to find it of central concern to a wide range of writers and scholars, each with their particular standpoint, be it cultural, political, historical, sociolinguistic or educational. Some writers are concerned to raise awareness of the implications of this relationship in relatively well-defined settings such as the workplace, the classroom, the negotiating table or the lawcourt.[1] Others have a more wide-ranging context when they take on the difficult and complex issues of linguistic imperialism and the cultural politics of English in its current world role.[2] The view that it is impossible to separate politics and language is at the heart of Cameron's work on language in society.[3] And for others a 'critical language study' focus is essential for understanding how language influences power relations in society.[4]

## 6.3   Some language and power issues

In this section we are going to look at four particularly contentious areas where the language/power interface is central: the power conferred by language choice;

[1] For examples here, see Graddol *et al.* 1994; Gumperz 1982; Scollon and Scollon 1995; Sinclair and Coulthard 1975; Sinclair and Brazil 1982; Wodak 1996.
[2] See Phillipson 1992, and Pennycook 1994.
[3] See Cameron 1985, 1995.
[4] See Fairclough 1989, 1991, 1992; Ivanic and Roach 1991; Clark *et al.* 1991.

the power conferred by ownership of knowledge about language (and disadvantages springing from lack of such knowledge); the power of standard language varieties; and whether English is a 'sexist' language, biased in favour of the male gender.

## 6.3.1 Language choice: manipulation and accessibility

We saw in Chapter 2, that principles of politeness and the need for tact often lead us to use language whose surface meaning masks the truth. And we are all, no doubt, aware of how we can vary the impact of what we say or write by our choice of words and structures. In English, we talk of people using *strong language* (when we may either approve or disapprove of its power), or the need *to tone something down* (when the meaning is that the language should be made less direct or confrontational). This we might think of as a relatively innocuous kind of manipulation.

But, as Crystal (1995:174–176) suggests, most of us are also aware that at times the ways in which language is manipulated may be more dishonest, and that it can often deliberately be used to mislead and cover up. Bolinger (1980:6) alerts us to this abuse of language with his compelling image of language as a 'loaded weapon', urging us to identify 'the concealed weapons as well as those worn on the hip' and to examine 'how some people use them to get the better of others'. We consider first some common ways in which language can be manipulated, and then we look briefly at two 'worlds' where we are regularly assaulted by 'loaded' language – those of advertising and the media.

### *Who manipulates language and how?*

**Euphemistic language**
English actually contains in its lexicon a number of words (*propaganda, misinformation, disinformation* and *doublespeak,* for example) which are used to describe language that is designed to mislead in some way. However, recognition of and agreement about such manipulation is an area fraught with difficulty, not least because judgements will always depend on individual political, ethical and moral standpoints. To take euphemistic language as an example: English is full of what most of us readily accept as useful ways of reducing the possibly offensive nature of certain direct expressions (see *The Oxford Dictionary of Euphemisms* for a whole bookful of examples):

| | | |
|---|---|---|
| *to die* | → | *to pass on* or *pass away* |
| *toilet* | → | *loo, restroom, bathroom* |
| *to urinate* | → | *to have a pee, to pay a call* |
| *a shortage of money* | → | *a cash problem* |
| *obesity* | → | *a weight problem* |
| *illegal narcotic* | → | *substance* |

Businesses and governments are also happy to use this strategy for their own advantage. Some relatively recent neologisms in the world of multinational business are *efficiency gains, rationalisation, delayering, delevelling* and *rightsizing,* all of which in some contexts are euphemisms for the unpleasant reality of firing employees.[5] Crystal (1995:174–176) provides a range of examples of language used for non-personal communication which is identifiable as manipulative. One rich area here is military doublespeak, where bombing raids manifest themselves as *air support,* or killing metamorphoses into *deprivation of life.* Expressions promoted by the nuclear industry offer further evidence where, for example, an explosion is presented in public as *energetic disassembly.* From the world of politics the phrase *being economical with the truth* has now entered the language[6] to mean not saying what actually happened, or lying. Such manipulation of language is one way of trying to present unpleasant or unpalatable matters in a more positive light, in some cases more transparently than others. It is not difficult to see that using an expression such as *collateral* when what is really meant is dropping bombs on people is an attempt to call upon language to reduce the power of reality – war, in this particular case. Whether people are actually deceived by such linguistic tactics is difficult to know. Linguists are presumably not alone in finding some of the official terminology of war tragically absurd, as when euphemistic phrases such as *ethnic cleansing* (killing people of a different race or religion) or *casualties resulting from friendly fire* (killing your own troops) are used.

These examples demonstrate two dimensions of power: the power of the language itself is seen in the direct, emotive impact of words such as *kill, bomb* or *war;* the power of language users – such as spokespersons of multinational business conglomerates, the armament industry or drug companies, or politicians and armed forces personnel – to influence public thought and opinion is seen in their attempts to mitigate or soften the power of the language itself by using terms which they hope will distance and disengage us from distasteful, unsavoury and sometimes, perhaps, morally questionable activities.

**Making language inaccessible**
A rather different type of manipulation can be seen in the way that language is sometimes made difficult to understand through being inaccessible. People are often placed in a relatively powerless position vis-a-vis employers, bureaucrats and lawyers because they are hampered – whether by design or otherwise – in their understanding of official communications by the opacity, or lack of clarity, of the language. Making language difficult to understand results in denying easy access to meaning, and is thus an imposition of the user's power over the recipient. Example 6.1 on page 187 contains some instances from a collection of official 'gobbledygook', where the complex and repetitive language, although its initial objective might ostensibly have been to make things clear, ends up by doing the opposite.

In 1990, the Plain English Campaign (a body campaigning to reduce jargon and simplify the language of official forms and documents) introduced a Crystal Mark scheme in the UK to recognise texts which had been written clearly. The scheme was intended to make the sometimes unduly complex, distant and

---

[5] *The Independent on Sunday,* 12 June, 1994, p.17
[6] As a result of political skulduggery in the UK during the Spycatcher affair of the 1980s.

## Example 6.1

**From the Department of Health and Social Security**
Where a married woman's own contribution record is not sufficient to give her a retirement pension basic component at the standard rate, her basic component may be increased by the amount of basic component to which she is entitled on her husband's contributions, subject to the combined basic component not exceeding the standard rate of basic component payable to a married woman on her husband's contributions.

*(Cutts and Maher 1984:38)*

**From the Agricultural Wages Board**
A year's holiday allowance will vary according to the number of days on which a whole-time or regular part-time worker is regularly required to work during a week, excluding Sunday and his weekly day-off and disregarding weeks in which he is allowed a holiday or in which a public holiday occurs, and where that number varies during any period of employment in a holiday year, it shall be ascertained by taking an average over that period and rounding it off to the nearest whole number, a half counting as one.

*(Cutts and Maher 1984:50)*

**From a Local Council Education Office**
If it is not possible by the date that the application form should be returned to this office to submit the necessary evidence to verify any information included on the form regarding the amount of income received by you and/or your parents or spouse during the relevant period, it is suggested that the completed application form should, nevertheless, be returned by the appropriate date and that evidence of income e.g. certificate of employer, Income Tax Form P60, Income Tax assessment Form, etc., should be submitted as soon as it is available.

*(Cutts and Maher 1984:161)*

impenetrable writing of employers, bureaucrats and lawyers more accessible.[7] Partly because of the efforts of the Plain English Campaign, perhaps, it is true that many official bodies in the UK have in recent years made considerable efforts to redress the balance somewhat by producing clearer public notices and less convoluted official documentation than in Example 6.1 above. Nevertheless, there often remains in the language of official communications a distinct sense of the distance between those with the power and those without. Example 6.2 on page 188 contains two versions of a letter with the same public function: to publicise the UK Inland Revenue's self-assessment system. The first version is that actually used by the Inland Revenue; the second is a suggestion for an alternative proposed by the Plain English Campaign.

[7] We should, however, note Cameron's comment that 'we cannot assume ... that plain language will be automatically transparent or that the alternative will be automatically misleading'(1995:71).

**Example 6.2**

---

### THE REVENUE VERSION

① Dear Madam,

② Self-assessment 1st payment overdue: £x
This includes interest to 7/5/97.

③ The total amount above is unpaid. Please pay it now unless you have done so within the last few days. You will find more information on the amount you owe and how to pay it on your Statement of Account.

If I do not receive your payment within 7 days I shall ④ start legal proceedings to collect the amount due.

This could result in: ⑤          ⑥

■ your possessions being seized, removed and sold at public auction, or

■ a court order or judgement against you.

It may also mean you have to pay costs.

⑦ Should you wish to discuss this matter further then ⑧ please contact this office immediately.

⑨ You are reminded that interest is charged on late payments and this increases daily.

Your sincerely (illegible signature) ⑩

---

### PLAIN ENGLISH VERSION

Dear Mrs Smith,

The new Self-Assessment system has now started. Please send your first payment for £x. This includes interest from Date A to Date B.

If you have already sent your payment, I am sorry for troubling you. If not, please pay it now. You will find more information on the amount you owe, and how to pay it, on your statement of account.

If I do not receive your payment within seven days, I will have to start legal proceedings to collect the amount you owe. These proceedings could include:

■ your possessions being removed by a bailiff and sold at public auction, or

■ a court order being made against you.

You could also have to pay costs.

Obviously we do not want this to happen. If you have any questions, please contact me immediately at the number shown above. Please remember that we increase the interest you have to pay each day.

Yours sincerely, (printed name)

---

*(The Times 15.5.97, p. 2)*

**Activity 79** ▷

---

Both versions of the letter in Example 6.2 on page 188 have the same purposes: to get people to co-operate with a new income tax self-assessment system, and to warn them about the negative consequences of failing to comply with it.

▶ Which version of the letter would you prefer to receive and why?
▶ Would you agree that the Plain English version has been successful in making the language of the original letter more accessible to the ordinary person? What is the evidence?
▶ Compare the two letters at the points indicated with numbers. How do the language choices made at these points in the two versions differ in terms of the way they indicate differences in status (and therefore power) between the sender of the letter (the Inland Revenue) and the recipient (a member of the public who has failed to comply with the law)? Are the power relations made more obvious in one version of the letter than in the other?

---

Despite examples from contexts such as that in Example 6.2, there are many areas of life where redressing the balance is extremely difficult, if not impossible. This is largely because certain types, forms and usages of language which reflect high prestige and status – and therefore power – are built into the system, the classic example here being the legal system. As well as being exclusive in the sense that not everybody can understand them fully, in Britain these forms and usages are so entrenched in the culture and traditions of the country that they are particularly hard to change (see 6.4.1 for further discussion).

**Some other techniques for manipulation**

Another avenue through which people with power can impose their way of perceiving things on the less powerful is not to allow their audience to question their assumptions, or, as Clark *et al.* (1991:85) put it, to make it difficult 'to challenge orthodoxies'. Example 6.3, from a British government official publication in the eighties, concerns the 'need' to cut the higher education budget. It illustrates how those with power (in this case, the government) establish that something is happening because it is necessary without explaining why (or whether) it *is* actually necessary. Neither do they allow those without power (the public) to question the assumption that there is a need to cut the higher education budget.

**Example 6.3**

Higher education is provided by universities, polytechnics, the Scottish central institutions and some 350 colleges and institutes of higher education, some concerned wholly with teacher training. The *need* to reduce the public expenditure on higher education has necessitated some restructuring of courses and departments in universities and other colleges.

(*Britain 1986: An Official Handbook. Central Office of Information:164, authors' italics*)

Incidentally, we might note in the above example, the 'ab-use' of language in the tautological 'the need ... has necessitated' – another example of how couching ideas in 'officialese' probably helps to mask unpleasant or politically unpopular policies: the language sounds authoritative, so people often don't bother to question it.

Another version of this technique is to use unsupported generalisations in putting forward a personal viewpoint. This might lend credence to ideas that really need to be challenged – or at least discussed. John Honey, for instance, a strong supporter of the concept and power of standard English, uses the terms *standard*, *educated* and *educatedness* extensively in his book *Language and Power* without giving precise definitions of what he means by the terms.

A final illustration concerns the introduction of a new word or a change in meaning of an established term by a body of authority, such as a public broadcasting body. This may represent an abuse for some people. Complaints to the BBC are a rich source for examples here, as when an irate listener wrote to complain about the weather broadcasts: *Why do weather forecasters insist on talking about 'interludes'? There is no such word!*

## The advertising world

In everyday usage we don't have to look very far to find examples of the potential of language to be used for manipulative purposes. Is the language of advertising, for example, designed simply to promote products or does it also mislead? Is it actually possible to promote *anything* in a genuinely neutral way? Dyer, in her book *Advertising as Communication* believes that it is not:

> Advertising language is of course loaded language. Its primary aim is to attract our attention and dispose us favourably towards the product or service on offer.
>
> *(Dyer 1982: 139)*

We might agree that advertisers and their highly competitive business techniques are clearly using language to persuade, but are they also, therefore, constantly guilty of attempting to mislead people? We might suspect that there are some quite frequent attempts to do so – why else are advertisers fond of words whose meaning is hard to tie down, such as *elegant, enchanting, intriguing* and *captivating* (Dyer 1982:149). Not all examples are quite as blatant as the advertisement quoted by Bolinger (1980:65), where the expression *fun-sized* is used to describe a chocolate bar which is actually just small, but a list of the most common adjectives used in advertising is revealing (*new* is a favourite, according to Dyer, but what does it actually mean – how new is new, and why is it important for things to be new?). Suspicions that advertisers may have agendas other than simple persuasion are reinforced by the existence of bodies such as the Advertising Standards Authority in Britain which tries to ensure that advertisements are reasonably truthful.

**Activity 80**

> Collect some advertisements from TV, magazines, newspapers, billboards and any other sources you can find. List some expressions that appear to be currently 'fashionable' in the sense that they are often used in advertisements. Think about why advertisers use them.

## The media world

Another 'world' where we recognise the power of language to mould opinion and thought – perhaps less blatantly than in some advertising – is that of the media. Sensational headlines 'grab' us, and we are forced to encounter information in the way a reporter or editor chooses to present it. An example here comes from the reporting of an incident which occurred in August 1997: the Russian space station, *Mir*, developed serious technical problems which at one point seemed likely to threaten the safety of the astronauts on board. Example 6.4 below contains two versions of how this situation was reported on two different UK news channels.

**Example 6.4**

The Russian space station, Mir, is *spinning out of control* ...

*(ITV News, 18/8/97)*

The Russian space station, Mir, is *drifting in space* ...

*(Sky News, 18/8/97)*

Both the images (italicised in the example) chosen by the two TV channels to convey this message to the public are powerful in their emotive evocation of impending danger or disaster. But which – if either – accurately reflects the truth? In the late 20th-century world of instant communication, the media have become such omnipresent purveyors of information[8] that we might perhaps be in danger of failing to realise the extent to which they hold us in their thrall.

Example 6.5 on page 192 is a reminder of the power of the press. The headlines, all of which come from a single edition of a local newspaper, may have been intended to pander to readers' seemingly insatiable appetite for sensation and vicarious thrills, but do they really present a true picture of life in the town?[9]

---

[8] *Television* was voted the word that best sums up the 20th century in a recent newspaper poll (*The Times*, 14 March, 1998, p.7).

[9] An additional 'power' element here is that of the compiler of this collage in his selection of headlines.

**Example 6.5**

## Assistant at DIY store attacked

# BIKE STOLEN

Robbers stole a £200 mountain bike from a teenager at the Sutton estate on Thursday

# PENSIONER ROBBED BY GUN GANG

## OAP guilty of manslaughter

## Bag snatch fails

A gang of youths tried to snatch the bag of a 35-year-old man as he walked in the underpass between Cross Street and Belview Way.

## Hit and run victim recovers

## EVENING HOLD-UP

## Firefighters called to suspected arson blaze

## POISON WARNING

# Cashpoint robbery

POLICE are looking for a robber who attacked a woman in broad daylight in a busy shopping street. The woman was knocked to the ground and the robber made off with the money she had just taken from a cashpoint machine.

## Thugs beat up man outside bank

## Prostitute damaged milk float

## Pensioner foils robbery

A brave pensioner threw a can at a would-be robber who threatened him with a knife and demanded money.

## Judge: 'I won't let crook go free'

# Police hunt attacker

Police are looking for a thug who kicked a teenager in the head giving him a fractured skull.

## Search on for car wreckers

# Man jailed for attack on woman

**Activity 81**

> Collect some data of your own from the media, such as those in Examples 6.4 and
> 6.5. You could, for example, take one or two news items on a particular day and
> compare how they are reported by different TV channels, different radio stations and
> different newspapers. Think about how the language choices (e.g. choice of lexis,
> choice of structure, choice of format, choice of image, degree of directness, degree of
> formality) exercise power over you – in the sense of how they affect the way you react
> to and understand the situations reported.

## 6.3.2 Knowledge about language

How do we recognise when language is deliberately being used to manipulate
what we think and believe? And who is in the best position to decide whether
and to what degree language is being misused or abused in this sense? The
answer, surely, is that we ourselves need to be able to exercise informed
judgement. The corollary of this for teachers of language is that their job entails
helping learners to react critically to what they read and hear. One of the key
issues related to language and power, therefore, and one particularly relevant for
language teachers, is this need for people to be informed about language.

### The need for knowledge about language

Knowledge about how language works and how it may be manipulated is seen by
many writers as an essential means of protection against, and more effective
response to language use and abuse. Bolinger (1980) is one such writer who
emphasises the power of advertisers and the military to use language to mislead
and misinform. But he also warns us to be careful about where we get our
language knowledge from, viewing certain self-styled language experts – or as he
terms them 'shamans' – with some distrust[10]. Pinker (1994:373) has a different
word for the same kind of self-informed expert: he calls them 'language
mavens'[11] and criticises them for being interested only in 'prescriptive rules of the
language [that] make no sense on any level'. Both suggest that more reliable
sources of language knowledge are rooted in less prescriptive approaches which
attempt to discover how people actually use and exploit the language resources at
their disposal.

But for many teachers of language this 'knowledge about language' dimension
of their work might present a certain problem: how much of this 'knowledge' is it
practicable or feasible to teach? The more one discovers about a language, the
more one becomes aware that teaching it almost inevitably involves reduction
and oversimplification (as indeed is the case with many other subjects). People
may feel that it is much easier to teach prescriptively from the 'rules' offered by
many learner-grammars and dictionaries than to muddy the waters with doubts
about their validity.

---

[10] Certain popular newspaper language pundits, whose columns, though entertaining, may not necessarily
be well-informed from a linguistics perspective, are given as relevant instances here by Bolinger and
Pinker.
[11] From the Yiddish word meaning *expert*.

## Whose version of the knowledge is best?

A further difficulty is to identify reliable sources of information. Knowledge about English is apparently easily available: it is one of the most investigated and written about of languages. Besides reference grammars and dictionaries, which range from the simple (and simplified) to the highly complex, there is also a vast number of books and articles dealing with questions of usage, correctness and standards, often with either an implied or a direct statement to the effect that a proper understanding of these bestows power on users. Many of these publications are simply guides to what is, or is supposed to be correct; others, often based on a literary, stylistic or etymological approach, discuss at length what should and shouldn't be happening to English (see Howard 1986). Other publications attempt to set up a framework for discussion of what should be considered educationally advantageous in the context of the forms and models of language that are taught (e.g. Honey 1997; Bernstein 1971).

One consideration for teachers is how to decide which kind of knowledge and/or source of information is the best for their specific purposes, and which kind of knowledge is required by their learners. Sinclair (1991:42) makes the point that any collection and presentation of language knowledge is arbitrary:

> How many words written *bow* are there in English? The *OED* lists seven head-words; *Webster's New Collegiate* gives five; *Collins English Dictionary* has three; and *Collins COBUILD English Language Dictionary* gives just one. They are all describing the same language facts.

## Activity 82

Look up the words *decline* and *charge* in different types of reference books (e.g. two different dictionaries) and compare how they explain their meanings and usage. Check how these reference sources help you understand this word as part of the English language by comparing the range of language areas they refer to: grammatical categories, transitivity, countability, collocation, meaning, connotations, likely contexts of use, synonyms and antonyms, formality and so on.

**Follow-up:** Explore some other language items in terms of how they are explained and represented in a variety of reference books, and consider which level of knowledge is relevant to you and your learners.

## A key to knowledge about society

There is another side to the importance of having as wide a knowledge as possible about language: such knowledge gives us insights into how society works. Halliday (1982, cited in Carter 1997:52[12]) recognises the hidden power this kind of knowledge might bestow upon its owners when he claims that it

[12] Carter was discussing here the descriptive, rather than prescriptive, methodology proposed by the UK Language in the National Curriculum (LINC) project, (see Carter 1990) for teaching knowledge about and awareness of language – a methodology which encountered considerable opposition from the government of the day, concerned as that government was with raising 'standards' rather than awareness.

might help to make them aware of the language-related inequities of society:

> More than any other human phenomenon, language reflects and reveals the inequalities that are enshrined in the social process. When we study language systematically ... we see into the power structure that lies behind our everyday social relationships, the hierarchical statuses that are accorded to different groups within society.

At the same time, a *lack* of such knowledge is dangerous in a quite different sense, for it might be equated with ignorance, lack of education and low standards. People may be led to believe they are socially inferior if their knowledge of language is impoverished:

> Are you embarrassed because your English isn't quite good enough? Are you mystified by grammar and punctuation? Can you spell correctly and use a wide vocabulary?
>
> *(Metcalfe and Astle, 1985, cover blurb)*

At the same time they – and the ways the language is taught – may become objects of scorn to those whose knowledge is superior:

> All the people I have in my office, they can't speak English properly, they can't write English properly. All the letters sent from my office I have to correct myself, and that is because English is taught so bloody badly.
>
> *(Prince Charles, heir to the British throne, quoted in Carter 1997:7)*

It is to this aspect of power – the power of standard varieties of the language – that we turn our attention in the next section.

## 6.3.3 The power of standard varieties

The 'ownership' or command of a standard form of English – to speak and write the language 'properly', as Prince Charles expresses it in the quote above – produces a wide range of emotions including admiration, fear and criticism. These emotions have varied with the historical and political perspectives prevailing at any given time, and standard English has been closely linked on the one hand with imperialism and elitism, and on the other, with social division and declining educational standards. In other words, the subject is an extremely provocative one, and views differ enormously.

### Standard or standards?

On the one hand, there is the school of thought that language and morality are dependent on one another and that the 'decline' of one inevitably includes the other. Thus, for some people *standard* is very similar to *standards*: if things are not 'correct' in a grammatical sense, then the natural progression is towards social as well as linguistic chaos. 'Bad' grammar, as Norman Tebbitt[13] sees it (his

---

[13] A former Chairman of the Conservative Party in Britain when Margaret Thatcher was Prime Minister.

thoughts on this subject are quoted in Chapter 5, page 182), can quite easily lead to crime, filthy appearance and general moral decline.[14] On the other hand, there is the view that people simply speak different varieties, each of which can be accepted in its own right: language and morality have nothing to do with each other. At the same time, there has always been a linguistic perspective that a standard form of the language is, or at least should be, identifiable and objectively describable.

There is no denying that the concept of *standard language* is a powerful one, even if extremely controversial and extremely difficult to define. Wilkinson (1995:23) claims that any definition is always determined by 'our own attitudes and prejudices', depending as it does on subjective assessments spread across a broad band of context, choice and usage. But ultimately the notion of standard language is a social issue, which is why it relates to power. It has to do with education, privilege and social inequality. The paradox is that Standard English – in any English-speaking country – is a 'minority variety' of the language, and yet the one that 'carries most prestige and is most widely understood' (Crystal 1995:110): the reality is that those who have been born or educated into it are largely those with power and influence in society.

## Standard written or standard spoken?

Before we can even try to consider concepts such as the acceptability or the role of 'non-standard' varieties of English, we need to confront the difficulty of describing what we mean by 'standard' English. What does it mean to speak and write 'properly'? Crystal (1995:110) includes grammar, vocabulary and orthography as the chief markers of the standard variety of English. The exclusion of pronunciation from this list underscores the fact that the word *standard* very often relates to written forms of language, which are relatively easy to observe and define; determining standard spoken forms is much more difficult. Also, until quite recently written forms were almost exclusively used as a basis for judgements on language (as well as for the creation of language teaching materials). It is only with increasingly sophisticated and accessible computer technology that the collection and analysis of spoken language has become much easier. At least we can now begin to describe spoken language and its grammar, even if it remains difficult to define a standard variety.

Example 6.6 on page 197 contains an extract from a recent novel.[15] The letter in this extract, written by one of the characters in the novel, highlights some of the points we want to make about the meaning, definition and power of standard varieties.

[14] See Carter 1997, Chapter 1, pp.5–12, and Cameron 1995, Chapter 3, pp.82–115 for further discussion of this alleged connection between 'standard' and 'standards'.
[15] Pat Barker 1994. *The Eye in the Door*, p.83, a novel set in the First World War period.

**Example 6.6**

Dear Winnie,

Don't worry about me pet I am orlrite Hettie come
home for Xmas and we had a good time even little
Tommy purked up a bit and you no what he's like you
notice this new year there wasnt the same nonsense
talked as there was last I think last year knocked the
stuffing out of a lot of people except that bloody bugger-
ing Welsh windbag he dont change his tune much the
poor lads

   Hettie made me go to the sales with her cos she new I
wanted a blowse there was a nice black one *no trimings*
but Hettie says aw Mam your making yourself an old
woman anyway you no Hettie I come away with a
navy blue with a little yellow rose on it I think it looks
orlrite cant take it back if it dont with it being in the
sale we bumped into Mrs Warner you no her from the
suffragettes and of corse she asked after you but she was
only standoffish you could see her wanting to get away
she says she thort to much was made of Xmas and turcy
was a very dry meat I says well Ive never tasted it so I
wouldnt no You no what Ronnie Carker used to say ...

*(Pat Barker (1994).* The Eye in the Door, *p.83)*

## Activity 83

> ▶ The variety of English in the letter in Example 6.6 above is meant to indicate that
> the writer comes from a social and educational background where 'standard'
> English is not the norm. How does the novelist represent the letter-writer's 'non-
> standard' variety? (Think about some differences between spoken and written
> language, conventions of written language such as spelling and punctuation and so
> on.)
> ▶ If this had been spoken language rather than written, would we still be likely to
> think of it as 'non-standard'? If so, why?

## 6.3.4 English as a 'sexist' language

Our fourth language and power 'issue' is the question as to whether English is a 'sexist' language. This question – and its implications – can provoke sarcasm, scepticism, rage and dismissal as well as more considered responses. However, language at least reflects the attitudes and values of the society in which it is used and possibly helps to perpetuate them. So, if people think that English-language-based societies do maintain some gender-discriminatory (or 'sexist') attitudes, it is not unreasonable to consider to what extent the language reflects them.

### Is there any evidence for gender bias?

According to the *Cambridge International Dictionary of English* (1995), sexism refers to 'the idea or belief that the members of one sex are less intelligent, able, skilful, etc. than the members of the other sex'. Other definitions refer to the oppression of members of one sex by the other. In theory, then, sexism (or genderism) can be seen as some kind of discrimination against either gender. In reality, of course, when the alleged sexism/genderism of the English language is discussed it is discrimination against females as built into the language that is of concern. Such discrimination is an aspect of power since it is a means of maintaining a power structure which favours males over females.

In 5.5.1 we drew attention to the development of a so-called 'gender-neutral' vocabulary. We can see this as one attempt to rid the language of gender bias in the sense that such words either replace a male-specific item (e.g. *fire fighter* for *fireman*) or deny the necessity to mark the gender of the occupant of a particular post (e.g. *headteacher* for *headmaster* or *headmistress*). However, as Cameron (1994:29) points out:

> the purely technical problem of avoiding he and man ... is not the underly-ing problem. The technical problem has to do with linguistic form: eliminating some forms and finding suitable substitutes for them. The real underlying prob-lem, however, is meaning. Unfortunately there is not a perfect mapping between the two. Gender-neutral forms do not always carry gender-neutral meanings; language can be gender free in the technical sense without being truly free of gendered connotations, and without being inclusive in the sense of including women.

Nevertheless, the fact that these changes are occurring in the language indicates that this is indeed a live sociolinguistic issue: we can readily hear and see how the language is adapting to changes in attitudes towards male and female roles in society. The tendency to question whether it is necessary or even desirable to mark the gender of a person in a particular occupation is also illustrated in changes in the use of the suffix *-ess,* the subject of the next activity.

## Activity 84 ▷

> ▶ Look at the following pairs of words and decide which of the 'female' items are:
> a) no longer in use
> b) still in use but probably disappearing
> c) showing no signs of disappearing
>
> | | | | |
> |---|---|---|---|
> | actor | actress | host | hostess |
> | author | authoress | manager | manageress |
> | clerk | clerkess | poet | poetess |
> | governor | governess | prince | princess |
>
> ▶ What do you think is the connection between changes in the use of *-ess* and attempts to eradicate gender bias from the language?

We can find further evidence for the claim that English does reflect and support gender-biased attitudes if we look at the associations (often negative) of certain words with female reference and the associations (often positive or neutral) of their male counterparts.

## Activity 85 ▷

> ▶ Consider the three pairs of words below, and think of any positive or negative connotations associated with them. Can you discern any pattern or general trend?
> a) bachelor/spinster    b) sir/madam    c) wizard/witch
>
> ▶ Can you think of any other such pairs with positive or negative connotations?

Another aspect of English usage which bears examination in this context is the 'natural'- or 'normal'-sounding order of certain words occurring in common collocations. McCarthy and O'Dell (1994:154) give examples of binomials, which they define as 'expressions (often idiomatic) where two words are joined by a conjunction (usually *and*)'. Among the many examples provided are some which are characterised by the use of near-synonyms (e.g. *pick and choose, peace and quiet*) and others with a common sound pattern (e.g. *part and parcel, wine and dine*). McCarthy and O'Dell point out that the order of the words in binomials is usually fixed. In the following activity you are invited to consider the order of words in expressions, which, while not binomials as such, are certainly in frequent use as common combinations.

**Activity 86** ▷

> ▶ Try saying the following phrases out loud and decide which ones sound 'natural' or 'normal' and which ones do not.
>
> | | |
> |---|---|
> | brothers and sisters | women and men |
> | light and dark | death and life |
> | rich and poor | queen and king |
> | sons and daughters | bad and good |
>
> ▶ Do you notice any patterns or trends in those that sound 'natural' with reference to connotations of the words and position of 'female' reference words?

### 'He or she'? Or 'she or he'? Or 'he/she'? Or 's/he'?

The use of *he* as a non-gender-specific pronoun is another area of English usage which has come under scrutiny in the 'English is sexist' debate. Crystal (1987:46) presents a list of alternative pronouns which have been proposed to replace this generic use of the male pronoun: *tey, co, E, ne, thon, mon, heesh, ho, hesh, et, hir, jhe, na, per, xe, po* and *person*. As Crystal comments, 'none of these has attracted widespread support'. This is hardly surprising, especially given the difficulties we would have in pronouncing some of them.

Nevertheless, it is the case that people have become conscious of the gender bias implied by the use of *he/him/his* with generic reference. In written English some people use combinations such as *he/she* or *he or she* to get round the problem. Some, perhaps in an attempt to redress the implied balance of power between the genders, prefer to reverse the order as in *she/he*. Many people feel quite comfortable using *they/them/their* with singular reference as in: *Every student has to buy their own books.* But other users, including some teachers, find this apparent breach of a grammatical rule unacceptable.

We have been looking at some instances of English usage where it is claimed that the language reflects society's power-related attitudes towards male and female roles. We have also looked at some attempts to rid the language of this bias. If nothing else, the discussion should have illustrated the *power* of this topic to provoke debate and discussion. At the same time, it is important to note that the changes in the language we have considered reflect attitude changes predominantly in cultures where English is spoken as a first language. As with the change towards use of the gender-neutral term *partner* (discussed above in 5.5.1), it would not necessarily be appropriate to transmit these language changes to learners in cultures where the corresponding attitudes and values are not current.

## 6.4 Asymmetrical discourses

In this section of the chapter we look at some instances of language-in-use to explore further how language reflects the 'power structure' in society that Halliday referred to (see page 195 above). We are going to be particularly interested in the *asymmetry* of the discourse in our examples of social interaction. The term 'asymmetry' here indicates that there is an imbalance in the discourse in that it is weighted or loaded in favour of the socially more powerful party.

In Chapters 2 and 4 we explored the idea that language as people use it is the end-product of the choices they make – choices of structure, vocabulary, delivery, presentation and response. We also saw that although in theory we are free to choose whatever language items we want and present them in whatever way we wish, in fact our choices are always constrained by the context in which we are using the language.

One extremely important factor in any context is the status relations between the interactants and another is whether they happen to have been born male or female. Our language use reflects and is reflected by the power we either wield, share or concede at any given moment in any given interaction by virtue of our status (including gender) vis-a-vis the other parties involved: consciously or unconsciously we use language to impress, influence, persuade, mitigate, dominate, control, mislead, evade, distort, be devious, mask intentions and otherwise manipulate an interaction. Such manipulations range from the overt to the almost imperceptible, and from the acceptable to the invidious and despicable.[16]

There is an extensive literature[17] on the intricacies and subtleties of the relation between language and power in different settings. These range from high-profile contexts where a power imbalance is anticipated (such as law-court exchanges between cross-examining barristers and defendants, or interrogations of suspects by police officers, or 'expert'/'layperson' encounters) to rather more low-key settings where more equal power and status relations would be predicted (such as conversations among friends). The discourses which are the outcomes of such interactions are defined by Pennycook (1994:32) as 'relationships of power/knowledge that are embedded in social institutions and practices'.

We will look first at some specific settings where we anticipate that the discourse will be asymmetrical, and then at some issues associated with the 'gender' debate in discourse studies.

## 6.4.1 Some settings and contexts

As illustrations of relationships where an imbalance of power is anticipated, we look briefly at interactions which take place in a medical setting, a legal setting and a classroom setting.

### A doctor/patient encounter

The consultation between doctor and patient which we first encountered as Example 1.2 in Chapter 1 provides us with a familiar setting where an imbalance

---

[16] Accounts and analyses of these areas can be found in Ng and Bradac 1993; Fairclough 1989; Kramarae *et al.* 1984; and Fowler *et al.* 1979.

[17] This includes research from the relatively new field of forensic linguistics which explores, among other things, potential abuse of power through language in the worlds of the police or the law (see for instance the example, in Coulthard 1992, of the way a police statement was constructed and used).

of power relations is probably considered the norm: after all, the doctor is the 'expert' in terms of 'privileged' (specialised) medical knowledge, while the patient is the 'layperson'. What we need to look at now is how the language and the structure of the discourse marks and sustains the power relations. Perhaps before you look back at the interaction in Example 1.2 and do Activity 87 you might like to think about your preconceptions of a doctor/patient consultation:

- Who is likely to control the interaction and why?
- Who is likely to ask the questions and why?
- What kind of outcome is likely?

## Activity 87 ▷

Look at the interaction in Example 1.2 (page 24).

▶ Who controls the interaction and how? Look in particular at the opening and closing sequences, initiation of exchanges, control of topic and adjacency pair responses. Think also about who keeps to, and who flouts, the co-operative and politeness principles (see Chapter 2, 2.3.1).
▶ Look at what the doctor says in turn 7. What do you think the doctor's intention might be here?

One reason why discourses such as that in Example 1.2 are asymmetrical is that the interactants belong to different 'worlds' in the professional sense – and possibly, though not necessarily, also in the social sense. The patient is excluded from the doctor's discourse world of 'medical professional', because he is not part of it, and has little experience or knowledge of it. He is not party to the expertise, experience, skills, expectations and language of that world.[18] At the same time, in both patient's and doctor's worlds doctors *are expected* to take control, ask questions, give explanations, provide remedies. They are expected to be in authority, to dictate, to be pressured – particularly perhaps in hospital contexts.

### Some close encounters of the legal kind

We see a similar thing happening in Example 6.7 on page 203, which comes from a legal setting where again, we would anticipate a power imbalance. Such settings are rich grounds for investigating the interface between language and power because when laypersons and legal professionals meet 'they bring to the encounter two different world perspectives which are expressed in the form of disparate discourses' (Hale 1997:197). The encounter is almost certain to be unequal because most laypersons continue to operate on the assumptions of the discourse of their everyday lives in a context – the legal one – where these are not valid. The discourse of the legal world is constrained by rules, rituals and assumptions which render anyone without knowledge of them relatively powerless. Example 6.7 shows, for instance, how *indirect answers*, which (as we saw in Chapter 2) are a common feature of everyday discourse, are unacceptable in court.

---

[18] Also, of course, because they are sick or ill, patients are by default in the role of help-seekers.

**Example 6.7**

> *(M is magistrate, W is witness)*
>
> M: What happened on this occasion to alter that?
>
> W: Um as a public officer um I consider the uh/
>
> M: No, I won't consider what you consider, was there a petition this night for those who weren't financial to be allowed to vote?
>
> W: We were only sticking to the uh/
>
> M: No, no, don't tell me that. Was there a petition that night by somebody that those who weren't financial be able to vote?
>
> W: Yes, there was.

*(Hale 1997:200)*

Example 6.8 on page 204 is another legal example which illustrates a rather different dimension of power: the power of an interpreter (I) in a court context. Here, the witness (W) is an uneducated Spanish speaker, appearing before an Australian court. In this particular case, not only do we have the asymmetry of the legal expert/layperson discourse, but also the imbalance brought about by the fact that the legal person (solicitor) is a native speaker of the language, whilst the layperson (witness) is not. The interpreter sees her role as being not only to translate meaning, but also to redress the imbalance somewhat.

Example 6.9 on page 204 shows a lawyer 'translating' client speech – typical of everyday, conversational, intimate, personal discourse – into more acceptable (and 'powerful') legal language – formal, less intimate, more impersonal, curt and cold. Example 6.10 on page 205 illustrates the contrast between 'powerless' and 'powerful' styles of client responses.

## Activity 88 ▷

- ▶ Look at the exchanges in Examples 6.9 and 6.10 on pages 204 and 205.
- ▶ Decide what features of the language could be said to characterise a relatively 'powerful' style in the legal context.
- ▶ Decide what features of the language could be said to characterise a relatively 'powerless' style in the legal context.

## Example 6.8

In Extracts I–III the interpreter translates the informal discourse of the witness into a more acceptably formal and therefore 'powerful' court discourse. Extracts IV–VI show the reverse happening, when the interpreter alters the court discourse of the solicitor (S) into language more akin to the everyday discourse of witness.

I   W:   No, No me recuerdo de eso ['No, I don't remember that']
       I:   No, I don't remember *him having said* that

II   W:   Así es ['That's right']
       I:   *Yes*, that's *the position*

III   W:   Sí ['Yes']
       I:   Yes *I said that*

IV   Solicitor: ...and you are the defendant now before the court.
       Interpreter: ...y usted es el que está aquí en la corte? ['and you are *the one* who is here in court?']

V   S:   Well, you agree that you watched him run away from the incident?
       I:   Pero usted lo vio cuando se arrancó del incidente ['But you saw him when he *took off* from the incident']

VI   S:   Can you tell the court to your best, to the best of your recollection, the best of your memory?
       I:   ¿Pero algo recuerda usted? [But you remember something?']

*(Hale 1997:204–207)*

## Example 6.9

Client:   ...whatever trouble he had he called me always you know and help clean up his mess ... even I was in the bath I had to come and bail him out somewhere the police got him

Lawyer:   you provided assistance to him on a number of occasions.

*(Maley et al. 1995:44–5, cited in Hale 1997)*

**Example 6.10**

> Q: Approximately how long did you stay there before the ambulance arrived?
> A: (Powerless) Oh, it seems like it was about, uh, twenty minutes. Just long enough to help my friend, Mrs Davies, you know, get straightened out.
> (Powerful) Twenty minutes. Long enough to help get Mrs Davies straightened out.

*(Conley et al. 1978:1381, cited in Hale 1997)*

## Classroom settings

The third type of context where asymmetrical discourse might be expected to be the norm is the classroom, teachers being 'authorities' and learners, to whatever degree, 'novices'. However, with certain 'communicative' language teaching methodologies demanding a degree of role change, language learning classrooms might become quite 'risky' settings for learners: established patterns and procedures might often give way to the unpredictable and unforeseen. When teachers relinquish their traditional roles of 'initiator', 'director' or 'fount of wisdom' and learners are required to take on roles of 'challenger', 'problem-solver' or 'independent learner', the chemistry changes, and those who have been accustomed to taking a relatively passive part in proceedings may feel uneasy at being required to be relatively more dynamic and assertive. In such contexts, it is a tricky business for teachers to get the balance right between controlling classroom interaction and taking a back seat.

Indeed, it could perhaps be claimed that one legacy of communicative language teaching methodology (as of recent general trends towards 'learner-centred' approaches, 'learner independence', 'negotiated syllabuses' and the like) has been to upset the orthodox conception of status relations between teacher and students. Roles have been re-defined, responsibilities re-distributed. Teachers now include in their repertoire of skills the 'mediating' and 'facilitating' of the learning experience. They are 'guides', 'mentors', 'classroom managers'. They are no longer 'dictators'; they do not necessarily dominate – or at least not overtly. Of course, this is by no means a universal picture, nor is there any reason why it should be. No one should have the power to impose a culturally alien methodology on teachers who might not necessarily wish to change their more traditional classroom style if they feel this to be more appropriate to their own context. Nevertheless, in any language teaching context, irrespective of the methodology chosen, we would argue that teachers need to be especially 'alive' to language and its power, not least because language teachers are the ones with the language power – not only do they have access to so many more choices than their learners, but they also possess the socially-conferred superior status in any discourse.

Equally important is awareness of the different interactional styles and conversational strategies stemming from the world's various cultures and languages.[19] We have already noted the potential for misunderstanding arising from differences in interpretation of politeness phenomena (2.3.1). Teachers of people learning to operate in a new culture and language also have to be sensitive to, and if necessary prepared to mediate between, different culturally-based expectations of how people will behave when they interact with each other through language. These interactional strategies range along a spectrum from strategies of 'high considerateness' to strategies of 'high involvement'[20], as represented in Figure 6.

| high considerateness ▓▓▓▓▓▓▓▓▓▓▓▓▓▓ high involvement | |
| --- | --- |
| orderly turn-taking, without overlap | co-operative overlap |
| aversion to interrupting current speaker | frequent interruptions |
| tolerance of silence between turns | discomfort with silence |
| relatively little use of gesture | noticeable use of gesture |
| agreed protocols for turn-taking | less obvious protocols for turn-taking |
| extensive use of backchannelling | |
| *said to be typical of many speakers of Asian languages* | *said to be typical of many speakers of Arabic and Latin languages* |

*Figure 6*

Though the characterisations in Figure 6 are undoubtedly stereotypical, they are still useful as pointers to potential misunderstandings, misinterpretations and asymmetries, especially in mixed language-background groups. And if, to the above *interactional* strategies, we then add cultural and individual differences in *language learning* strategies – such as the willingness to take risks and experiment with language, or the willingness to 'lose face' by making mistakes – we have an exciting cocktail of power ingredients to enliven the dullest language classroom. We should also note that the 'riskiness' of communicative methodology might tend to favour the more extrovert interactional behaviours, and thus present teachers with another factor to take into account. Example 6.11 on pages 207 and 208 contains a transcribed 'snapshot' of classrom interaction which illustrates some typical classroom power dimensions language teachers might like to think about.

---

[19] See, for instance, Smith 1987; Valdes 1986; Wiseman and Koester 1993.
[20] The terms here originate from Tannen 1984(a), and were used by Dr Virginia Lezhnev in a presentation at a CIEE (Council for International Educational Exchange) conference in London, February, 1998.

## Example 6.11

This example is a transcription of interaction in an elementary level language class of adult learners – within the age-range of early to late twenties. The focus is on a vocabulary recycling game. MI and M2 are male students from Oman; F1 is a female Japanese student; F2 is a female student from Oman: T is an English-mother-tongue female teacher. Turns in the interaction are numbered.

| | | |
|---|---|---|
| 1 | T: | OK let's just do a couple more + Shinobu again +++ now + easy one *(writes word on board)* |
| 2 | M1: | yes ++ yesterday I bought some fruit it is very very not tasty because ++ because it ⊡was |
| 3 | F1: | ⊡food |
| 4 | M2: | yes fruits |
| 5 | F1: | ++fruits |
| 6 | M1: | yes + sometime sometime you bought sometime you buy fruit from shop then you get some fruits it is not ready to eat ++ |
| 7 | T: | ↓ good ++ |
| 8 | F1: | +ah |
| 9 | M1: | ⊡no |
| 10 | F1: | ⊡fruit ne + |
| 11 | M1: | it is not yet ready to eat need days or couple of days then ready to ⊡to |
| 12 | M2: | ⊡to eat it +++ |
| 13 | T: | ↓ what part of speech |
| 14 | F1: | what part ⊡of |
| 15 | M1: | ⊡adjective |
| 16 | T: | adjective |
| 17 | F1: | ++ so ++ uh ++ |
| 18 | M2: | it can |
| 19 | T: | ↓ no need to look it up ++ good definition + when something is ready + when for example a pear is ready to eat we'd say it is +++ |
| 20 | M2: | it is |
| 21 | T: | this word |
| 22 | M1: | ++ specially we say for the fruit |
| 23 | T: | fruit in particular yes ++++ |
| 24 | T: | ↑ No ++ |
| 25 | F1: | ↓ No ++ |
| 26 | T: | ↑ Do you know the word in Japanese ++ |
| 27 | F1: | ++ uh ++ uh ++ mm ++ |
| 28 | T: | ↓ OK ↓ CHECK |
| 29 | T: | ⊡RIPE |
| 30 | M1: | ⊡RIPE |
| 31 | F1: | ah + yes |
| 32 | T: | ↑ remember |
| 33 | F1: | ↑ ripe is much + like + mature |
| 34 | T: | it's like well yes mature is well yes it's like mature but maTURE we use for example ⊡for cheese |
| 35 | M1: | ⊡for children |
| 36 | T: | children + wine + RIPE ⊡we |
| 37 | M2: | ⊡wine |
| 38 | T: | use for fruit + ready + good ++ *(knock at door)* |
| 39 | M1: | ↑ the wine also mature or not mature the wine |
| 40 | T: | yes we can ⊡use |

41  M1:                    ⌐when you use in your own when you use in your what ++ I don't know why can be mature or
          not mature wine + the liquid   ⌐because it's
42  T:                                     ⌐it's
43  M1:                              already
44  T:   yes but yes but sometimes you need to leave wine for a length of time you leave it to make  ⌐it
45  M1:                                                                                               ⌐ya ya
46  T:                                                                                                ⌐really good
47  M1:                                                                                               ⌐ya ya ya ya
48  T:   ↓right + ↑Mohamad ++ ↓good MORning Abir *(laughter when Abir arrives late for class)* or good
          afterNOON + right + mm ++ OK *(writes next word on board)* ++++
49  M2:  more asset ++ more asset asset
50  T:   no you're confusing it with that other  ⌐word
51  M2:                                           ⌐yesterday yes
52  T:   I think Shinobu knows this word
53  F1:  ++ aya *(sighs)* ++
54  M1:  I know this word I think
55  T:   *(laughs)* he knows it without looking
56  M1:  I have pain in my leg
57  T:                        ⌐yes yes
58  M1:                       ⌐straw + ⌐sore
59  T:                                 ⌐sore + well done *(general laughter)*
60  M2:  ++ ↓my turn
61  T:   ↓your turn + ⌐last one
62  F2:               ⌐why + why you are upset
63  T:   ↓no no no + I'm I was just wondering where everybody was at the beginning of the lesson
64  F2:  'cos I went to change my passport because I lost it and I didn't and I don't because yesterday no chance to
          change it and anybody get it he can use it in bad way and they can report about me to the embassy
65  T:   ↓so you sorted it out
66  F2:  yes + fine
67  M1:  ↑you did
68  F2:  yes
69  T:   do you know do you know where Kawtha is
70  F2:  no no I'm worry about her Sair do you know do you know where she is she didn't come here
71  T:   no
72  M2:  no I don't know
73  F2:  maybe she's sleeping or doing her object
74  M1:  I think maybe she ⌐was
75  F2:                    ⌐she was not in computer room she ⌐didn't
76  M1:                                                      ⌐Abir yesterday he said she said until nine o'clock
          I'll stay here in computer room about ⌐Sue or
77  M2:                                         ⌐she wasn't sleeping
78  T:   Penny says she's finished her project ++
79  F2:                                   not this ⌐one
80  M2:                                            ⌐file + file + on Sue + one file Sue file
81  T:   ↑the Sue file is it + thank you Abir + OK right well maybe if she isn't here ↑give a ring to her family
          just to do a time check + ↑check she's OK ++ ↓ OK *(moves on to next word)*

                                                                                    *(Authors' data)*

**Activity 89** ▷

Look at the transcription of the classroom interaction in Example 6.11 on pages 207 and 208 in terms of the power relations between the various participants. Then answer the four questions below, thinking about discourse elements such as:

▶ turn-taking
▶ initiation/closure/change of topics
▶ initiation/closure of exchanges
▶ interruption of current speaker
▶ allowing current speaker to hold the floor

a) Who controls the interaction? What discourse clues lead you to make your decision about this?
b) Is there any evidence that the two male learners (M1 and M2) take a more dominant role than the two female learners (F1 and F2)? What discourse clues lead you to make your decision about this?
c) Is either of the two male learners more dominant than the other? Is either of the female learners more dominant than the other? What discourse clues lead you to make your decisions about this?
d) If you were the teacher of this class, what sorts of considerations would you have to bear in mind if your aim was to help the learners interact with each other in English in as authentic and natural a way as possible?

**Follow-up:** Record some classroom interaction from one of your classes, and analyse it in terms of the interactional strategies we have been thinking about. How does your analysis reveal power relations between you and your learners and between different learners?

## 6.4.2 Gender-based discourse

As might be expected, the 'gender issue' has generated a rich and extensive literature, and gender has already been mentioned as a factor influencing language use (see 5.5.1, 6.3.4). Here, our focus is on gender-based differences in spoken interactional styles and strategies.

### Do men and women speak differently?

One of the major problems in making any claims about whether differences in the ways men and women talk can be ascertained and if so, described, is that any differences which do emerge might be attributable to many other factors beside gender: age, social class and status, personality, educational background and ethnicity, to name but a few. Nevertheless, there is a very considerable body of sociolinguistic research which suggests that broad distinctions can indeed be made between male and female patterns of talk, and between male and female ways of interacting in speech.[21]

[21] See Coates 1998, for an account of these differences in her survey of seminal research papers in this area.

One set of claims – often referred to in the literature as *dominance* theories – suggests that, in mixed speech, women and men do not have equal rights to the conversational 'floor':

• male speakers tend to dominate in mixed speech, i.e. they take an unequal (larger) share of the turns in interaction[22]
• male speakers tend to interrupt female speakers in mixed speech, i.e. males attempt to deprive females of the right to speak
• male speakers may use non-co-operative strategies to establish dominance in everyday domestic interaction, i.e. they fail to respond, they interrupt, they delay response or they are silent

Another strand of research is concerned with *differences* in conversational style, and major claims here are as follows:

• women tend to be more sensitive than men to the 'face' needs of others, i.e. they tend to be more sensitive to politeness strategies
• women tend to both give and receive more compliments than men, i.e. they see compliments as less face-threatening than do men
• women's talk tends to be more co-operative than competitive, whereas the reverse holds true for men, e.g. women tend to use mitigated forms such as 'let's ...' whereas men prefer to use strong directive forms to establish control

## Activity 90

Check out the classroom interaction in Example 6.11 on pages 207 and 208 in terms of the above *dominance* and *difference* theories. See if you can find evidence to support any of the theories.

**Follow-up:** Collect some interactional data of your own and look for differences in the way women and men interact, both in mixed groups and in single-gender groups. Consider to what extent these differences might hinge on factors other than gender – personality, ethnicity, age and status of interactants and context of interaction.

## If men and women do speak differently, does it matter?

Many international students of English learn the language because of its perceived importance in global contexts such as those of business, communication, academic study, scientific research, technology, politics or diplomacy. Coates (1998:295) terms such contexts collectively as 'the public domain'. She claims that it is 'a male-dominated domain, and the discourse patterns of male speakers have become an established norm in public life'. If women wish to succeed in this domain, therefore, the implication is that they need to adopt more assertive, 'masculine' – adversarial and information-focused – styles of discourse. However, there is a growing body of research which suggests that a more 'female' style of interaction – more co-operative, less confrontational,

[22] According to some recent research, this tendency extends to interaction on e-mail discussion lists (see Herring *et al.* 1998).

and taking more account of others' 'face' needs – is more successful than the 'male' style in certain contexts such as doctor/patient relationships, or collaborative research, or teaching. Despite this, though, it still appears to be the case that in many public work-related domains, it is women who have to adapt their style to that of men.[23]

Other research on gender-related matters has attempted to establish whether the so-called 'typical' features of female speech and interaction strategies do actually correlate with lack of power. For instance, women's speech has come to be characterised as relatively 'powerless' because of claims that women tend to use 'hedges' (expressions of tentativeness) or tag questions (said to indicate lack of assertiveness) to a much greater extent than men. Such views have been challenged, and refuted, with many researchers arguing that linguistic forms matter only insofar as they have a cultural value attached to them; they do not, of themselves, have any power-related meaning. Also, and not less important, the 'folklinguistic' view of women's speech which labels it as 'disfluent', 'non-logical' and 'non-competitive' has been shown to be seriously flawed, not only on the grounds that the stereotypes of both male and female usage simply do not hold up in the face of the evidence, but also that the all-important factor of contexts of utterances has been insufficiently taken into account in much past research.[24]

In this book, we have had room for no more than a very superficial glance at this enormously complex aspect of language and power. But as language teachers, it is worth reminding ourselves that gender and its embedding in the language adds a further intricate dimension to our learners' language learning experience. We need awareness not only of the gender 'baggage' brought by each individual learner, but also of how that relates to aspects such as:

- the cultural norms of the target language, and how these compare with norms in learners' origin language
- the frustrations brought about by a probable mismatch between learners' L2 proficiency and their ability to use desired interactional strategies
- the methodology being used by the teacher, and how this may infringe learners' gender-related norms of behaviour
- learners' different goals in learning the language

## 6.5   English as an international language (EIL)

The final aspect of the language/power interface that we consider here is one that is particularly relevant to teachers of English, namely the influence English currently wields by virtue of its status as a global language. Apart from the consequences of sheer numbers of speakers speaking a common language, there

---

[23] Coates 1993 and Gumperz 1982 report research on these issues, and Scollon and Scollon 1995, bring an intercultural perspective to the discussion.
[24] See for instance Cameron 1985; Mills 1995.

are challenging implications of the spread of English that exercise politicians, historians, educators, economists and other specialists. First, though, we look at the position English currently has as the world's major international language, with particular reference to the following:

- the extent to which English has spread and how it has spread
- attitudes towards English as an international language

## 6.5.1  The spread of English

It is generally accepted that English is currently the most widely used language in the world in terms of the number of countries where it is the first or second language of the population, where it has some official status, or where it is the major foreign language taught in schools. In a 1998 BBC broadcast (*Analysis*, 12.3.98) it was stated that by the year 2000 there would be one thousand million people learning English, four hundred million speaking it as a second language and another four hundred million speaking it as their mother tongue. These figures are based on estimates, rather than precise calculations, and should be treated with due caution. Nevertheless, it is difficult not to be impressed by them and they certainly suggest that English has acquired a powerful, perhaps dominant, position in the world today.

It is thus not uncommon nowadays to hear English referred to as a global language. Crystal (1997b:2–8) discusses what the term 'global language' might mean. Among the points he makes is that a language can be said to achieve global status when its special role is recognised in every country. Special roles here include:

- the mother-tongue use of a language
- being accorded official status in a country
- being the major foreign language taught in a country's schools

Given this definition, English clearly is a global language.

### Reasons for the spread

There are generally considered to be two main causes of the world-wide spread of English and the continuing expansion of the English-speaking world: first, Britain's colonial history, which saw the movement of British English speakers to territories around the world; and second the economic power enjoyed by the USA in the 20th century. There have, of course, been other contributory factors in the spread of English. Along with the economic and political aspects of colonialism, there was also the spread of Christianity and a European style of education, both of which were promulgated through the medium of English. Nowadays, countries where English is the mother tongue (particularly the USA), as well as wielding economic power, have enormous global influence in areas of technological development and everyday cultural matters.[25]

[25] For instance, the range and influence of CNN (the USA-based TV news station) news coverage world wide (see Pennycook 1994: Chapter 2 and pp. 39–40, for a detailed discussion of the influence of western culture), the 'cocacolarisation' of the world, the global spread of UK, US and Australian soap operas.

One perhaps not immediately apparent mechanism whereby English maintains a powerful position in countries where it is not the mother tongue is suggested by Vicki Munro (1996). She discusses the influence of graduate students returning home after completing their studies in English-medium institutions in other countries (in Munro's study, in the USA) to take up senior positions in government, education, business or other professions. Such students, Munro concludes, can have an enormous influence on the use of English and, indeed, on language policy, in their countries:

> If the respondents are ever in a position to do so, they may very well support in their country an official language policy which encourages the inclusion of English (and specifically AE [American English]), whether as a second or preferred foreign language.
>
> *(Munro 1996:341–2)*

## *Present facts and future possibilities*

Graddol (1997a) provides a comprehensive and informative survey of the current position of English as a world language and assesses its future in the light of present knowledge about global trends in other domains[26] which are likely to impinge on EIL. He suggests that English retains its current hegemony as the dominant working language in international organisations, financial institutions, scientific publishing and book publishing in general largely because of the economic, technological and cultural influence of the USA. Once this influence declines, however, the picture may be very different.

In the 21st century, the future of English may be dictated by the majority of people and institutions who use it as a *second*, rather than a *first* language. Indeed, according to Graddol, there is a growing belief that 'the future will be a bilingual one' in which those who speak only one language will be at a severe disadvantage. His argument is that English has spread so extensively in the 20th century largely on account of 'economic rationalism'. The 21st century, however, may see significant 'social value shifts' which:

> would foreground the complex ethical issues associated with the world domi-nance of a single language and cause a reassessment of the impact of English on other cultures, national identities and educational opportunities for the world's non-English speaking citizens. The economic argument for English may also be challenged as developing countries make more careful evaluations of the costs and benefits of mass educational programmes in the English language.
>
> *(Graddol 1997a:4)*

The prediction here seems to be that the current 'global wave of English may lose momentum' and be replaced by a new language hierarchy for the world, with a larger group of languages at the apex, but fewer at the base than is the

[26] Such domains include demography, the world economy, the role of technology, globalisation, the 'immaterial' economy (language-related service industries), cultural flows (how language will change in a relatively borderless world) and global inequalities.

case at present: 'No single language will occupy the monopolistic position in the 21st century which English has – almost – achieved by the end of the 20th century' (Graddol 1997a:58–60).

## 6.5.2  Attitudes towards EIL

Whatever the future role of English may be, the current fact of the matter is that English has, by dint of historical circumstance, become – at least in terms of international communication – the world's most powerful language. But, as we have noted many times, language cannot be divorced from its cultural trappings, and though English may be perceived as a useful – and indeed indispensable – tool for access to information, knowledge and power, the accompanying cultural baggage may not be welcomed. This is how a Malaysian graduate student at a UK university comments on the attitudes towards English in her country:

> In Malaysia, there exists the state of ambivalence about the importance of the English language and its role in the Malaysian society. While on the one hand it is regarded highly as the language of knowledge and information, on the other, *it is feared for its power* in disseminating a cornucopia of information regarding anything western. Evidence from the media shows how, at times, there is this deep-rooted anger for the colonial masters; while, at other times, there is the national urge to quickly be very much like the colonialists themselves, adopting their language and gaining their knowledge.
>
> *(Mobel 1999:9, emphasis added)*

It is not surprising that the dilemma described by Mobel should exist in the post-colonial circumstances of her country. The histories of former colonies provide many examples of the role language has played in movements to dislodge the power-wielding colonialists. And the language policies developed after independence have often been designed to cement political independence with a coherent sense of national identity, expressed through the promulgation of a national language.

It is not only in colonial situations that we see instances of a dominant group within a country establishing and maintaining power over other groups where the language of the former has been both a means of establishing power and a (much resented) symbol of that power. Zentella (1997), for instance, provides a detailed account of the effects of 'growing up bilingual' on members of a Puerto Rican community in New York. Her research documents 'a stigmatised group's attempts to construct a positive self within an economic and political context that relegates its members to static and disparaged ethnic, racial and class identities' and foregrounds 'the high price they pay when their new syntheses are disparaged and assailed'(pp. 2, 13).

Resentment may also be aroused by the fear of linguistic and/or cultural invasion emanating from one country to another where there is no recent history of a dominant/subordinate relationship between the two. A *Guardian* newspaper article (5.2.98) reported 'increasing clamour' in Germany 'against the rape of German by English'. Sources of 'the cultural English onslaught' were cited as 'Hollywood, transnational industry, advertising, the Internet, pop music'.

It is unlikely that the anxious Germans referred to in the newspaper article would feel that the very survival of their mother tongue is at risk because of the spread of English. However, extinction is the fate envisioned by some writers for some languages as a result of the spread of English. Pennycook (1994:14) cites Day (1980, 1985) as the originator of the term 'linguistic genocide' in his study of Chamorro[27] in Guam and the North Marianas. Day's view was that, given the continued control of the islands by the USA and the accompanying dominance of English, Chamorro would eventually have no native speakers. Similarly, Phillipson (1992:106) refers to the work of Calvet (1974) on the tendency of French to 'eat up' languages in the French empire. Phillipson translates Calvet's French term as 'linguistic cannibalism'. English, in its role of influential global language at the end of the 20th century may indeed be destined to cut a swathe through the world's wealth of languages. But we should not discount the fact that nothing remains constant, and the status of English today may not necessarily be that of tomorrow.

Activity 91 is framed around two extracts from Pennycook (1994) which summarise two general, basic but contrasting opinions (not, it should be noted, necessarily those of Pennycook himself) on the spread of English.

## Activity 91

The extracts below offer two contrasting opinions on the spread of English and its influence as an international language. To what extent does your experience as a learner, teacher and user of English match either of them?

### Extract 1

By and large, the spread of English is considered to be natural, neutral and beneficial. It is considered natural because, although there may be some critical reference to the colonial imposition of English, its subsequent expansion is seen as a result of inevitable global forces. It is seen as neutral because it is assumed that once English has in some sense become detached from its original cultural contexts (particularly England and America), it is now a neutral and transparent medium of communication. And it is considered beneficial because a rather blandly optimistic view of international communication assumes that this occurs on a co-operative and equitable footing.

*(Pennycook 1994:9)*

### Extract 2

... its [English's] widespread use threatens other languages; it has become the language of power and prestige in many countries, thus acting as a crucial gatekeeper to social and economic progress; its use in particular domains, especially professional, may exacerbate different power relationships and may render these domains more inaccessible to many people; its position in the world gives it a role also as an international gatekeeper, regulating the international flow of people; it is closely

---

[27] An indigenous language

> linked to national and increasingly non-national forms of culture and knowledge that are dominant in the world; and it is also bound up with aspects of global relations, such as the spread of capitalism, development aid and the dominance particularly of North American media.
>
> (Pennycook 1994:13)

## 6.5.3 Ownership of the language

One of the implications of EIL is that the wider its spread, the more diverse its ownership. As we saw in Chapter 5, English is an extremely flexible language with a great propensity to change and be changed. Its spread during the 20th century has meant that as it has been 'taken into the fabric of social life' in many diverse cultural contexts (Graddol 1997a:2), it has diverged considerably from the language spoken in so-called 'inner circle'[28] contexts. The predictions are that in another twenty years or so, EL2 speakers will outnumber EL1 speakers to the extent that:

> the centre of authority regarding the language will shift from native speakers as they become *minority stakeholders* in the global resource. Their literature and television may no longer provide the focal point of a global English language culture, their teachers no longer form the unchallenged authoritative models for learners.
>
> *(Graddol 1997a:3, emphasis added)*

Henry Widdowson, in a plenary address at the annual IATEFL conference in 1993, argued that:

> mutual intelligibility cannot be established by the conservation of language forms: it can only come about as a function of their use by a kind of communicative ecology. *The native speakers of English have no special rights or responsibilities in this regard,* and to put language in their custody is self-defeating.
>
> *(Widdowson 1993:7, emphasis added)*

Indeed, so prevalent has the theme of 'ownership' of English become, with its attendant concerns over the relationships between language and identity (Norton, 1997), the socio-cultural identities and practices of teachers (Duff and Uchida, 1997) and the linguistic profiles and language learning needs of EL2 students (Leung *et al.* 1997), that it has been the focus of much recent discussion in ELT forums. EL2 teachers are being required to be much more critical about what they teach, how they teach it, and their rationale for teaching it.[29]

This probable shift in English's centre of gravity away from EL1 speakers has fundamental implications for the ELT profession:

---

[28] i.e. contexts where English is spoken as the first language (see Kachru 1985)

[29] See, for instance, the spring and autumn, 1997 editions of *TESOL Quarterly*; the 1998 and 1999 special-topic issues of *TESOL Quarterly*, on Teacher Education and Critical Approaches to TESOL, respectively; and *IATEFL Newsletter*, Issues 126, 136.

- Standard English will no longer be the exclusive province of either US forms or UK forms, but rather a 'World Standard Spoken English' will evolve (Crystal 1997a:11)
- future goals in ELT will include the command of a range of varieties of the language
- 'authentic' sources of 'real' English will not be exclusively EL1 varieties
- teachers will need to teach a 'negotiated form of International English', where the cultural values embedded in the language are appropriate and acceptable to all participants (Hollett 1997:18)
- the cross-cultural negotiation of meaning, and communication strategies in 'lingua franca' English contexts[30] will need to assume greater importance in both teaching and research (Graddol 1997a:13)

Knowledge about the language is increasing all the time, as are new ways of looking at language. Much current research and analysis relies on computer power to amass and sort huge databases of authentic usage, predominantly from British or North American contexts, and particularly expanding our notion of 'grammar' by extending this to include a grammar of spoken discourse. However, as Prodromou (1996:372)[31] suggests, not all teachers and learners may wish or need to have language which has come from authentic sources, especially Britain-based colloquial ones:

> One ... wonders whether informal British English is perhaps a variety of the language which most students are unlikely to encounter for extensive periods, let alone have to produce, simply because they do not belong to the micro- or macro-culture of the British native speaker.

In other words, the English as it is known and presented in many of today's ELT materials might need radical re-thinking and re-viewing; the 'power' of mother-tongue speakers might be dissipated; and the current debates over 'standard' English might come to be seen as rather irrelevant in world terms.[32]

## 6.6 Empowerment of learners

'Empowerment' has become a well-established theme in educational and language teaching circles over the last decade or so, and it is perhaps fitting that it should provide the focus for the end of our 'power' chapter. Francis Bacon's aphorism[33] – 'knowledge itself is power' – points to one implication of the current

[30] i.e. contexts where English is used as the lingua franca – or common language – between speakers from different EL2 backgrounds
[31] In correspondence in *ELTJ*, 50/4:369–373. See also the 'Octopus/Hydra' debate in relation to global English and new knowledge about the language in IATEFL newsletters 135 and 137.
[32] See articles by Rampton, Phillipson, Medgyes and Alptekin, all reprinted in Hedge and Whitney 1996.
[33] Bacon, F. (1597). *Meditationes Sacrae: 'Of Heresies'*.

educational notion of empowerment: teachers, initially the *power-holders* – as possessors of knowledge – become *power-sharers* as that knowledge becomes owned and utilised by learners.

We are going to end our book by looking briefly at four language-related contexts involving empowerment: learning the genres of a second culture; critical language awareness; independent learning; and the notion of learners as explorers of language.

## Learning the genres of a second culture

Learners of English who are learning the language in order to become members of an English-speaking community need knowledge of the language which will equip them to operate effectively within that community, and enable them to take a full part in social, political and educational life. This has been the thrust of much of the genre-based work springing from contexts such as those involving ethnic-minority groups in Australia and the USA: people need awareness of, and ability to operate within, all the spoken and written discourse types, or genres, of their second or adopted culture.[34] As we have noted, though, there is certain disquiet at the price people have to pay in terms of identity adaptation; a development here might be that, once people become empowered through understanding how English works in their new communities, they will utilise that knowledge to assert rights to an alternative identity, not necessarily one that has been assimilated into the new culture.[35]

## Critical Language Awareness (CLA)

Another increasingly prominent theme is that of the need for a 'critical language awareness' strand in language teaching contexts.[36] This theme is associated particularly, though not exclusively, with those contexts where international students study through English in an English-speaking environment; they are thus required to operate within a culture which may be not only socially and linguistically, but also academically, unfamiliar and even alien. CLA entails – as part of a general sensitivity to language – the particular understanding of how underlying ideology, beliefs and attitudes are encoded in text; how socio-historical contexts and socio-cognitive processes are inevitably bound up together in the production and interpretation of text; and how learners can exploit this kind of understanding for their own purposes. Such awareness empowers people to 'take control of their writing', to 'challenge orthodoxies' and to 'overcome the dilemma of whether to conform or not' to conventional academic practice (Clark *et al.* 1991:85) – or in other words, to have a voice of their own.

We could also add to this list acquiring the confidence to question and challenge 'authorities' in spoken settings such as seminars or lectures – a quality seemingly highly valued in English-based academic environments. Students

[34] See the work of Christie, Hammond, Halliday and Hasan, Martin and Rothery in the Australian context; that of Kaplan, Connor and Zentella in the USA context; and that of the LINC project in the UK context.
[35] See Zentella 1997.
[36] See Clark *et al.* 1991; Ivanic and Roach 1991; Fairclough 1991; Jin and Cortazzi 1993; Pardoe 1994. A warning note is sounded by Atkinson 1997.

coming from cultures where it is not so highly valued – or indeed positively discouraged – may find themselves at a disadvantage unless they are 'empowered' through increased awareness of the new academic conventions and expectations.[37]

This process of awareness is not only one-way, however. Equally important is the need for lecturers and faculty in such contexts to be 'alive' to cultural differences in learning styles and strategies, assumptions and expectations about roles of teachers and learners, and classroom behaviours.[38]

## Independent learning

A third, more general, context of empowerment is that of independent learning. Encouraging learners to become less dependent on teachers and classrooms and more responsible for their own learning is a familiar theme in ELT.[39] It seems likely to continue to grow in importance in our computer-transformed world, for just as computer technology has already changed the way people interact with each other in many areas of their lives, so it is quite possible that it will bring about equally great transformations in teaching and learning.

We have referred in several places in the book to the potential that increasingly sophisticated computer technology offers us, not only for gathering and processing information about language, but also for innovation and exploration in language teaching and learning methodology. Learners have independent access to the language they are studying through a wide range of computer-based reference resources and tools; networking and conferencing facilities provide new avenues for distance learning and group interactions; and e-mail and Internet settings are motivating possibilities for extending communication beyond the bounds of the traditional language learning classroom.[40]

## Being an explorer of language

Technology may bring new dimensions to the language teaching/learning process and may thus help teachers by widening their options. But it cannot replace them. Teachers will always be the vital human link between the language and the person who wants – or needs – to learn it. Our thesis in this book has been that we can never know enough about language; that it is, in effect, a life-long learning process for those who teach it. It seems to us that a major corollary of this standpoint is that teachers should perceive themselves not as founts of received wisdom about language, but rather as those who help their learners to become, like themselves, explorers of language.

In order to 'own' a language, one's knowledge has to be internalised, to come from oneself. From their broader knowledge base, teachers can open up choices for learners, they can indicate possibilities, but they cannot ultimately choose. Only the language user can do that. Our final example, Example 6.12 on page 220,

[37] See Bashiruddin *et al.* 1991.
[38] See Kinnell 1990; Blue 1993; Donald and Rattansi 1992; Harris and Thorp, 1995; Hedge and Whitney 1996.
[39] See Ellis and Sinclair 1989; Pemberton *et al.* 1996; Lee 1998; Tudor 1996; IATEFL Newsletter 139, October 1997; and the newsletters of the IATEFL Learner Independence Special Interest Group.
[40] See Sperling 1998, for a guide to ELT resources on the Internet.

## Example 6.12

In this transcription of part of a writing conference, three people (Y and M, Japanese teachers of English, studying on an educational exchange programme, and V, their tutor) are discussing part of M's written text about how groupwork can be implemented in the Japanese teaching context.

Y:   There's one thing I really don't understand very well ... 2nd paragraph, the last bit

V:   Mm, this is exactly the bit that I've commented on too!

Y:   *(reads)* '**Groupwork should be conducted in a student-centred way. This seems to be beyond what one teacher can tackle**'...

V:   Yes that was the bit that I ...

M:                                    Me too! *(laughter)*

Y:   Great minds ...!!

V:   I think I know what you mean, though, well at least I'm guessing. In this case, well no, am I guessing or inferring ...

M:   Inferring ... mm

V:   No I'm not inferring.

Y:   Predicting?

V:   No, I'm imagining really, imagining what is in your mind and what you want to say.

M:   So, this is the only sentence in the conclusion I'm NOT happy with.

V:   Good, OK, so let's do something about it.

Y:   So you mean, you need other teachers' help?

M:   Help, yes.

Y:   Or consensus?

M:   Mm ... and that will link 2nd and 3rd paragraphs.

V:   Yes, exactly. So what's the problem, what do we need to add?
     *(long silence)*

V:   You could just add something at the end couldn't you? *(reads)* '**This seems to be beyond what ONE teacher ...**' – you need to make a contrast between <u>one</u> teacher and the idea of <u>teachers getting together</u> and discussing ideas in the 3rd paragraph, don't you ... So, '**This seems to be beyond what one teacher can tackle by?** ... **by?** ...

Y:   themselves?

V:   Yeh, that would make the idea a bit clearer, wouldn't it?

M:   '**by themselves**'?

V:   '**by themselves**' or '**on their own**' ... *(then follows long discussion on concord between 'one teacher' and 'themselves')* ...

V:   Or there's another expression you could use.

Y:   '**alone**'?

V:   Yes, even a word like '**alone**' would make that idea clearer, I think. Or do you know the expression '**single-handed**'? ... *(then follows long discussion of 'single-handed' – origins, meaning, other expressions with this meaning of 'hand' etc.)* ... so that use of the word '**single-handed**' might be possible here.

M:   Just putting '**single-handed**' after '**tackle**' is all right?

V:   Yes, that would make your idea clearer.

M:   *(writes)* '**single**' and hyphen? '**handed**'?

V:   Yes, that's right.

Y:   Mm ...

V:   So, '**This seems to be beyond what one teacher can tackle on their own**' or '**This seems to be beyond what one teacher can tackle single-handed**'.

M:   I prefer '**single-handed**'.

V:   Yes.

Y:   Mm.

M:   New vocabulary!!

*(Authors' data)*

shows teachers/learners exploring the language, and the highlighted turns in the exchange illustrate what seems to us to be the kind of inquisitive and perceptive mindset that frames 'ownership' of knowledge about the language.

Rees (1997) argues that 'the teacher impervious to change should be placed in a cell rather than in a classroom; inertia thus confined cannot sap the profession of its dynamism'. He goes on to invite 'the energetic teacher, eager to develop as a professional ... to explore a grid of intersecting avenues in the search for self-awareness and enlightenment'. We hope that our book will have made a contribution to the language awareness strand of professional development by providing a tool for teachers to become such explorers.

## Key references

Bolinger, D. (1980). *Language – The Loaded Weapon*. London: Longman.

Cameron, D. (1995). *Verbal Hygiene*. London: Routledge.

Graddol, D. (1997a). *The Future of English?* British Council.

Hedge, T. and N. Whitney (Eds.) (1996). *Power, Pedagogy and Practice*. Oxford: Oxford University Press.

Pennycook, A. (1994). *The Cultural Politics of English as an International Language*. Harlow: Longman.

Phillipson, R. (1992). *Linguistic Imperialism*. Oxford: Oxford University Press.

# Commentaries

## Activity 1

The ease with which we can understand the texts in Examples 1.1–1.4 and place them in their cultural context will depend on our exposure to and familiarity with the culture of late 20th-century Britain. Below are some suggestions for the kinds of knowledge one might need to understand them.

| Example | Source and context | 'Knowledge of the world' required to understand them |
|---|---|---|
| 1.1 | Front page article from *The Sun* (26.10.96) | *The Sun* is a daily tabloid (popular) newspaper in Britain. The language is likely to be emotive, colloquial and direct (e.g. *raging* comic *flattens* TV critic ... ; *sulky loudmouth* Lewis-Smith ...). The paragraphs are likely to be short, giving descriptive or factual information rather than evaluation or analysis; and the whole report is likely to be a rather sensationalised account of events. We also anticipate that reports will be likely to concern gossip and scandal connected with media, film and sports personalities, or people in public life such as members of the British royal family. |
| 1.2 | Consultation between hospital doctor and patient *(authors' data)* | There may well be some similarities between cultural experiences of interactions such as the fairly universal doctor/patient consultation. Therefore the general context will probably be familiar, though the details of expectations about how the consultation is carried out may not. This particular example shows a rather stereotypical encounter of unequals – doctor firmly in control of the exchange, patient very much at the mercy of the doctor's decisions about the diagnosis and treatment. |
| 1.3 | Part of a railway timetable | Among other things such as familiarity with place names and distances, we need to understand the tabular layout, the conventions of the 24-hour clock, the conventions of abbreviations (e.g. *a* = arrive, *d* = depart); we also need to know that the order of the stations in the left-hand column is not necessarily the order of the journey, and that train timetables in Britain are not consistent throughout the week or year. |
| 1.4 | Horoscope column in a daily newspaper (*The Express*, 18.12.98, p. 58) | Again, as in Example 1.2, the general concept (here, of horoscopes) is probably a fairly universal one. Here, where horoscopes are concerned, our knowledge of the world tells us that many people believe in the power of astrologers to predict what's going to happen to them in the immediate future, according to the star sign under which they were born. In the particular British |

daily newspaper context of this example, one would need in
addition to understand that most of such newspaper horoscope
predictions are concerned with personal relationships, love, money,
fame and fortune; that most of them are so general as to be
nonsensical; and that a lot of people regard horoscopes as a bit of
harmless fun.

'Textual' features of layout certainly help us to recognise and understand the
texts in Examples 1.3 and 1.4, whilst the typefaces and layout of the article in
Example 1.1 enable us to place it as coming from a tabloid newspaper – e.g. the
attention-grabbing huge font-size of the headline, or the capitalisation of
attention-grabbing action verbs in the third paragraph.

## Activity 2

| Example | Context<br>e.g. who? to whom? where? when?<br>why? how? about what? | Language Features<br>e.g. formality? explicitness? topic?<br>layout? |
|---|---|---|
| 1.5<br>*(Authors'*<br>*data)* | • domestic, informal spoken family interaction between people who know each other well<br>• probably in the kitchen, during the preparation of a meal<br>• face-to-face interaction, apart from imposition of non face-to-face interaction by telephone call<br>• topics related to everyday domestic activities and the immediate setting and environment | • language typical of informal conversational interaction – false starts; incomplete structures; overlaps; interruptions; no special theme; lots of interweaving, negotiated topics<br>• much implicit reference because conversation anchored in immediate surroundings |
| 1.6<br>*(Authors'*<br>*data)* | • spoken language occurring in the form of a monologue – i.e. one speaker is allowed the right to 'hold the floor' (see 2.3.2) without interruption for a very extended 'turn', in this case a formal academic lecture by a lecturer to a group of students<br>• interactants do not know each other well<br>• interaction takes place in a formal setting – probably a lecture theatre<br>• face-to-face interaction<br>• topic abstract and prescribed by title of lecture (Mythology and the Media) and nature of interaction | • although the language is characterised by many of the features common to spoken language, it is nevertheless more formalised than the domestic interaction in Example 1.5 – for instance, it is consciously structured, and there are clear 'signposts' to keep listeners 'on course'<br>• little reference to immediate environment<br>• much emphasis on explanation of unknown facts and theories – language therefore more explicit than that of Example 1.5<br>• topic coherent and unified, because of the nature of the 'speech event'; consciously organised and constructed progression of ideas |

| 1.7 (Addo, M. 1998) | • written article published in some kind of academic forum – a journal, perhaps, or a conference paper<br>• written by a legal academic for an unknown legal audience<br>• purpose: (a) to argue a case for the answer to the question in the title and thereby (b) to further writer's reputation and support his standing within legal academic community<br>• topic: extremely specific and 'narrow' in the sense of being addressed to an audience with specialist knowledge of topic | • language extremely formal and 'academic' – sentences with complex sentence structure, many embedded clauses, extensive use of passive and 'distancing' constructions, nominalisations, non-colloquial vocabulary, hedging and qualifying constructions<br>• language extremely explicit, with care taken to ensure references are understood clearly<br>• topic presented in explicit and coherent framework of logical argumentation<br>• layout conforms to conventions of academic article |
| 1.8 (*Authors' data*) | • postcard<br>• written by colleague on working holiday to fellow colleagues – writer and readers know each other well<br>• purpose: to maintain and affirm friendship, and 'keep in touch'<br>• topics conform to stereotype of context – brief, evaluative comments on places visited and experiences | • language informal and in semi-note form – abbreviated structures typical of written contexts where space is at a premium<br>• language immediate and personal – underlying context of writing does not need to be made explicit<br>• layout constrained by template imposed by postcard itself and immediately recognisable as such |

It might be possible to use texts like those in Examples 1.5–1.8 for teaching purposes such as: illustrating differences in 'genre' or text-type; examining different registers and types of language occurring in different circumstances; discussing some of the differences between spoken and written mediums; looking at format and layout (in the case of Examples 1.7 and 1.8). Example 1.6 could possibly be used for authentic academic listening practice (assuming the original recording was available), and Example 1.5 might be useful for drawing attention to the importance of various paralinguistic features of spoken language. All could be used to clarify the notion of 'discourse' (see Chapter 2). However, one would need to take learners' proficiency levels into consideration, as authentic texts such as these could cause frustration at more elementary levels (with the possible exception of Example 1.8).

## Activity 3

Activities 1 and 2 have already introduced eight very different texts illustrating the variety of text-types produced by different contexts of language use. Four more are illustrated here in this activity.

| Example | Source/origin | Contextual and formal factors |
|---|---|---|
| **1.9** *(Authors' data)* | • *poem* (consciously patterned in structure and layout) <br> • written by child (handwriting that of 'learner writer') | • written language, but full of informal expressions <br> • assertive and forthright style <br> • child's school workbook (consciously crafted artistic presentation) <br> • purpose probably to fulfil teacher-assigned task; possibly also to amuse – writer conscious of what *should* be done vs what is actually done <br> • context: formal education, evidence of accomplishment of learning (i.e. child has acquired knowledge of poetry *genre* and conventions of cursive script; also aware of meaning, significance and conventions relating to [New Year's] '*resolution*') |
| **1.10** (Dickens, C. (1843). *Martin Chuzzlewit*: 122–123) | • extract from *novel* (written representation of spoken interaction and actions among characters in imagined setting) <br> • novel not contemporary (certain usages have a non-contemporary 'feel' to them, e.g. *declared* [2], *round-robin* [18]) | • written, but including a variety of ways to represent spoken language: *direct speech* (indicated by conventions of punctuation, e.g. 'Who is severe?' [4]) and *indirect speech* (indicated by function verb *declared* and transformation from present tense of speech into past tense of reported speech, e.g. *Mrs Todgers ... declared she was quite afraid of her, that she was. She was so very severe.* [1–3]) <br> • style: language chosen to convey the possibly flirtatious relationship between the two characters, whilst at the same time retaining a strong sense of the author's 'voice' as manipulator of the characters <br> • anyone familiar with classical English literature will recognise the source of this language as a work (*Martin Chuzzlewit*) of the Victorian novelist, Charles Dickens – largely on account of the idiosyncrasy of Dickens' style <br> • purpose: to entertain, amuse and comment (indirectly) on life, society and the human condition <br> • context of *extract*: respectable Victorian household (in this case an eccentric London boarding-house); context of *novel*: produced for publication in serial form in popular mid-19th-century periodical <br> • social usage in extract: dialogue meant to represent genteel, middleclass, probably middle-age social interaction; social usage of *novel*: popular form of entertainment (and social commentary) for educated classes from 18th century on |
| **1.11** (BBC TV, 24.4.96) | • weather forecast, live broadcast on breakfast TV (topic explicitly introduced, and supported by extensive references to weather-related vocabulary) | • spoken, recorded in front of camera to unknown audience <br> • style: mixture of formal (Isobel invited to take the floor for an extended turn, with a formal purpose – to give the weather forecast) and informal (she tries to convey the information in a friendly, chatty way); always veering towards the tentative – an appropriate strategy in view of the fickleness of weather systems <br> • context: TV studio presentation with visual aids in the form of charts |

- purpose: to inform public (within very restricted timeframe – 50 seconds, in this case) of what some would regard as essential information

**1.12**
*(Authors'
data)*

- personal *telephone conversation*

- informal spoken interaction between two people who know each other well – lots of deictic references which need no explanation (e.g. *it's me again*) and 'incomplete' structures (e.g. *don't know + usual probably*)
- purpose: mainly transactional (i.e. practical – to get B to take the meat out of the freezer)
- context: domestic situations relevant to lives of interactants (e.g. the chickens have laid three eggs)
- personal usage: use of variety of greeting and leavetaking conventions (e.g. *Hi!*, *OK*, *Ciao*)

## Activity 4

**Example 1.13:** *E-mail.* As mentioned in the text, this relatively new electronic medium straddles spoken and written language: *spoken* in that it utilises informality, and shared knowledge between interactants such that a kind of dialogue, or conversation results; *written* inasmuch as the medium is graphic, not oral. It retains some conventions of standard written layout (e.g. memo conventions of headings), but invents new conventions (e.g. sets of arrows to indicate chronology of messages).

**Example 1.14:** *voice* (recorded for radio broadcast) *transcribed.* This example shows the increasing difficulty of understanding a spoken message written down, as the transcription becomes what phoneticians call 'narrower' (i.e. more detailed and with more features displayed). Yet even a narrow transcription is not a totally accurate representation of the original spoken language: precise length of pauses or changes in speed and loudness, for example, are not marked in the transcription. In general, even with training, it is extremely difficult to capture accurately what is said and turn it into a written equivalent. This observation also reinforces the point that the average 'conversation' as represented in play scripts or language learning materials frequently bears little resemblance to the real thing (though it can, of course, be argued that play scripts and language learning materials have quite different purposes and contexts of use from real-life conversations, and are therefore not intended to be 'real'). For a detailed guide to phonetic and phonemic transcription conventions see Roach 1991.

**Example 1.15:** *comic* [from *The Beano*, 26.10.96] Comics mix graphics and text to tell a story. The written language is not intended to represent 'real' speech and it poses no particular problems for understanding, provided you are familiar with the conventions of English (language) comics where the norm is to start in the top left-hand corner and read from left to right. This example also shows us where our knowledge of the world (and in this case, particularly the English-reading world) helps us to understand a text, usually without us even thinking about it.

If we use the term *medium* in a very broad sense, as we have done here, to cover a range of contextual factors, some other mediums we could add to the list – you can probably think of many more – are: advertisements (on TV, in magazines, on billboards); political speeches; sermons; prayers; lectures; walkie-talkie messages; intercom announcements; notes; lists; newspapers (daily, weekly, evening, weekend, national, regional, etc.).

The narrower the specification of medium, the more obvious it becomes that the audience and purpose of the communication will affect how the message is conveyed via the chosen medium.

Coulthard (1985:49) has a pertinent observation on the development of new mediums:

> The development of radio and television has created a situation in which some speech events have enormous unseen and unheard audiences, which subtly affect the character of the event. What is superficially a round-table discussion or a cosy fireside chat can in fact be an opportunity to attempt, indirectly, to sway a nation's opinions. The channel itself has even allowed the creation of new speech events, the sports commentary and the quiz show, with their own highly distinctive stylistic mode and structure, prescribed participants, typical setting and key.

Indeed, it could even be said now that the (unseen and unheard) audiences for these radio or TV speech events are as much part of the 'events' as the actual interactions between the participants.

## Activity 5

Here are a few of the main points we might note about each of the letters in Example 1.16 which seem to us important in understanding how writers express attitude.

| | Attitude expressed | Language features relating to expression of attitude |
|---|---|---|
| **a** | • *irony* (flippant and serious) in response to ridicule expressed in letter of November 28<br>• *support* (for Victim Support scheme)<br>• *anger* (that people underestimate distress caused by minor crimes) | • ironic use of *delighted* and *advantageous position*<br>• anger expressed through inclusion of phrase 'what to *some* would be considered ...', with implication that a lot of others might have a different opinion<br>• support expressed through positive associations of *emotional support* and *practical help* |

| | | |
|---|---|---|
| b | • *irony* (flippant)<br>• *ridicule* of the apparent devaluation of the notion of counselling | • irony expressed in conscious exaggerated naivety of last sentence (*what could possibly be said*)<br>• juxtaposition of concept of counselling and theft of virtually valueless items |
| c | • *irony* (flippant) | • juxtaposition of initial 'serious' tone of *in these days of moral confusion* – leading readers to expect serious topic – and actual, ridiculously lightweight, topic<br>• implied contrast between the religious and commercial concepts of 'love' |
| d | • *complaint* and *indignation* at misrepresentation of financial activities of local football club | • serious and orderly organisation of each misrepresentation, followed by factual refutation<br>• strength of feeling indicated by use of emotive words like *guesstimates, saddened* – also use of graphic devices such as inverted commas in *guesstimates* and italicising of *not* for emphasis<br>• indignation creeps in through the shift to direct address in paragraph 5 in contrast to the polite impersonal address of paragraph 1 |
| e | • *disapproval, anger, indignation* | • disapproval shown by explicit reference to various antisocial behaviours (*urinating* and *vomiting* in public)<br>• anger or indignation expressed through sarcastic reference by means of inverted commas to what is normally a positive term – *mature* – and rhetorical question form of final sentence |
| f | • *outrage, anger* | • strength of feeling expressed through choice of emotive words – *infuriating, smug, forcibly, redundant*<br>• also through departure from normal sentence structure in first and last sentences<br>• also through the ironic recognition of bureaucratic hypocrisy – how language is manipulated so as to mask unpleasant truths with euphemisms (*forced retirement* or *redundancy = setting you free* or *early retirement; inadequate compensation for loss of salary and pension = being cushioned*) |
| g | • *support, approval* | • positive evaluation (*worthwhile*) of contribution made by book to understanding psychology of child killers like Mary Bell |
| h | • *support, congratulation* | • explicit expression of congratulation in *applaud* and *courage*<br>• support expressed through reasoned, non-emotive argument, rehearsing the justification for publication of controversial book in controversial circumstances |

## Activity 6

Here are some suggestions for criteria to judge the effectiveness of various types of messages. Note, however, that these are broad and general – it would be difficult to judge how effective any message is without full knowledge of its specific context.

| | |
|---|---|
| *a legal document* | is it comprehensive and explicit? does it plug all possible 'loopholes'? is it legally sound? |
| *a business letter* | is sufficient contextual information given? is it courteous? is it clear and concise? |
| *an advertisement* | does it grab our attention? is it informative? |
| *a university lecture* | is it well-organised and clearly presented? can the audience follow the argument? can they hear it? will they remember it? |
| *a safety routine in-flight announcement* | can the audience hear it? are the instructions easy to understand? is enough information given? are there appropriate visual clues to accompany the message? |
| *a CV* | does it create an immediate positive impression? is it clear and well-presented? does it contain the essential and appropriate information? |
| *a dictionary entry* | does it give us the information we want? is it easy to find? is the language of explanation accessible? is it comprehensive enough? |

## Activity 7

*The recipe* here is singularly ineffective: no quantities are given, nor any instructions for preparing the ingredients. In fact, so much culinary knowledge is taken for granted, that as it stands, the recipe would be of no use to anyone without such knowledge.

*The health warning on the cigarette packet* (Example 1.17): the effectiveness of such messages as deterrents (presumably their major function) is questionable, although it is clear that, in Britain, they have had to become more strongly worded to conform with legislation: compare current warnings such as that in the example – where the verb *damages* is not softened with a modal verb – with earlier ones such as *Smoking **Can** Damage Your Health*. It is also difficult to know precisely what the purpose of the message is, since the main objective of the tobacco industry is to sell tobacco products. On the one hand, the tobacco industry does not want the health message to be given; on the other hand, it is obliged to conform with legislation to warn people of the dangers of smoking. What we have here, perhaps, is a case where the attempt to force the industry to make the message more effective may paradoxically have reduced its effectiveness, in that it may not perform its ostensible deterrent function. There may also be a degree of cynicism involved, since the likelihood is that people will choose to ignore it, a factor known to all parties concerned.

*The prohibition from walking on the grass* (Example 1.18): very effective, (a) because of its originality (completely different from the standard *Keep Off The Grass* prohibition); (b) because the message is based on an *appeal* (although this is only implied); (c) the language of the message is a clever play on the colloquial expression *my feet are killing me*.

*The party invitation* (Example 1.19): very effective – fulfils its function in an efficient, clear and attractive way, and since interactants are well-known to each other, all necessary information is included.

*The charity appeal* (Example 1.20): functionally effective, in that all necessary information and details for becoming a member or supporting the charity are there, but a fundamental problem is that a crucial piece of information is missing – nowhere is the acronym BUAV (the charity's name *The British Union Against Vivisection*) explained. This might put potential supporters off (even though the purpose of the charity is made clear) as might the rather obscure condition in the last sentence of the *'Member's Agreement and Guarantee'*. Please note that this is not the current registration form for BUAV.

## Activity 8

'Rules' are as follows:

'Conditional Sentence Type 1': verb in main clause 'future', verb in conditional clause 'present'
'Conditional Sentence Type 2': verb in main clause 'conditional', verb in conditional clause 'past'
'Conditional Sentence Type 3': verb in main clause 'conditional perfect', verb in conditional clause 'past perfect'

None of the other 22 ways of expressing condition in sentences 4–25 actually use exactly the same exponents as are presented in the 'rule' sentences, nor are the structures exactly parallel. Probably the 'rules' are helpful in getting learners to understand the varying degrees of possibility in which conditions might or might not be fulfilled, but it is clear that many other areas of 'structure' are involved in expressing condition apart from the rule-based relations between tenses in the three prototypical sentences, among them modality, the subjunctive, word order, clause order and lexical exponents for condition (*whether, otherwise, provided that, whatever*). Thus to leave learners with the impression that once they had learned the rules in sentences 1–3 they would have '*done*' condition, would indeed be misleading! (See Maule 1988, and Lewis 1986, for further discussion of this, and also 3.5.3 for more on the 'reduced model' of grammar.)

## Activity 9

A more 'appropriate' order for jumbled text 1 would be: (ii) Thank you.
(i) You're welcome. This is because these two utterances form an 'adjacency pair' (see 2.3.2) where the preferred response to an expression of thanks is acknowledgement. This exchange is a very common one in all types of contexts where we want to show appreciation for someone's help.

If the text remained in its jumbled order, we could interpret the first remark *You're welcome* as a sarcastic indication that someone who had been helped had *failed* to show appreciation. *Thank you*, in this case might be either a belated appreciation, or an equally sarcastic indication of the inadequacy of whatever service had been offered.

A more 'appropriate' order for jumbled text 2 would be: (iv) There was severe traffic congestion yesterday during morning rush hour, following a serious accident. (iii) A maroon Renault, driven by a local businessman, swerved out of control, crossed the highway divider, and crashed head-on into the oncoming traffic. (i) Miraculously, none of the drivers in the cars involved in the collision was seriously injured. (ii) Police and ambulance services were soon at the scene, though it took several hours before traffic returned to normal.

This is the order which follows the *chronology* of the events and thus gives a straightforward narrative account – it is in fact the order in which the events were reported in a newspaper account of the accident the following day. Another structural pattern we can see operating here is that *general statements come before detailed ones* – the general context precedes the specific details.

If the text remained in its jumbled order, we could still understand what happened, despite the 'abnormal' order of the sequence. But we would be likely to interpret it as coming from a novel or sensational report, rather than a factual account, since the writer would be teasing us by not revealing from the start what had happened, and therefore drawing us more imaginatively into the text. Changes would have to be made, though: the tense of the verbs in sentence (iii) would become past perfect, and sentence (iv) would have to be either completely re-cast or omitted.

## Activity 10

Some language items which might be 'new' to people unfamiliar with the *Internet* or the *Web* could include:

| | |
|---|---|
| *cool* | used here to mean up-to-date, recent, fashionable, à-la-mode, the thing to have or be seen as having or knowing about |
| *sites* | used here to mean spaces, areas, page(s), features, entries or places where specific information can be found on the Internet or Web |
| *download* | used here to mean to be available for you to access on your computer |
| *plug-in* | used here to mean a program you install that allows you reach parts of the Internet your standard software cannot cope with |
| *streaming* | used here to mean that you can see video or listen to sound more or less instantly on the Internet, without having to copy everything to your computer first |
| *multimedia* | used here to mean that, in addition to text, your computer allows you to have animations, video and sound as well |
| *Web* | the now commonly accepted term for the electronic information system that enables people to have instant access to a huge range and variety of information from sources all over the world via their own computer |

Here's a brief comparison between the two texts in Example 1.22 along certain language parameters. The major reason for the differences is historical: Text A was written in the 17th century (from *The London Gazette*, June, 1685), whilst Text B comes from a 20th-century racing publication (*Sporting Life*, 20 December, 1996).

|  | Text A | Text B |
|---|---|---|
| **Vocabulary items** | • Gentlemen<br>• The Plates ... will be run for ... | • punters<br>• ... attempts timber ...<br>• ... who saddled Royal Gait to ... glory |
| **Formality** | • This is to give notice to ... | • ... warned punters to hold fire on ...<br>• ... will have his fingers firmly crossed ... |
| **Time expressions** | • heretofore<br>• the first Tuesday in August next<br>• The Plates ... will be run for the 25th of July next | • ... on Monday week |
| **Graphic conventions** | • capitalisation of verb *Run*<br>• no longer current representation of 's', as in Old-Hor*f*e-Cour*f*e | |
| **Grammatical forms** | • ... which hath been run for upon ...<br>• ... the Ormskirk Plate ... is now put off to ... | |

## Activity 12

As far as the CP is concerned, both speakers probably obey the quantity and relevance maxims.

Speaker A also probably obeys the manner maxim.

However, B most certainly flouts the quality maxim, and probably also the manner maxim, since she knowingly gives false information, and her choice of the word 'fine' makes her answer neither entirely clear nor unambiguous.

Both speakers are clearly obeying the PP: A wants to give B the option to respond negatively, so that an apology could be offered if necessary; B wants to make A feel good, and wants to avoid imposing on A (by avoiding a potential loss of face). Both maximise the expression of polite beliefs, in carrying out this social etiquette routine.

In this case, the PP can be seen to be the stronger in the conflict between the CP and PP. It certainly helps to explain why B flouts the CP; it also underlines the importance of relevance theory, as in this context it was in B's best interests not to upset A, and therefore to tell a lie.

## Activity 13

If you use a 'buddy' tape, it would be interesting to monitor your own language use in the speech event 'discussion' which you will have recorded on the tape. Incidentally, the same principles of recording and analysis of data could be used with students to help 'immerse' them in discourse and give them exposure to 'real-world' language.

Below is an example of the kind of *checklist* you could use to keep track of what was happening in various interactions. The main objective here would be to observe the differences between the interactions.

|  | Interaction 1 | Interaction 2 | Interaction 3 |
|---|---|---|---|
| Where did it take place? | | | |
| How many people were involved? | | | |
| What was the status relationship between interactants? | | | |
| What kind of 'speech event' was it (see 2.3.2)? | | | |
| Was the language mainly transactional or interactional (see 2.3.6)? | | | |
| How carefully did you have to think about the language you used? | | | |
| How explicit did your language need to be? What was the extent of the shared knowledge? | | | |
| Did the agenda change at all during the interaction? If so, how and why? | | | |

## Activity 14

Below are instances of language use in both examples which seem to us to flout maxims of the CP and PP. We should note, however, that, as is the case in many language teaching materials, students are given no information about the supposed context of the interactions represented (although the cartoon accompanying Text B in the original suggests that Noriko and Chuck belong to a gym club and meet as they are leaving/going to their respective sessions). Without knowledge of the status/age/socio-economic backgrounds of the speakers, or the purpose and circumstances of what they say, the exchanges are inevitably artificial, because it is virtually impossible to know if the language is appropriate or relevant.

|  | Text A | Text B |
|---|---|---|
| Quality flout | Possibly ll. 16 and 20 – maybe Mr D and Miss E are simply being polite | |
| Quantity flout | l. 1 – why does the teacher need to give this information – unless the purpose is to establish power relations right from the start (NB use of the definite article *the*)? l. 1 – does the teacher really *not* know who the other people are? ll. 3, 5 – does the teacher doubt the truth of what the class has said in l. 2? ll. 9, 11 – can the teacher really *not* figure this information out? ll. 15, 19 – does the teacher really want to know this information in the | Possibly ll. 1, 2 – would we normally give surname and country in this rather casual encounter? This may, of course, be more customary in American English than in British English. Possibly l. 4 – the *and* and *Chuck* sound either redundant or superior – unless Noriko was intending to assert her status as teacher |

233

light of the other questions forming the interrogation?

ll. 21, 23 – does the teacher doubt the truth of the students' replies in ll. 2, 4, 6, 10, 12?

| | | |
|---|---|---|
| **Relevance flout** | ll. 1, 3, 5, 9, 11, 15, 19, 21, 23 as for **quantity** We could say that the whole interaction can *only* be considered relevant if the sole purpose is to teach question and answer structures, and vocabulary items – in terms of anything else, the language used is patently irrelevant | |
| **Manner flout** | ll. 4, 8 – unnecessarily long-winded, unless students want to question the intelligence of their teacher ll. 14, 18 – would we normally give our titles in this kind of classroom context? (NB date of publication 1938 – a much more formal era?) | |
| **Politeness flout** | l. 1 – do we normally start a conversation by asking someone *what* they are? ll. 3, 5, 7, 9, 11, 21, 23 – by these questions the teacher implies that students must be either idiots, liars or both ll. 13, 17 – rather impolite to ask this question so late in the exchange | Possibly ll. 1, 2 – would we normally give a stranger so much unsolicited information without being asked? Possibly l. 8 – *by the way* makes the question seem almost unimportant possibly l. 12 – *Hey* might be considered a somewhat impolite way to address someone one has only just met – though perhaps the intention is to inject some humour – but then, *why* should Chuck want suddenly to join Noriko's class? |

If we think about the two texts in terms of teaching agendas, clearly there are justifications on the grounds of structure and vocabulary practice (dare we say 'drill'?) in Text A, and provision of a model in Text B for students to practise the function of introducing themselves.

## Activity 15

Although A's use of *he* to refer to the passerby might appear not to show due deference to a member of an older generation, it could be argued that A was not including the passerby in the conversation at that point. Also, to have used an alternative term like *that gentleman* would from A's point of view probably have seemed artificial and unnecessarily long-winded. The most expedient word in the immediate context was *he*. As for *Cheers, mate*, A probably chooses this informal and idiomatic exponent for acknowledging appreciation

- to indicate solidarity with the passerby (despite generation difference)
- because this usage means that he is aware of adult, British, middle/lower class male usage in situations of *camaraderie*, and that he has become socialised into his culture to the extent that this expression is part of his repertoire

So, although it might, in other contexts, and in other cultures, have infringed politeness maxims, here this usage seems quite acceptable, and even touching.

## Activity 16

One 'conversation' centres round whether the chop is cooked or not. Another centres on the coincidence that C and B have identical tape recorders. The third focuses on who should answer the telephone. As for the individual 'agendas' of the four interactants, here are some possibilities:

- A (*mother*) wants to make sure her daughter is fed on time, and possibly to implicate B in not having been very cooperative in this respect.
- B (*father*) is passing the pre-suppertime hour in casual chat with houseguest. He also wants to know whether it's necessary for him to take the phone call. At the same time, there seems to be quite an interesting desire to transfer responsibility for action (seeing if the chop is done, getting daughter to come and eat, answering the phone) to other people!
- C (*houseguest*) is oiling the social interactional wheels by contributing a story about her tape recorder, warning of possible oversight on B's part about the tape recorder recording, and mediating in the domestic dispute over whose fault it is the chop is taking so long to cook.
- D (*daughter*) is performing the function of conveyor of messages.

## Activity 17

Although there are lots of instances of informal usage and 'idiomatic' language (e.g. ll. 5–6, 16, 31, 32), the dialogue is clearly 'scripted' and not 'natural' if we think in terms of authentic interaction. Some features common in authentic interaction, but *not* present in Example 2.6, are:

- false starts
- overlaps
- interrruptions
- grammatical inconsistency, inaccuracy, incompleteness
- unclear sentence boundaries
- repetitions, hesitations, pauses

## Activity 18

Examples of the six types of adjacency pairs from Examples 2.5 and 2.6 are given in brackets.

| | preferred response? | dispreferred response? |
|---|---|---|
| question (2.5:19) | a relevant answer, whether right or wrong (2.5:22) | silence; another question(2.5:20); an irrelevant answer |
| offer (a 2.6:7 b 2.6:18) | acceptance; thanks (a 2.6:8,10) | refusal (b 2.6:19) |
| accusation (2.5:1) | acceptance of blame | non-acceptance of blame; counter-accusation (2.5:2) |
| greeting (2.6:1) | return of greeting (2.6:2) | ignoring of greeting; impolite or brusque response |
| apology (2.6:25–26) | acceptance of apology (2.6:27); indication of forgiveness | refusal to accept; insult; threat |
| assessment (a 2.5:27–28; b 2.6:16) | agreement; justifiable difference of opinion (a 2.5.34?; b 2.6:17) | outright opposition or disagreement (2.5:34?) |

The probable response to 2.5:42 (and the preferred one) would have been along the lines of: *Hello! I'm fine, thanks. How are you?*

The adjacency pair notion is probably extremely useful for helping students cope with everyday interactions and transactions in 'social English' contexts – interacting with host families, for instance; dealing with shops and banks; making telephone calls and so on.

## Activity 19

The standard opening and closing in all these *speech events* would probably include *Good morning/Good afternoon/Hello* or equivalent and *Goodnight/Goodbye/Thank you* or equivalent. These formulaic expressions will be taken as given – although we might note that even here there are difficulties for students: being clear for instance about the difference between *good evening* (usually opening and very formal) and *goodnight* (usually closing and neutral on the formality/informality scale). The table below contains examples that the authors have come across, but it would be interesting for you to add to the list from your own observations in your personal data collection (see Activity 13 above).

| | opening? | closing? |
|---|---|---|
| **a lesson** | ... Today we're going to look at ... ... What I'd like to do today is ... | Right. We'll have to leave it there for today. See you tomorrow/next week. |
| **a service encounter** | ... Can I help you? | Thanks very much! /Have a nice day! |
| **a telephone enquiry** | ... I wonder if you could help me. I'd like to know ... | Thanks very much/ Thanks for your help. |

| | | |
|---|---|---|
| a GP/patient consultation | ... Right, what can we do for you today? | Come back and see me in two weeks' time ... |
| a TV newscast | ... The headlines tonight: ... | ... That's all from us. We're back again at ... |
| a job interview | ... I'm ... and this is my colleague ... We'd like to ask you first of all about ... | ... Thank you very much. We'll let you know as soon as possible ... |

## Activity 20

| | Text A | Text B | Initiator |
|---|---|---|---|
| a) opening of ordering sequence | l. 1:May I take your order, please? | ll. 16–17: I want, they don't do cider, and I don't want a beer [<s 03> Hi] don't do cider, do you? | Text A: Waiter<br>Text B: Customer |
| b) closing of ordering sequence | l. 12:Thank you | l. 46: Thanks | Text A: Waiter<br>Text B: Customer |
| c) ordering of food | l. 2: I'd like a ... please<br>l. 5: I'll have ... | l. 21: I'll have ...<br>ll. 22, 29: Can I have ...<br>l. 33: I'll have ... | Text A: Waiter customer's order is (response to waiter's question)<br>Text B: Customer |
| d) ordering of drinks | l. 11: I'd like a ... please | l. 17: Don't do cider, do you?<br>l. 38: d'you have, er have you got ...<br>l. 44: Can I have... | Text A: Waiter (customer's order is response to waiter's question)<br>Text B: l. 17 – Customer l. 38 – Waiter (customer's order is response to waiter's indirect speech act in l. 37, realised by simple statement of topic 'drinks')<br>l. 44 – Customer |

In Text A it is clearly the waiter who controls the interaction, initiating and closing the whole speech event and also the sub-units within it – which are all examples of adjacency pairs of questions seeking information and preferred responses, i.e. the waiter gets the information he needs.

By contrast, in Text B, it is the customers who are obliged to take charge – the waitress simply waiting until they say something. Not once does the waitress ask them what they want – except indirectly in l. 37 – all her questions are simply to ascertain details of cooking preferences. Here is an interesting example of how the 'rules of the game' are so transparent to all participants in the interaction that the major moves in the sequence do not need to be expressed explicitly – as they are in the scripted dialogue of Text A.

Text A, although it contains certain colloquialisms such as *OK* (l. 6), and the single word response in l. 9, is much more formal than Text B. There are many more polite forms such as *May I ...?, I'd like ..., Would you like ...? ... please.* Also, most of the exponents chosen for performing the different functions in the interaction are direct.

In Text B, by contrast, many of the exponents are indirect (e.g. l. 17, l. 18, l. 37 and l. 39); many of the vocabulary and structure choices reflect spoken, rather than written language (e.g. l. 1 – I'm *gonna* have ...; l. 16 – to *do* cider; l. 32 – *though* occurs at the end of the clause; l. 38 – *d'you have ...?* l. 43 – *loads of* ice); and there are the usual features of spoken interaction such as non-marking of sentence boundaries, overlaps, pauses, fillers and so on. (The glossary in Carter and McCarthy 1997, has a very useful summary of features of spoken discourse.)

## Activity 21

Topics in Example 2.5 include:

- the chop and whether it is cooked
- the story of how the tape recorder caught fire
- ascertaining the identity of the telephone caller
- the surreptitious recording of the conversation
- deciding who should answer the phone
- preparing the daughter's meal

Topics in Example 2.8 include:

- reincarnation
- Speaker B's knowledge of horses (as a possible example of reincarnation)
- Speaker B's father
- superstition

Example 2.8 is probably more coherent in terms of topic than Example 2.5 because of the nature of the two speech events involved: Example 2.8 is a radio chatshow with a chairperson whose role it is to make sure that the conversation is reasonably coherent, and to steer speakers back on course when they wander from the topic (as Speaker B does); by contrast, Example 2.5 is casual domestic chat where several topics can be pursued at the same time, and where there is no pre-specification of role.

## Activity 22

Here are some possible interpretations of the question forms (though of course they can only be guesses, as we cannot get inside the heads of the speakers to know *exactly* what they meant).

| l. 1 | ↑isn't her ↓CHOP done yet | A expresses surprise or irritation that chop isn't cooked, possibly implicating B. | l. 26 | ↑can you go and TALK to him | B requests A to take the phone call, implying that this would be the best course of action. |
|---|---|---|---|---|---|
| l. 6 | ↑can you ↓GET it | B requests (or perhaps even orders) D to answer the phone. | l. 34 /35 | ↑can you put HER + it's ↓REAdy I think + ↑can you put the ↓SWEET corn on | A requests B to co-operate in getting daughter's meal, possibly expressing irritation that she's expected to do everything – answer phone, take responsibility for meal, make sure chop is cooked, etc. |
| l. 12 | ↓who's that on the PHONE | B asks for information; possibly wants to confirm that D has complied with request. | l. 36a | can you send her ↓IN here | B requests A (possibly in return for A's request in ll. 34/35) to carry out an order on his behalf. |
| l. 13 | can you tell ↓DAD it's JACKie | D conveys information. | l. 36b | ↑can I put the ↓WHAT | B asks for clarification, because message has not been heard. |
| l. 15 | did you ↓KNOW your tape was reCORDing | C warns B of a potentially negative situation, or possibly accuses him of playing a trick. | l. 37 | do you think it ↓IS ready | C expresses doubt, and possibly cautions against eating the chop without further cooking. |
| l. 19 | when did you put this ↑CHOP ON | A asks for information; she possibly expresses disbelief. | l. 40 | what did she ↑SAY | B asks for clarification, because message has not been heard. |
| ll. 20/ 21 | what ↓TIME is it | B tries to find rationale for absolving himself from blame. | l. 42 | how are ↑YOU | A starts telephone conversation with formulaic greeting. |

What is worth noting about the use of the modal verb *can* is that in every instance in this particular random snatch of conversation its major function is that of requesting, ordering or instructing, and has little to do with the often suggested primary, 'basic' meanings of ability, possibility or probability.

| l. 6 | ↑can you ↓GET it | request, instruction, indirect order | l. 34 | ↑can you put the ↓SWEETcorn on | request, instruction, indirect order |
|---|---|---|---|---|---|
| l. 13 | can you tell ↓DAD it's JACKie | request | l. 36a | can you send her ↓IN here | request, instruction, indirect order |
| l. 26 | ↑can you go and TALK to him | request, suggestion | | | |

Even this short extract reveals that a range of five different structures is called upon to perform the function of requesting someone to do something, with varying degrees of politeness (least polite are probably ll. 2. and 23; most polite is probably l. 32) It is also interesting to note that in every case where the modal *can* is used – except one – the pitch direction in the intonation unit is downward, not upward – indicating a mix of request/instruction/order. The exception is l. 26, where the function is a mix of request/suggestion.

| l. 2 | have a ↓LOOK at it | imperative | l. 26 | ↑can you go and TALK to him | question with modal *can* |
|---|---|---|---|---|---|
| l. 6 | ↑can you ↓GET it | question with modal *can* | l. 29 | hang ON a MINute | imperative |
| l. 12 | hang on | imperative | l. 32 | you'd better go Carolyn | *had better* structure |
| l. 13 | can you tell ↓DAD it's JACKie | question with modal *can* | l. 34 | ↑can you put the ↓SWEETcorn on | question with modal *can* |
| l. 23 | have a ↓LOOK at it | imperative | l. 36 | can you send her ↓IN here | question with modal *can* |
| l. 25 | it's ↓COLin | declaratory statement (implication: 'tell me what to do next' or 'come and talk to him') | l. 40 | what did she ↑SAY | question (implication: 'please repeat what she said because I didn't catch it') |

# Activity 23

The two places where the surface meaning seems to be at odds with the underlying meaning are indicated in (1) and (2) below.

> The format of the workshop allows for a restricted number of 20 *non-speaking participants*[1] who are expected to participate actively in the discussions. Participance will be accepted on a *'FIRST COME, FIRST GO'*[2] basis.

1 Is it likely that participants will not be capable of speaking (cf. non-English-speaking = not able to speak English) and, even more remarkable, how can a non-speaking participant be expected to participate actively in discussions? But ...

Inferences from background knowledge of academic conferences in general tell us that at conferences there are usually invited speakers – the 20 participants will not be expected to perform this role, but merely to listen to the speakers and discuss what they've heard afterwards.

2 How can one both come first and go first? But ...

Inferences from background knowledge of this specific conference tell us that it's in Holland, so participants who apply first (the idiomatic expression *first come, first served* is relevant here) will be those who have the *first* chance to *go* to Holland.

## Activity 24

When we first encountered this text as Example 1.20 in Chapter 1 (page 46), we noted that any understanding of it would have to be firmly rooted in shared cultural background knowledge and cultural assumptions about the role of charities in society (in general) and about the argument over whether it is ethically justified to exploit animals for scientific and/or commercial purposes (in particular). Armed with this knowledge, we could predict that:

- the *purpose* of the appeal will probably be to ask for money – either in the form of donations, or getting people to become members
- the intended *audience* is probably people who are relatively well-off, with money to spare to support charities; people with consciences about human exploitation of animals; animal lovers in general; people with strong feelings about any kind of suffering and cruelty
- the kind of *language* used is likely to be emotive and persuasive – appealing to imagination and heart, rather than intellect and head

In the opening section of the appeal we have examples of three different channels of reference: *deixis* (i.e. using the immediate context of the discourse to take linguistic shortcuts); *shared knowledge*; and *inference*.

| Item in text | Channel of reference | Meanings | What helps us to infer the meaning |
|---|---|---|---|
| 'us' (1), 'we' (3) | deixis | the people who run BUAV and who are issuing this appeal | the immediate context – charity appeal, which charity? someone is responsible for the appeal, and BUAV is presumably a collective group, because it's a registered charity: charities like this need more than one person to run them, therefore they refer to themselves as 'we' and 'us' |

| 'help laboratory animals' (2) | shared knowledge | animals used in scientific research laboratories | general knowledge that animals are often used in scientific research |
|---|---|---|---|
| | | laboratory animals need help because they have no power to change their situation themselves | general knowledge of conditions in which laboratory animals are kept (in cages, strapped to machines, etc.) |
| | | (financial) help to campaign to change public opinion (and the law) | general knowledge that campaigns to change public opinion and long-established practices are costly |
| 'this suffering' (4) | deixis and inference | the suffering of the animals experimented on | association of deictic 'this' to *implied* outcome of 'painful and unnecessary experiments' (pain leads to suffering and suffering can lead to death) |
| 'this vital work' (5) | deixis and inference | campaigns for fund-raising and awareness-raising to change public opinion | to the people who run BUAV these campaigns are considered 'vital' – a good example of persuading your audience by assuming that they agree with your point of view |

**Follow-up**: Here are a few suggestions for pre-reading activities:

- bringing a collection of charity appeals to class, and asking students to find common patterns in format, content, organisation of information, and type of language used
- using these observations as a basis for discussion of purpose, audience and language of charity appeals in general
- thinking about the word *vivisection*, and getting students to discuss their reaction to it
- discussing the various reasons why animals are used in scientific research
- thinking of various types of research and their respective end-products (drugs, cosmetics, etc.)
- eliciting opinions about the justification for using animals in different research contexts
- comparing public opinion in Britain with that in students' home countries

And for post-reading:

- discussing the effectiveness of the language choices made in the BUAV appeal
- discussing the extent to which students feel the appeal accomplishes its purpose

## Activity 25

| A | Referent? | Referent explicit? | Referent implicit? |
|---|---|---|---|
| a | addressee (B) | | ✓ |
| b | either addressee and speaker (C), or speaker's family | | ✓ |
| c | speaker's family | | ✓ |
| d | model of B's tape recorder | | ✓ |
| e | C's tape recorder | | ✓ |
| f | the sound of the phone ringing | | ✓ |
| g | the phone – i.e. speak into the receiver to find out who's calling | ✓(?) | ✓ |
| h | C's tape recorder | | ✓ |
| i | a particular wire in the tape recorder's electronic circuitry | | ✓ |
| j | a particular place in the tape recorder | | ✓ |
| k | the wire and/or the tape recorder | | ✓ |
| l | C's tape recorder | | ✓ |

| B | Referent? | Referent explicit? | Referent implicit? |
|---|---|---|---|
| m | premise | ✓ | |
| n | accountability | ✓ | |
| o | public bodies | ✓ | |
| p | participation ... government | ✓ | |
| q | people who are governed | ✓ | |
| r | proposition | ✓ | |
| s | to curb open debate | ✓ | |
| t | matters of public interest | ✓ | |
| u | principle of open debate | ✓ | |
| v | European Court of Human Rights | ✓ | |
| w | Article 10 | ✓ | |
| x | European Court of Human Rights | ✓ | |
| y | freedom of expression | ✓ | |
| z | European Court of Human Rights | ✓ | |

The writer of Text B makes doubly sure that readers will understand references to the European Court of Human Rights and the European Convention on Human Rights by giving extensive documentation backup in footnotes, and also by indicating that the short forms of these two names, enclosed in brackets – (the Court) and (the Convention) – will be used to refer to these two entities in the rest of the paper without their having to be made explicit each time.

## Activity 26

The table below the text suggests items in the student's writing which could benefit from being clarified. Of course, we are not suggesting that a teacher would necessarily want to highlight all these items at the same time (this would probably be far too much for a student at this level of proficiency to cope with all at once), but we *are* drawing attention to (a) the enormous complexities of reference systems in English and (b) the more general writing problem of making sure that readers have enough information to process intended meanings.

In [1]**arranged marriage**, parents find [2]**a consort** instead of [3]**the person** [4]**oneself**. In such a case that people eager to get married but there is no [5]**lover**, people go to [6]**agent** of arranged marriages. Some people [7]**are forced** to see each other and they have to marry [8]**him/her**. I agree with [9]**an arranged marriage is good** in thinking that seeing [10]**each other** with a view to marriage [11]. [12]**Arranged seeing each other** is a good occasion to meet [13]**new person**. Recently [14]**group meetings** are on increase. [15]**Some of group meetings** have a purpose to get [16]**his wife** or [17]**her husband**. However [18]**other** are also just entertainments like [19]**dance parties**. I approve that if [20]**they** can make [21]**good relationship**, there is no problem in an arranged marriage.

| Item | Unclear reference? | Lack of shared knowledge? | Possible questions for student to answer |
|---|---|---|---|
| 1 | ✓ | | Do you mean all arranged marriages? Or all arranged marriages in Japan? Or a specific arranged marriage? |
| 2 | ✓ | ✓ | A consort for whom? What is the role of this person? Is the meaning of *consort* the same in Japanese as in English? |
| 3 | ✓ | | Which person is referred to here? |
| 4 | ✓ | | Are you referring to yourself, or to anybody? |
| 5 | | ✓ | Is the meaning of *lover* the same in Japanese as in English? Is this the most appropriate word in the context of marriage? |
| 6 | ✓ | | How many? One, or more than one? |
| 7 | ✓ | | Who forces them? |
| 8 | ✓ | | Which person is referred to here? |
| 9 | ✓ | | Whose idea is this? |
| 10 | ✓ | | Which people are referred to here? |
| 11 | ✓ | | What comment do you want to make about 'seeing each other with a view to marriage'? Is the idea complete? |
| 12 | ✓ | ✓ | Which people are referred to here? Who arranges this? How is it organised? What form does it take? Does it happen more than once? |
| 13 | ✓ | | How many people are referred to here? |
| 14 | ✓ | ✓ | What kind of group meetings? Does this expression refer back to 'arranged seeing each other'? |

| 15 | ✓ | | Which group meetings – do you mean all group meetings in general, or the group meetings that you've just mentioned? |
|---|---|---|---|
| 16 | ✓ | | Whose wife is referred to here? |
| 17 | ✓ | | Whose husband is referred to here? |
| 18 | ✓ | | What does *other* refer back to? How many are you talking about – only one, or more than one? |
| 19 | | ✓ | What kind of occasion is a 'dance party'? How formal is it? How many people go to it? Where is it held? What kind of music? What kind of dancing? How long does it last? Who organises it? |
| 20 | ✓ | | Which people are referred to here? |
| 21 | ✓ | | What does this expression refer to here? To a particular kind of relationship needed for marriage? |

# Activity 27

Text A: You could draw attention to aspects of the discourse such as:

- the juxtaposition of the very long list of side-effects with the very short end question – the inference being that the question is clearly not intended to be taken seriously, but rather to point up the dangers of taking the pills;
- the negative associations of both the general word *side-effects* and the specified medical conditions;
- the ironic naivety of the end question, flouting as it does the co-operative principle's maxim of quality, in that although the ostensible function of the question is to seek advice, this is not its force.

Text B: You could draw attention here to how the force of the message depends almost entirely upon the writer simultaneously

- flouting the quality maxim – the writer is patently *not* thanking Lucy Pinney for having told him the ending of a film he wanted to see, *nor* making a genuine request for information about the ending of a famous murder mystery play;
- adhering – ostensibly – to the manner maxim: the language is clear, unambiguous, and not unnecessarily long-winded.

In addition, of course, one would need *shared general knowledge* that people often write letters to newspapers to protest, or voice criticism; that newspaper letters often end with some kind of 'punchline'; that people often use irony as a linguistic tool for making a point in newspaper letters. One would also need *shared specific knowledge* about medical conditions in the case of Text A, and, in the case of Text B, that *The English Patient* is a film with a particularly convoluted storyline, and that *The Mousetrap* is the longest-running murder thriller in London's West End.

## Activity 28

- (1) in this context it is highly unlikely that it is the speaker who's being trained; therefore *my trainer* must refer to the person who trains his horses
- (2) the speaker admits to not knowing anything about horses, and therefore it is presumably difficult for him to appreciate subtle differences between the twelve horses, whereas to the trainer such differences are immediately apparent; one of the purposes of a trainer taking an owner round to see his horses is to inform him about the specific circumstances of each horse, so *it* must refer to the horse being pointed out at any given moment
- (3) probably *it* refers back to the absurdity of a successful racehorse owner not knowing anything at all about horses – one would expect just the opposite
- (4) since a horse can be neither a coal merchant nor a bookmaker, *he* must refer to the speaker's father, though, grammatically, the nearest referent is *horse*

Items requiring culture-specific knowledge would probably include:

- racehorses and racing (notice the speaker assumes we understand he's talking about racehorses)
- carthorse
- coal merchant
- bookmaker

The speaker's fairly broad northern English accent would probably enable us to place him as coming possibly from a working-class background, perhaps a northern mining community. This would underscore the contrast with his now presumably relatively wealthy position (he now owns twelve racehorses) along with the upper-middle class – or even aristocratic – racing fraternity.

## Activity 29

In the right column are just a few of some of the more common formal markers of the basic logical relations in the left column.

| so | therefore; consequently; as a result; accordingly; thus; hence |
|---|---|
| but | yet; however; whereas; nevertheless; by contrast; rather; at the same time; whilst; conversely |
| and | in addition; moreover; furthermore; besides; similarly; equally |
| because | on account of |
| or | alternatively; rather; otherwise |

## Activity 30

| Point in text | What is the relation? e.g. result, reason, example, contrast, alternative | How is the relation marked? | | |
|---|---|---|---|---|
| | | not explicitly marked | marked with a punctuation symbol | marked with an explicit logical marker |
| A1 | result | ✓ | | |
| A2 | reason | ✓ | | |
| A3 | result | ✓ | | |
| B4 | contrast | | | however |
| B5 | example | | : | |
| B6 | alternative | | , | |
| B7 | alternative | | | or |
| B8 | result | | | thus |
| B9 | contrast | | | rather than |

## Activity 31

| Text A | | Text B | |
|---|---|---|---|
| what we're going to DO is … | marked (i.e. not usual) *what … is …* structure, plus stress on auxiliary verb *do* to highlight intention | Today, I'd like to talk to you about group discussions | polite structure to introduce intention |
| what do we mean by this idea of myth ↓OLogy what is myth ↓OLogy … | repetition of major question to be discussed | I want first of all to deal with … | list and order marker |
| ++ ↑I'm going to ↑START by looking at | pause, upward pitch movement, and stress | then I want to… | list and order marker |
| what do we actually ↓MEAN by this ↓TERM what ↓COULD it mean + um ↑+ | repetition of major question to be discussed, stress on key words | next I'll go on to … | list and order marker |
| IN this lecture I'm ↓NOT trying to put across to you the ideas that … | stress and downward pitch movement to outline *opposite* of what lecturer intends to do | and then finally I'd like to … | list and order marker |
| ++ ↑what I'm trying to ↓DO is | pause, upward pitch movement, and stress, underlining what lecturer *does* intend to do | Firstly, then, let's look at … | list and order marker, plus structure to invite audience to comply with speaker's programme |

247

| | | | |
|---|---|---|---|
| ++ OK ↑so let's START with some of the more theor↓ETical stuff +++ | pauses at either side of the language chunk, upward and downward pitch movement, and stress | | |
| +++ um↑ the first thing about mythOLogy is is that is A ↓STRUCTured ↓SYSTem ++ | pause, upward pitch movement to signal new chunk; stress and downward pitch movement on key terms | | |

Of course, it is true that some of the features of spoken language apparent in Text A (stress, pauses, pitch movement) would become apparent if students listened to the tape accompanying Text B. Nevertheless, Text B still does not contain many of the features typical of spoken language which are so abundant in Text A:

- unclear sentence boundaries (in the sense of the grammar of the written language)
- grammatically incomplete sentences (in the sense of the grammar of the written language)
- redundancy and repetition
- implicit connections between ideas

Text B, by contrast, is very orderly, grammatically 'correct', compact. The sentences are sometimes quite complex, with qualificatory phrases and 'asides', typical of academic written text (e.g. ... secondly, *and perhaps more importantly,* their purpose) and embedded clauses or phrases, also typical of academic written text (e.g. The traditional differences *which are still accepted by many lecturers,* are firstly the size of the group and secondly, *and perhaps more importantly*, their purpose ...); logical markers are often explicit; the vocabulary and structures used are generally more formal, more distant and less immediate than those of Text A; finally, there is virtually no inbuilt redundancy – perhaps one of the most common features of spoken language.

## Activity 32

*(The writer has been discussing objective features of alienation at work)*

... These can be considered the *objective* features of alienation. Much discussion, however, extends to considering how far the *objective* features of alienation result in *subjective feelings* of *deprivation* or *estrangement*: a *sense of a lack of wholeness*, a *sense of frustration* or of *a loss of humanity*. Thus many people come to feel that their lives and work are *controlled* by *material things* rather than by *processes* which are ultimately of *human* origin.

| Words/phrases establishing contrasts | Words/phrases establishing supports | Words/phrases supporting negative meaning of 'alienation' |
|---|---|---|
| objective/subjective | subjective feelings / sense | deprivation |
| material/human | deprivation / a lack of wholeness | estrangement |
| things/processes | estrangement / a loss of humanity | lack of wholeness |
| | a sense of frustration | frustration |
| | | loss of humanity |
| | | controlled by material things |

## Activity 33

| Resolution | Organisational features |
|---|---|
| I'll tidy my tray<br>And bring my book every day.<br>I'll stop bugging my brother<br>And be kind to my mother.<br>I won't be rude<br>Or get in a mood.<br>I go to bed at seven<br>Instead of eleven. | • text arranged as eight-line stanza of four two-line couplets<br>• each line has two beats (or stresses)<br>• each two-line couplet ends in words that rhyme<br>• lines 1–3 contain examples of sound patterns (alliteration in *tidy* and *tray*; *bring* and *book*; *bugging* and *brother*<br>• each couplet contains two 'resolutions', formulated with parallel structure using modal verb *will* indicating intention (with the exception of the final one – perhaps an orthographic oversight?)<br>• words and images reflect theme: 'good' things to be done – tidy, (remember to) bring, be kind, go to bed early – vs. 'bad' things to be avoided – bugging a brother, being rude, getting in a mood, going to bed late |

## Activity 34

In the second draft, the writer changes the organisation of the information and highlights the point to be stressed as follows:

• the point the writer wants to stress comes at the beginning, rather than the end, of the paragraph
• it is evaluated (i.e. the writer makes a judgement about it – *The **most serious** [problem] is ...*) rather than presented merely as a fact (as in the 1st draft – *Not a few Pachinko players are addicted to Pachinko ...*)
• the rest of the information is presented as examples or evidence to show the dangers of addiction and is linked to the controlling idea with markers and linking devices like *This has resulted in ..., In one case ..., In another case ..., These accidents ....*

*The principle of organisation* could be identified as moving from a general point (various problems are caused by Pachinko) to specification of the most serious problem (addiction) to even more detailed specification of results of this addiction. Thus we move *from general to particular*, a pattern claimed to be common in academic writing in English. In Japanese, by contrast, it is claimed that a common pattern is often the reverse: detail to general conclusion.

The second draft paragraph is also a good illustration of another common organisational pattern: *Situation* (the popularity of Pachinko has brought various problems); *Problem* (the most serious problem is addiction, which can result in tragedies like parents neglecting children and letting them die in fires); *Solution/Response to Problem* (setting up of nurseries – in this case this is not a solution to the major problem, addiction, but rather to one of the associated problems); *Evaluation* (too early to say whether such measures will be effective). See Hoey 1983, for detailed discussion of this pattern.

To a reader familiar with conventions of organisation in Anglo-American academic writing, the second draft probably puts the writer's point over more clearly than the first, because of the various highlighting devices mentioned above.

## Activity 35

It seems to us that Text A is the more 'authentic' because:

- it attempts to replicate a natural mix of interactional and transactional language (it contains an initial exchange of greetings, and a 'leavetaking' sequence in addition to accomplishing the inviting function);
- it sets up a context (telephone conversation between two named persons);
- it has more 'colloquial' language;
- it attempts to give the two interactants some kind of personalities – Anna insists on paying for Tony and Tony accepts!

Text B, by contrast, seems rather cold and impersonal, largely because the focus is obviously on the (bolded) formulae and structures which can be called upon in this type of situation (even so, some of these seem to our ears distinctly strange: how often do we issue invitations by saying *I'd like to invite you to a party on Saturday?*), and there is a noticeable lack of any kind of interactional language.

## Activity 36

Questions relating to the *point in a teaching programme* at which you might think it appropriate to consider discourse competence:

- Is discourse competence something which can only be considered when learners have already reached a certain level of proficiency in, and acquaintance with, the basic 'nuts and bolts' of syntax and lexis, or is it something which ought to be incorporated right from the start?
- If the former, what would the 'right' level of proficiency be?

Questions relating to *ways* in which discourse competence is acquired:

- Is discourse competence something that can be taught, or is it rather gradually acquired through the natural process of increasing exposure to the language?

- Should teachers make a conscious effort to include *discourse awareness* in their teaching programmes?

Questions relating to the *constraints* of materials and teaching contexts:

- What happens if a teacher is restricted to using only prescribed textbooks and materials which are controlled and graded for pedagogical purposes and which therefore do not expose learners to large-scale authentic use of the language?
- How can teachers who themselves perhaps do not feel confident about their own discourse competence in the language they are teaching find ways of giving their learners access to it?
- Does a focus on discourse competence necessarily mean that teachers should base their teaching on authentic materials?

**Follow-up**
Here are some areas for consideration:

- using role-play, or simulation-type activities, where learners have to use the language they know to accomplish tasks or fulfil functions
- using projects in which learners have to interact with each other in order to accomplish actual goals or solve actual problems – thus encouraging a mix of transactional and interactional language
- using off-air recordings or film/video clips to let learners see how people interact with each other in authentic target language encounters and contexts
- using off-air recordings or film/video clips to expose learners to a wide range of spoken genres
- 'immersing' learners in discussion of their own discourse in the classroom through the use of taped classroom interaction and/or feedback from teachers, thereby increasing exposure to the target language by extensive and intensive listening
- using extensive reading programmes to encourage familiarity with different types of written texts

## Activity 38

The range of meanings of the word *grammar* in the examples is very wide. Suggestions for the meanings are:

a) the person was talking about informal / or non-standard spoken usages such as we <u>was</u> or it's hot, <u>innit</u>?
b) a book containing rules and a description of patterns in the Romanian language
c) grammar here is being confused with just one part of the structural system, namely morphology (see note below for point c)
d) a reference book containing guidance and rules of structural patterns (Murphy 1994, or Swan and Walter 1997, or *COBUILD Grammar* for instance in an ELT context)
e) the word here refers to the development of an EL1 child's language and the way patterns and structures and communicative skills are acquired

f) the meaning is not absolutely clear but the teacher who was speaking seemed to be saying that they no longer taught structures in the classroom but concentrated instead on functions (apologising, asking for things and so on)

g) traditional grammar, including the dividing up of decontextualised sentences into constituent parts (parsing)

h) a highly theoretical grammar (book); it could actually be a concept as much as a reality (it would be extremely difficult to write such a book)

i) the subject of grammar: grammar can be considered to be a subject in its own right in the same way as botany or literary criticism or algebra

j) the method of using translation (and précis) often from written literary texts as the basis for learning a foreign language

Most of the contexts are real or based on real data, i.e. they are taken from conversations or were overheard as comments. Some of the examples include standard reference terminology, e.g. e, f, h and j.

a) an EL1 teacher talking (at a party) about her teenage children's use of language

b) used in a description of a university lecturer's research

c) a view sometimes put forward by people in reference to English morphology, which is not complex in the same way as for instance German or Russian where the endings of words change according to the gender and case (see footnote in Section 3.4.2 on p. 115)

d) an instruction from an EFL teacher to a student

e) part of a written description of the process of child language acquisition

f) an EFL teacher talking about the functional approach

g) an EL1 parent speaking about their experience at secondary school

h) gloss of a typical written description of a theoretical linguistic grammar

i) a teacher talking about how grammar is systematic

j) a comment by one of the authors about their language learning experience at school

# Activity 39

Here are some suggestions for definitions of 'grammar' to match the views in the five extracts:

## Extract 1

Grammar is a sociolinguistic concept: 'an attempt to describe the system of communication' which everybody 'possesses'.

## Extract 2

Grammar is based on sentence structure and the way words group together and form themselves into sentences.

## Extract 3

Grammar is 'the way in which a language is organised'.

## *Extract 4*

Grammar is rules and correctness.

## *Extract 5*

Grammar is an educational and socially valuable and valued discipline which is enhanced by the study of Latin.

# Activity 40

Children learning English (and any other language) as a first language encounter many examples that appear to them to be inconsistencies in language patterns. They – the learners – have to deal with these as part of the learning process. Most of the 'mistakes' here are based on usages which sound familiar to the child but in fact are not the ones they think. A confusion might be a better way of describing them. A purely structural analysis fails to capture fully the entertaining and amusing aspect of children learning language(s). Learning by analogy is a recognised and vital part of language acquisition.

a) The child is confusing the preposition *ahead* with the probably much more familiar noun *head* (and the indefinite article).
b) The pronunciation of the letter W̲ (double u) sounds like *double you* to the child, who replies – logically enough – *double me*.
c) Not all words have opposites; there is no opposite form of *outskirts* in English (although if there was *inskirts* might be a good one). Children display considerable inventiveness in their use of language.
d) This is similar to the first example above. The child knows the noun *jar* and is confusing it with the much less common adverb/preposition *ajar* (slightly open). The meaning and structure of the child's reply is impressive.
e) Agreement between singular and plural (concord) is a difficult area. The problem is not helped here by the linguistically unusual singular/plural pattern of *mouse/mice*. The child is making a very reasonable conclusion as to what the plural of *mouse* might be in English.
f) The negative of *had better* is not *bettern't*; the child thinks, again a reasonable conclusion, that the verb in the sentence is *better*. The analogy is with *you shouldn't do that* where it is possible to reduce the negative particle *not* to *n't*. The negative of *you had (you'd) better* is *you'd better not*.
g) By analogy the irregular past participle of *break* could be *brokened*; the child might be thinking of a verb like *ruined* perhaps but in any case has successfully managed to put the right ending on the (wrong) word.
h) The message here is that comparisons are confusing: the child is confusing comparative *bigger than* with superlative *the biggest*, a very common mistake amongst learners of all ages.

## Activity 41

There are several main areas where EL1 children have difficulties. They are relatively easy to identify and include:

- problems of regular and irregular forms, e.g. nouns
- singular and plurals of nouns and verbs forms
- confusions over lexical items, e.g. words that sound similar
- confusions over grammatical items such as past tense forms
- 'knowledge of the world' problems (Lucy and the well-done steak)
- a tendency to join ideas together with no sentence breaks (a feature of emergent writing)
- handwriting which is still identifiable as that of a child learning to write

While some problems overlap (e.g. difficulty with irregular forms) and some of the above look at first sight as though they are shared by adult EL2 learners, in fact it seems unlikely that L1 children learning their mother tongue encounter the same kind of difficulties as adult L2 learners. The basis, environment and type of learning are all so different that comparisons are hard to make; children learn languages in ways which are unlike those used by adult learners (they are not worried about mistakes, for example) and in an L1 situation the child is usually exposed to very large quantities of language input. Compare the typical school or adult situation in L2 learning contexts and it is not surprising that some of the children have already mastered elements which cause great difficulties for some older L2 learners (articles for instance). The message is perhaps that if you want to learn a language in a reasonably painless way, then do it when you are young. On the other hand, it is arguable that an adult's knowledge of the world is much more highly developed (the same may be true of written skills as well) and that therefore adults have some considerable advantage in the skills they bring to learning another language.

## Activity 42

There are a number of differences between spoken and written language (look back to 1.3.3. for more details). Some basic points which it is useful for learners to be aware of include:

- formal and formal features, e.g. contracted forms, colloquialisms, etc. in speech
- writing tends to be organised predominantly in sentence units while speech is more flexible
- writing is more permanent

The answer to the second question depends a lot on the situation in which the language is being taught. In general it might be useful to have some informal examples in learning materials so that learners can be made aware of the flexibility of spoken language. The kind of conversations often presented in teaching materials tend not to expose learners to much of this. In fact there are often various different ways of doing things even in quite basic spoken language (e.g. expressing thanks, or agreeing and disagreeing). There is a tendency for teaching materials to present language as *one form* = *one meaning*, a potentially misleading language fact.

## Activity 44

It is very difficult to say precisely whether something fits into a certain category, not least because a major element – context – is often missing. Although these pairs look like *either/or* categories, in fact many of them represent a scale: it is usually easy to identify things at either end but the middle area is often rather grey. Some of them are also descriptions which are more easily verifiable (e.g. *non-native*), while others may be much more subjective or judgmental (*wrong*, for example). The descriptions which are subjective may well overlap: for instance what might be acceptable for one person might not be for another and so on. Context is also very important.

Some interesting grammatical features are underlined. The words in italics at the end identify a general area for discussion.

a) <u>People happy are</u>. *(word order)*
b) She <u>brang</u> the book downstairs. *(past tense form)*
c) The shirt <u>ironed</u>. *(verb category)*
d) He <u>said her</u> some terrible things. *(wrong verb choice)*
e) They <u>must to</u> go. *(modals)*
f) I <u>seen</u> them yesterday. *(non-standard past form)*
g) There are <u>less</u> apples on the trees this year. *(quantifier/determiner)*
h) We were checked <u>and stuff</u>. *(informal spoken use)*
i) He <u>don't</u> know <u>nothing</u>. *(lack of agreement between subject + verb; non-standard 'double' negative form)*
j) There was <u>this</u> frog sitting on the pond, a <u>sort of</u> china frog. *(story-telling style; informal spoken form)*

Points to consider:
a) The sentence breaks a basic rule of word order in English (subject verb object). It's hard to see how it might be labelled 'correct' unless we look at a very small category of usage such as poetry.
b) It may not exist as a verb form in standard (adult) English but it is a typical example of child language development; by analogy with the verbs *sing* or *ring* for example (*sang* and *rang* in the past). The interesting question is whether it can be considered 'wrong'.
c) Transitive verbs like *iron* require an object. Compare a sentence like *the car stopped* where the verb type will allow this form without any problem.
d) English has two verbs – *say* and *tell* – where the meaning is similar but the grammar is different. You *say something to somebody* but *tell somebody something*. If a learner's L1 only has one form, the confusion is obvious.
e) The verb *must* here is a modal verb and the full infinitive with *to* is not used after modals.
f) Standard English demands *saw* as the past tense of *see* but a number of varieties have this form, particularly in informal spoken situations. An

interesting comparison can be made between non-standard forms and learner errors.

g) Traditional grammars will give the rule *less* for uncount nouns (*less sugar*) and *fewer* for count ones (*fewer bananas*). In this context English, certainly spoken English, seems to be changing and moving towards the single form – *less* – for both types of nouns. This may be unpopular with some users but language change is hard to halt. (cf. Activity 72 in Chapter 5).

h) *... and stuff* functions as a sort of informal spoken version of *etc.*, assuming that the listener is aware of the possible details. It performs a useful function in spoken English (though some EL1 speakers may disapprove of it). This is an interesting example of a form that doesn't usually find its way into teaching materials.

i) Both these examples are stigmatised (i.e. criticised as being non-standard) although equivalent forms occur in other standard forms of some languages (Spanish, for example, uses a double negative construction as the norm). In spoken varieties of British English both are common.

j) The *this* here is used as a story-telling device and is typical of this style (it is used in joke-telling as well). In the appropriate style it is acceptable. *Sort of* is again a very common 'filler' heard in spoken English. It seems to be functioning as a type of explaining device in this example.

## Activity 45

a) Adverbs of time, manner or place will fit (e.g. *late*, *quickly*, *here*). Adverbs are an open class: they are easy to form and there are lots of them. New ones can usually be formed from the adjective base + *ly*.

b) The word class is determiners, although not all of them will fit (*a*, *the*, *one*, *my*, *no* are all possible). The sub-groups (e.g. articles or possessive pronouns) belong to closed sets; try inventing a new article in English and you'll see why they are described as 'closed'.

c) A verb in its participle form, e.g. *standing*, or *arriving*. It could be the past participle (*stopped*) but note how the context governs how few words are semantically possible. The grammar (the preposition *at*) also reduces the possibilities. Verbs are part of a big open class.

d) A noun. An open class with lots of members. The potential to admit new members is large: new nouns enter the English language all the time (see Chapter 5 for more details).

e) The base form of a verb (an appropriate one presumably). Usually the infinitive form without the *to*.

f) Most of the group of 'wh–' question words will fit (*who*, *why*, *where*, etc.). Called interrogatives or just question words, they are a small closed set.

g) Modals (*must*, *can*, *should*) or the auxiliary *do* will fit. Both are closed sets. Note that full verbs (*eat*, *talk*, *go*) are not possible. Not all English verbs behave in the same way.

h) It might be the same noun as example *d* but it's unlikely. The gender change will probably affect the choice of noun.

i) An adjective (*big, striped, Siamese*). An open class. Here the possibilities are only limited by the features displayed by cats and how much you know about felines.

j) The past form of an auxiliary verb (*was*) fits to help form the past continuous. You could also try a gerund form with a verb such as *likes*. Or even a full verb in the past tense (*died*, for example). The auxiliary is part of a small closed set. The main verbs are severely limited either by the grammar (verbs which can be followed by *-ing* forms) or the meaning/context.

k) Either a preposition (*in* or *down?*) or a verb form with *-ing* that would fit (e.g. *watering* or *clearing* or *weeding*). Prepositions are a biggish group but on their own they are a closed set.

l) Both are pronouns (a closed set) but the big question is which one(s)? Purists might insist on *him* but the most likely possibility – in British English – seems to be *them*. Other forms either sound clumsy (*him or her*) or imply you know the sex of the caller. English lacks an unmarked third person singular pronoun so it's not surprising that the plural is used if you want to sound 'neutral'. Language and social change both have a related part to play here (see Chapter 5 5.5 for more information).

## Activity 46

The approach is one which follows a functional view of grammar (see text for definitions):

- Who did something to someone else? *Robert had already got up <u>to bring the others a cup of tea</u>*;
- How did someone do something? *William gave his teeth <u>a specially hard brush</u>*;
- Who had something done to them? *<u>Charles, John and Andrew</u> (the cup of tea)*;
- Where did something happen? *Once on a rainy day <u>there were</u> four small bears <u>in bed</u>*.

## Activity 47

Both these examples are from structurally based teaching materials which highlight the particular structure or structures to be practised and learned. The grammar in Example 3.12 includes *here* and *there*; *these* and *those* and *wh-*question forms (*what* and *which*). Example 3.13 contains a large number of examples of the present progressive tense (*is doing*).

Neither example makes any attempt to be realistic – the dialogues are scripted in order to present the grammar.

One of the main problems with the structural approach is its over-concentration on the forms of the language with little useful practice on where or when such forms might be used (the unrealistic dialogues give no clue to real contexts).

## Activity 48

The fact that delexical verbs (Example 3.15 on page 124) do not often appear in teaching materials is not particularly strange. Most teaching materials are based on written rather than spoken language and it is in spoken language that such verb forms are mostly found. Similarly, teaching materials often choose a formal type of example and delexical verbs are probably best classified as informal usage.

There is no doubt about their usefulness in general, for several reasons:

- they appear frequently
- they are less formal (sometimes the formal equivalents are over-formal e.g. *to bathe* instead of *to have a bath*)
- they generate other similar forms
- they are based on very common verbs
- the pattern itself is not a particularly complex one

Example 3.14 on page 123 is a good instance of language which might be useful in certain circumstances, e.g. for teachers or advanced learners, but is probably not relevant to the majority of learners. However, as a grammatical fact it is a useful one, and the existence of such language information in reference books is helpful.

## Activity 49

The first two definitions (Trudgill and Wardhaugh) are relevant in describing the doctor's use of language in that he does use vocabulary associated with his occupation and his role in the exchange with the patient. See, for example, turns 15, 17, 19, 21, 23, 29. However, these definitions provide a rather thin description. They say nothing about the doctor's purposes in talking to the patient.

The fourth definition, given by Bell, promises a 'richer' description since it refers to the use to which language is being put in particular situations. Unlike the first two definitions, this one encourages us to consider the doctor's purposes. Among the purposes we can identify are the following:

*eliciting information*: see the doctor's turns between 7 and 27;
*eliciting details*: see turns 11, 17, 19;
*informing patient about action*: see turn 29.

In Chapter 4, section 4.2.1 we referred to the overlap between the terms *register* and *style*. In this example of 'medical' English we can see that the doctor uses several expressions that might be considered as 'informal' in style: see, for example, turns 5, 7, 13, 29. It seems likely that the doctor is consciously using a rather informal style with a particular purpose in mind: that of attempting to lower the tension of the occasion for the patient. Sounding less formal and more friendly might help to reassure the patient or, at least, make him feel less anxious. Reference to the 'stylistic' choices made by the doctor thus becomes part of a meaningful description of his use of language, just as much as reference to his use of non-technical vocabulary associated with illness and the fact that he uses a lot of question forms. If we are right in assuming that choosing informal expressions is linked to attempting to lessen tension, then we should add *reassuring the patient* to our brief list of the doctor's purposes.

## Activity 51

The definitions and examples we have considered in 4.2.1 should suggest the following broad categorisation:

terms referring to *user: accent, dialect and idiolect*
terms referring to the *use* to which language is put: *style, register and jargon*

## Activity 52

Given the context described (a large mixed gender congregation in a working class district), the use of the phrase *good chaps* seems rather out of place. *Chaps* is not normally used to refer to females nor, probably, to working class males. The overall tone of the utterance might also be considered less solemn than that often encountered in a church.

It is possible that the priest was hoping to come across as friendly and approachable by sounding less formal (or solemn) than his listeners might have expected. It is questionable whether this was actually the impression he made.

## Activity 53

The words which convey a positive attitude are *articulate, eloquent* and *fluent*. The others, with the possible exception of *posh*, are negative. *Posh* could convey either positive or negative feelings. It often indicates a negative attitude towards RP compared with regional accents. On the other hand, it might convey an almost admiring attitude towards the use of standard pronunciation and grammar.

Linking these words to particular features of language use is not a straightforward task, not least because their meanings are difficult to pin down. *Articulate, eloquent* and *fluent* are often used to refer *to* the range and precision of a person's use of vocabulary and grammar, with *fractured* possibly meaning the absence of these qualities. The other negative words are particularly vague in meaning when applied to language use and may refer to any or all features.

## Activity 54

Other factors which influence the way we react to varieties of our own language include:

* our general attitude towards non-standard use of language
* how different the particular variety is from standard use or from our own variety

- how easy or difficult we find it to understand a variety
- associations we may have formed between particular varieties and various personality traits

It is difficult to say which factors are more influential than others. They all contribute to a cumulative effect on our reactions to particular varieties, but the most powerful factor is probably the first one in the above list: our general attitude towards non-standard use of language.

## Activity 55

Instances of non-standard usage in Examples 4.3–4.6:

### 4.3

The *Not to* structure would conform to standard usage if it was preceded by an expression such as *Guests are requested*.

Three adjectives are used which would probably not occur in an EL1 text of this kind: *disgusting, loathsome* and *demoralizing*. Possible alternatives would include *disruptive, unpleasant* and *inappropriate*.

We might also wonder what other items are referred to in *Animals, birds, etc.*

### 4.4

The second sentence of this example presents the most difficult problem for the reader. If the intended meaning is that the level of the sea has lowered over the years and that, consequently, Kumkapi is further away from the sea than it used to be, we are left to wonder about the meaning of *after the sea was filled*. In the third sentence, standard EL1 usage would express the meaning of the adjectival phrase *nearly beside the sea being* rather differently: e.g. *our restaurant, which is still quite close to the sea* and *these* would be preferred here to contrast with *those* in the first sentence.

### 4.5

We might question the appropriacy of the adjective *great* as used in this situation, but it is the noun used by the policeman *(unlawf)* which is clearly non-standard. *Offence* is a likely EL1 alternative.

### 4.6

The student is presumably apologising for *being* late and her excuse is that she has had to walk to school.

## Activity 56

In a very formal situation we would probably not choose to thank someone with exponents a), b), g) or j). These four exponents seem more appropriate to everyday informal situations and are marked by their brevity and apparent lack of grammatical 'completeness'. The formality of a situation tends to influence us towards using more structurally complex exponents for expressing gratitude, which approximate more closely to the rules of standard grammar.

## Activity 57

Situational features which influence our choice of exponent to express strong feelings include:

- the general relationship between us and our listeners
- the feelings we have towards the listeners at the particular time
- our feelings about the topic
- our feelings towards what others have said
- the psychological aspects of the situation: e.g. degree of urgency or pressure of time

## Activity 58

The stylistic labels employed in 4.7, 4.8 and 4.9 are useful to the extent that they help learners to become aware of the range of exponents available in English for giving advice. On the other hand, there might be a danger in fixing labels to exponents in this way. It is difficult to lay down rules for appropriacy as it is such a dynamic and variable aspect of language use, especially in the spoken form, influenced, as we have seen, by a range of situational factors. Giving an exponent a stylistic label is influenced by the subjective views of the person doing the labelling. It is not certain, for instance, that all users of English (EL1 or EL2) would agree with the order of tentativeness presented in 4.7. In 4.8 the distinction between 'General' and 'Informal' is not immediately clear and is potentially confusing.

Since Example 4.10 is concerned with a more specific area of language use (written academic English) the information provided is probably more accessible to learners as well as having greater potential usefulness. However, an examination of this example reminds us of another aspect of appropriacy of language use: the fact that what is considered appropriate or inappropriate changes over time. Learners are informed in this example about the tendency for formal writing to be more impersonal in style to the extent that personal pronouns are avoided. There are those who cling to this convention, but as Ivanic (1990:126–7) points out, there has been a movement away from it, with a growing acceptance of a more personal style in academic writing.

## Activity 59

The discussion presented in Section 4.4 was intended to bring out the complexity of situational factors as they influence the language choices we make. One problem we might identify in the task given in Example 4.11 is that seven situations (A–G) are offered, each of which is characterised by a single factor. The lack of further information about the situations and the fact that the two invitations have different purposes make it a bit difficult to complete the matching task. For example, both invitations could be appropriate to Situation A or F. Also, it is not entirely clear which invitation is more appropriate to 'feeling very nervous' (Situation C). We might also wonder about the likely effect of the illustrations on learners' responses to the task: do they accurately represent the feelings described in the situations?

## Activity 60

Given the information and instructions in the rubric of this task, we could certainly make a case for the 'correctness' of the proposed answers. On the other hand, it is questionable how far these answers reflect actual usage. Can we be certain that *increased* is necessarily better than *gone up* in Sentence 1 without seeing the rest of the text from which the sentence has been extracted? We might have similar questions concerning the answers given for Sentences 4, 9 and 12. All four of these sentences could have come from spoken language, in which case it would be difficult to say that the phrasal verb was not appropriate. In Sentence 6 we could well imagine a situation in which a speaker would choose *consumed*, perhaps to heighten the effect of the message. In Sentence 11 *disappoint* and *let you down* are both such frequently used expressions that it could be difficult to find a stylistic difference between them.

## Activity 61

### Is it possible to teach appropriacy?

There is no right or wrong answer to this question. It is certainly a challenging exercise to undertake, as the discussion in the final section of Chapter 4 indicates. A major problem is the lack of solid, accessible and reliable information on appropriacy which can be structured and organised for teaching purposes. A further difficulty is that appropriacy matters are securely anchored in the cultures of language users and that, without an understanding of those cultures, appreciation of what is appropriate or inappropriate in the use of language is probably impossible to attain.

On the other hand, it is essential for learners to be aware of the fact that effective use of a language involves more than control of its formal systems. We are all learners in this area of language whether we are teachers, students, EL1 or EL2 users and we are unlikely to achieve a state of full or perfect awareness of appropriate language use: appropriacy, above all aspects of language, does not stand still. What we can do is keep our ears and eyes open to the shifts and movements in how language is used in real person-to-person situations.

## Activity 62

### Example 5.1

The appearance of the text makes it initially difficult to identify any words from modern English. There are, however, a number of examples of recognisable similarities:

- *he, me, ure* (pronouns) (ll. 3, 5, 10, 13, 15, 16)
- *her = here* (l. 6)
- *fram = from* (l. 8)
- *ealle = all* (l. 12)
- *oft = often* (l. 13)

## Example 5.2

By the Middle English period the language has many more recognisable elements, including some forms that are the same as in modern English:

- *Whan = when* (l. 1)
- *Aprille = April* (l. 1)
- *with* (l. 1)
- *March* (l. 4)
- *droghte = drought* (l. 4)
- *roote = root* (l. 4)
- *bathed* (l. 7)
- *every* (l. 7)
- *in* (l. 7)
- *of* (l. 10)
- *which* (l. 10)
- *is* (l. 10)
- *the* (l. 10)
- *flour = flower* (l. 10)

## Example 5.3

In this example the word *nearly* has changed from Dickens' use of *closely* to mean *almost* in modern English. Note, however, that some of the meaning is maintained occasionally in certain modern contexts, for instance in the expression *near relatives*.

The word *station* in the extract has the sense of (social) *position*, a meaning that is no longer used except in formal language or occasionally in idioms (e.g. *to be above one's station).*

# Activity 63

A modern letter would probably differ in a number of ways, not all of them linguistic (the concept of 'apprentices' for instance, or the name of the school certificate).

Particular changes would include the layout, format and typeface of the letter. Modern business letters have a very different look about them, for instance in the way the paragraphs are aligned.

It is actually quite difficult to rewrite the letter: the language and style and layout can be changed but the message may perhaps be one that is no longer appropriate or relevant (or even present) in modern society. Try collecting some examples of modern business and commercial correspondence and see how they differ from this, or other, older examples. Even the medium itself (writing, posting and receiving personal letters) is perhaps somewhat reduced in modern technological societies. The impact of e-mail for instance on business communication has been far-reaching.

The reasons for the changes therefore include technology, style and cultural and social changes. You could reasonably ask whether such types of letters still exist. If you want to try to say why the letter has an 'old-fashioned' feel to it you would need to refer to some of the points above.

## Activity 64

| Russian | *glasnost* | German | *hamburger* | Inuit | *kayak* | Arabic | *algebra* |
|---|---|---|---|---|---|---|---|
| Japanese | *karate* | Hindi | *juggernaut* | Welsh | *corgi* | Czech | *robot* |
| Spanish | *sombrero* | Portuguese | *bossa nova* | Aborigine | *kangaroo* | Turkish | *kebab* |
| Italian | *spaghetti* | French | *crocodile* | Chinese | *kung fu* | American Indian | *chipmunk* |

Some of the ways you might have used to match the words with their origins include your knowledge of the world (a *chipmunk* is a North American animal) or language knowledge, for instance the fact that Arabic nouns often begin with the *al-* prefix.

## Activity 65

Not all the expressions in the list appear in learner dictionaries: the following is a list of those that appear in current versions of both the *Longman Dictionary of Contemporary English* (LDOCE) and the *Cambridge International Dictionary of English* (CIDE). Definitions which appear in only one of the dictionaries are indicated by ^ (LDOCE) and * (CIDE).

*blag*^
*bum bag*
*callanetics**
*cardboard city*^
*diffuser**
*fatwah*
*geeky*^
*karaoke*
*lager lout*
*Lambada*
*eco-friendly*
*mad cow disease*
*motormouth*
*sicko**

Some of the other words may be included in the dictionary but in a different form: for instance *dreads* is not in either dictionary but *dreadlocks* is in both.

The *Chambers (1998) Dictionary of English* is a much bigger L1 source (it has over 300,000 definitions) but even in this dictionary not all the words appear. The ones missing from Chambers are: *agg, all-seater, Balearic, basho, B-boy, bimboy, daytimer, Deep House, jheri curl, noodle western, skippy, skorts.*

## Activity 66

The semantic area of food and drink vocabulary is a productive one to look at because there are lots of new examples which have come into English from other languages and cultures. There are several reasons for this, including a heightened interest in the UK in different types of food and the existence of ethnic groups who have continued to use their own foods. Supermarkets, food markets in cities and the establishment of ethnic restaurants (Thai and Balti for instance) and takeaways are also contributing factors.

Some other recent examples which have entered common usage in the language via the same cultural and culinary routes are: *cappuccino* (Italian); *tapas* (Spain); *humous* (Mediterranean and Middle East); *nachos* (Mexico); *dim sum* (Chinese).

## Activity 67

Various methods for coining new expressions have been used in the article including back-formations and affixation (see 5.4.1). Using words which already exist but with a slightly different meaning is also typical of many news stories, e.g. calling Margaret Thatcher *Mother*.

- a *spin nurse* is, by analogy, a sort of female spin doctor (this refers to spokespersons who 'spin' stories and media comment, usually of a positive political nature)
- *off message* (used adverbially) is the opposite of *on message*, i.e. something which has not been specially written or vetted by the spin doctors
- *corralled* means put into a pen (the word comes from an enclosed area for horses); adding *slightly* to it gives it a strange sense (usually something is either in a corral or it isn't) and gives it a meaning of 'constrained to a certain degree'
- *Mother* is an example of a common word given a special meaning for the context or situation
- *briefette*: the suffix *ette* usually meaning small has been added to the noun *brief* (for *briefing* meaning giving instructions)
- *muffins*: a pejorative, presumably with gender and sexual implications (see also *crumpet* as a derogatory term for women)

## Activity 68

McChicken and McLibel are both also used in the texts.

The ability of proper names or parts of them to enter the language as affixes is well established; another example in English are words using the suffix -*gate* from the American political scandal known as *Watergate* (giving *Irangate*, *White Watergate*).

The converse process is where the name forms the main part of the word and affixes are then added to the name (names of politicians figure prominently in this process, e.g. Thatcherite, Thatcheresque, Reaganomics, Gorbymania and so on).

## Activity 69

Advantages could include:

- the range and variety of available materials
- the number of different skills and subskills that can be practised (reading and listening for instance)

- accessibility to different forms and genres of English
- ease of access
- support for learning via on-line dictionaries and reference materials
- information about language and languages

Some disadvantages:

- the huge range is potentially overwhelming: where do you start to look, for example?
- the accessibility of technology
- cost
- application to classroom methodology

## Activity 70

Some of the words, or parts of words, have other uses and meanings in English (e.g. *surfing*, *mouse*, *page*); others are more specifically linked to new technology, e.g. *Netcast*. Some words combine common terms (e.g. *café*) with technology affixes to create new forms: *cybercafé*, *webcrawler* or take words with a known meaning (e.g. the verb *to browse* meaning to look through something), extend their meaning and convert the form to a different grammatical category (the verb *browse* takes on a noun form: *browser*). Knowing or working out what the words mean depends very much on your knowledge of the medium they are describing. Dictionaries struggle, understandably, to keep up with innovations relating to modern technology, which is why they have to be updated regularly.

## Activity 72

### Example 5.10

The determiners *fewer* and *less* have traditionally been used with countable and uncountable nouns respectively. This difference seems to be disappearing in spoken British English and the form *less* is now used for both. This is perhaps by analogy with the determiner *more* which is used to show an increase in something and which has the same form for both count and uncount nouns: *more fruit, more apples*.

### Example 5.11

The lack of a neutral singular pronoun in English causes difficulties in some contexts. Spoken and written British English have started to allow the plural pronoun form *them* with a singular subject and verb (*someone* and *phones* in this instance). If you want to maintain the neutral possibilities in this sentence without using a plural form, you would need to use the somewhat clumsy *him or her*.

### Example 5.12

In spoken English the form *there's* is often used to refer to plural forms (although grammar books will say that English has *there is* for singular and *there are* for plural). This may be another example of the language removing an unnecessary redundancy, cf. French or Spanish where one form is used for either singular or plural). There may also be phonetic considerations – perhaps *there's* is easier to say, especially before an /s/, e.g. *there's some people who agree with that.*

## Activity 73

### Examples 5.13 and 5.14

Shakespeare uses questions forms such as *Will you sit?* and *Comes the King back?* which are no longer used in standard modern English and also old forms such as *hast* and *thee*. The Jane Austen extract has some grammatical and lexical forms which are unlikely to be found to any great extent in modern English; for instance *exclaimed on the greatness of the match* (l. 6) and *a career of conjugal felicity* (l. 20). Literary style is also a contributing factor.

### Example 5.15

The use of informal dialogue (one of Iain Banks' strengths as a writer of modern English) as well as the situation and some of the cultural items mentioned give this extract a much more contemporary feel (the Range Rover for instance) as does the use of the swear words in lines 22 and 35.

## Activity 76

- headmistress – *headteacher*, or *head*
- actress – *actor*
- weather man – *weather person/forecaster*
- usherette – *attendant*
- single mother – *single parent*

## Activity 79

We imagine that most people would probably prefer to receive the Plain English Version of the letter, because it addresses the recipient as a person who may have overlooked some important obligations rather than as an offender against the law. The Plain English Version has made the language of the Revenue Version less formal, less impersonal, less curt and cold, and thus more accessible to the ordinary person because it reads more like a personal letter than an official document. It has also put the sender and receiver on more equal terms by including names and making it easier for the receiver to find information they may need to put the problem right.

Here are some specific comparisons of language choices at ten points in the texts:

| | Revenue Version (RV) | Plain English Version (PEV) | Comment |
|---|---|---|---|
| 1 | Dear Madam | *Dear Mrs Smith* | personal address of PEV indicative of more 'equal' status |
| 2 | Self-assessment 1st payment overdue: £x | *The new Self-Assessment system has now started. Please send your first payment for £x.* | RV version in note form; no explanation<br>PEV version version in full sentences; explanation of situation and polite request |
| 3 | The total amount above is unpaid. Please pay it now unless you have done so within the last few days | *If you have already sent your payment, I am sorry for troubling you. If not, please pay it now.* | RV version implies receiver is in the wrong<br>PEV version implies receiver may not be in the wrong, and offers apology if this is the case. |
| 4 | ... I shall start legal proceedings | *... I will have to start legal proceedings* | choice of modal *shall* in RV suggests strict imposition of authority<br>PEV's *will have to* is softer, and suggests a note of regret |
| 5 | This could result in ... | *This could include ...* | RV's *result in* indicates definite outcome<br>PEV's *include* leaves outcome more open |
| 6 | ... your possessions being seized, removed and sold ... | *... your possessions being removed by a bailiff and sold ...* | RV's *seized* suggests aggression<br>PEV's *your possessions being removed by a bailiff* adds a human element and possibly makes the unpleasant procedure sound less alarming |
| 7 | Should you wish to discuss ... | *Obviously, we do not want this to happen. If you have any questions ...* | RV: impersonal, formal and uninviting<br>PEV: personal and showing concern with receiver's situation |
| 9 | You are reminded that interest is charged ... | *Please remember that we increase the interest you have to pay ...* | RV: stark, formal, impersonal<br>PEV: softer, more personal |
| 8 & 10 | ... contact this office ... (illegible signature) | *... contact me at the number shown above ... (printed name)* | PEV: identifiable person as sender, and telephone number |

Power relations between sender and recipient are more blatantly expressed in RV than PEV, largely because RV makes no effort to consider the 'face' of the receiver, or to be tactful (see 2.3.1).

## Activity 82

*Cambridge International Dictionary of English* gives two definitions for the verb *to decline*: to go down (1) and to refuse (2), with a similar 'go down' meaning for the single noun entry.

*Collins COBUILD English Dictionary* gives five definitions of *decline*:

1. verb: to go down
2. verb: to refuse
3. noun: a decline in something e.g. quality
4. phrases such as *in decline/on the decline*
5. phrase: *(to fall) into decline*

*Chambers Dictionary*, 1998, gives a number of definitions, including those above. The first three mentions (the verb is given first) are:

* to fail or decay
* to stoop or condescend
* to draw to an end

The first three noun definitions are:

* a falling off
* deviation
* decay

All three dictionaries give a variety of meanings (verb and noun) for the word *charge*. The word is a good example of polysemy in English in that it has a number of different meanings (to ask, to order, to accuse, to control, to move forward) and it can fit into various grammatical categories (e.g. to charge, a charge, to take charge). The grammar information and examples of contexts given in the learner dictionaries are more helpful than the L1 dictionary (*Chambers*) which simply lists the definitions.

Sinclair (1991), Chapter 3, provides a breakdown of the various meanings and contexts of the word *decline*, emphasising the multiple meaning of many words in English and the difficulty – especially for dictionary compilers – of deciding which is the basic, core or most common meaning. It is clear from Sinclair's description that it is very difficult to say with authority which meaning is actually the 'first'. You could try the same exercise with the following words:

* bank
* right
* back
* take

## Activity 83

Among the devices used by the novelist to represent this variety of non-standard written language are:

| | |
|---|---|
| 1. Non-standard sentence punctuation | e.g. *Don't worry about me pet I am orlrite Hettie come home for Xmas* instead of *Don't worry about me, pet. I am orlrite. Hettie come home for Xmas.* |
| 2. Non-standard spelling | e.g. *orlrite* instead of *all right* |
| 3. Non-standard structure | e.g. *Hettie come home* instead of *Hettie came home* |
| 4. Inclusion of 'taboo' and slang or colloquial expressions | e.g. *except that bloody buggering Welsh windbag* |
| 5. Non-standard sentence structure | e.g. *there was a nice black one no trimings but ...* instead of *there was a nice black one, which had no trimmings, but ...* |
| 6. Written form represents spoken pronunciation | e.g. *aw Mam **your** making yourself an old woman* instead of *aw Mam **you're** making yourself an old woman* |
| 7. Lack of explicit reference | e.g. *I come away with a navy blue* instead of *I came away with a navy blue **blouse*** |
| 8. Recounting of incident as if in spoken language | e.g. *she says she thort to much was made of Xmas and turcy was a very dry meat I says well Ive never tasted it so I wouldnt no* instead of *She said she thought too much was made of Xmas and that turkey was a very dry meat. I said: "Well, I've never tasted it, so I wouldn't know."* |

Devices 4, 5, 7 and 8 in the table above are common features of spoken language and would therefore be less likely to be thought of as 'non-standard' if this had been spoken language. It is devices 1, 2 and 3 (punctuation, spelling and standard structure) which mark 'standard' written language, but even here, if this had been spoken language, device 3 ('non-standard' structure) might be acceptable in certain local 'varieties' of the language.

## Activity 84

Opinions are likely to differ on this question, but it would probably be agreed that *clerkess* is no longer in use; *authoress* and *poetess* are used very rarely, if at all; the use of *governess* is probably restricted to references to the days when the role of tutoring and assisting with the upbringing of the children of wealthy families was an occupation available for young women.

With *actress* and *manageress* we see examples of the growing tendency for the -ess suffix to be dropped: the need for and desirability of labelling members of these professions as male or female has been questioned.

The 'female' items in the remaining pairs – *hostess* and *princess* show no real sign of disappearing from use. It may be that specific roles are associated with occupants of these positions so that it is still necessary to distinguish them linguistically from their male counterparts.

The general point is that the use of a suffix attached to the 'male' item to indicate 'femaleness' is felt by some people to be demeaning to female members of a profession or occupation. It seems to suggest that 'maleness' is the norm and 'femaleness' the exception and somehow less highly regarded.

## Activity 85

When we consider these three pairs of words it is clear that any negative connotations they have are associated with the female item in each pair.

- The word *spinster*, as well as referring to an unmarried female, has negative connotations in that being a spinster is sometimes seen as a state to be pitied. *Bachelor*, on the other hand, does not have such negative associations. The *bachelor-life*, in fact, is regarded by some as an enviable way of life.
- Whereas *sir* is only used as a respectful term of address for males, *madam* can be used to refer to a woman in charge of a brothel. It is also sometimes used to refer to an annoyingly precocious young girl: e.g. *She's a right little madam*.
- *Wizard* is often used to describe a man with exceptional talent in a particular field, whereas *witch* is used about a woman whose main characteristic is malevolence.

These examples are taken from an article written in 1989 by Patricia Kaye (*ELTJ*, 43/3:185–191). She provides other pairs of words or phrases where the female item has negative associations, including:

- king/queen
- courtier/courtesan
- old man/old woman

## Activity 86

The argument is that we tend to put the male item first in male/female pairs and, similarly, the 'positive' item precedes the 'negative' in the other pairs. If this is true, then the phrases in the left-hand column should sound more 'natural' than those on the right. The problem with this argument is that this tendency, if it exists, is not altogether consistent. Try these:

mothers and fathers?     or     fathers and mothers?
uncles and aunts?     or     aunts and uncles?

Does the argument still stand?

## Activity 87

It is clear that the doctor controls this interaction. This is what we would probably expect, given the situation, with the patient lying in bed, waiting for things to happen and probably feeling somewhat anxious and ill-at-ease.

The doctor initiates all the exchanges, which are mainly adjacency pairs, and controls the development of the interaction at every stage, from turn 3, where he sets the framework for the interaction, through all changes of topic (see, for example, turns 11, 15, 21, 23, 25 and 27) to turn 29, where he indicates that the interaction is coming to a close.

Given the constraints operating in this situation, particularly the time factor, with the doctor having to be fairly brisk in order to allow time for other patients on his list, and the psychological setting, with the patient's sense of anxiety, we could argue that both participants generally keep to the co-operative and politeness principle. However, in turns 22 and 23, it seems that the patient is not being entirely clear and unambiguous, while the doctor might be seen as not allowing the patient sufficient time to complete his response to turn 21.

In turn 7 the doctor is following a convention typical of this type of doctor–patient communication, where the overall purpose is for the doctor to elicit the details and history of the patient's symptoms. The convention is for the doctor to 'offer the floor' to the patient: i.e. to pose a general question which allows the patient to start talking about their condition in whatever terms they choose. In this example the doctor has chosen to do this in a very general and possibly non-alarming way.

## Activity 88

In general terms the process of making the language more powerful (i.e. what fits the courtroom situation) is partly one of *formalisation*:

> *... provided assistance to him ...*
> *... on a number of occasions ...*

The process also involves *reducing the amount of language* and *removing elements of redundancy* such as hesitations and repetitions (*like it was, you know*). There are some forms in the less powerful version which are non-standard/false forms (*he called me always ... and help clean up his mess*) and there are examples of colloquial usage (*get straightened out*). The powerful versions have *more similarity with features of written language* (discrete identifiable units for instance).

Both the 'powerless examples' are comprehensible but are not formulated in the language in which many interactions take place in courtrooms, i.e. they do not adopt the often highly formal grammatical and lexical conventions found in legal exchanges. The language thus marks the speakers of the 'powerless' forms as outsiders, in a sense. If you compare the courtroom language with that of a casual conversation between friends, it is clear that the situation/context is extremely important and that the general discourse on the part of those working in the system is not the same as those who may come into contact with the system (witnesses, or the accused, for example). What effect this may have on the proceedings is extremely difficult to evaluate: is there any chance that those who use 'standard' forms of the language are more likely to receive lighter sentences for instance?

## Activity 89

a) T controls the interaction for the most part, in the role of conductor of the class. Total number of teacher turns is 32 out of 81 (about 40%). She:

- initiates/closes/changes topics (turns 1, 32, 48, 61, 69, 81)
- initiates/closes exchanges (turns 1, 28, 48, 52, 69, 78, 81)
- nominates speakers (turns 1, 48, 52)
- gives hints, clues to encourage students to remember the words (turns 13, 16, 19, 26, 28, 32, 50, 52, 55)
- evaluates students' contributions and actions (turns 7, 38, 48, 50, 57, 59, 81)
- gives explanations and clarifications of students' contributions or questions (turns 23, 34, 36, 38, 40, 44, 46, 50)
- exerts authority through humour (turns 48, 55)
- asserts pastoral responsibility to check that students are not having extra-curricular problems (turns 63, 65, 69, 81)

b) In terms of number of turns, the male students have a more dominant role than the female students: M1 and M2 between them account for 30 out of 81 turns (about 37%), compared with 19 out of 81 (about 23%) on the part of F1 and F2. However, we should note that F2 only joined in the class at turn 48. After turn 48 F2's contributions account for about 24% of the total.

c) In terms of types of contributions, we might say that M1 appears to be more dominant than M2 in that he is usually the first to respond to T's initiation of exchange or topic (turns 2, 6, 9, 11, 15, 22, 30, 35, 43, 45, 47, 54, 56, 58) or to respond to a fellow student's initiation (turns 67, 74 76), and he initiates exchanges with questions and demands for explanation (turns 39 and 41); M2, by contrast, often echoes or supports (turns 4, 12, 18, 20, 37, 51, 72) with the notable exception of turn 60, where he demands a turn. M1 and M2 are both from Oman, so cultural interaction norms are less likely to play a role in the differences between them than individual strategy differences, e.g. willingness to take risks and make mistakes.

As for the female students, F1's turns account for only 13% of the total; she speaks only when directly asked to take a turn, and many of her turns contain repetitions, pauses, hedges and sighs. This may be to do with her insecurity in the language, her interactional strategy repertoire or the expectations of her culture (Japanese) about appropriate student behaviour. F2 (from Oman) appears to take a much more assertive role in proceedings, once she arrives for class: she challenges T in turn 62 with a direct, unsolicited question; gives a detailed and confident explanation or justification for her absence (turn 64) and takes a leading part in the discussion about the whereabouts of her fellow student (turns 70, 73, 75, 79).

d) As the teacher of such a class, with a mixture of nationalities, personalities, interactional styles and language learning strategies, one would have to take care not to let the naturally dominant members have everything their own way. In this example, T probably tries to do this by making sure that F1 has a fair chance to take part, by giving her supportive hints and clues, and by putting the more dominant members in their place with a carefully judged measure of good-natured sarcasm and humour.

## Activity 90

In terms of *dominance* theories, it does appear that the males dominate in that they take a larger share of the turns in the interaction (excluding those of the teacher) – 61% of total student turns. There is also some evidence of male interruption of female speech (turns 4, 15, 35, 37, 41, 45, 47, 51, 58, 76, 80).

In terms of *difference* theories, F1's style seems to be more hesitant and less assertive than that of either M1 or M2. However, F2's style seems more akin to that of the two males.

It is very difficult to draw any conclusions from such a short interaction, and in any case, the differences in interactional style may have much more to do with individual language proficiency, personality, age, cultural behavioural norms and the classroom context than with gender.

# References

Addo, M. K. (1998). Are judges beyond criticism under Article 10 of the European Convention on Human Rights? *The International and Comparative Law Quarterly*, 47:425–438.

Aitchison, J. (1991). *Language Change: Progress or Decay?* (2nd edition). Cambridge: Cambridge University Press.

Alptekin, C. (1996). Target-language culture in EFL materials. In T. Hedge and N. Whitney 1996.

Aspinall, T. and A. Capel (1996a). *Advanced Masterclass CAE*. (Student's Book). Oxford: Oxford University Press.

Aspinall, T. and A. Capel (1996b). *Advanced Masterclass CAE*. (Teacher's Book). Oxford: Oxford University Press.

Atkinson, D. (1997). A critical approach to critical thinking in TESOL. *TESOL Quarterly*, 31/1:71–94

Austen, J. (1814/1966). *Mansfield Park*. Harmondsworth: Penguin.

Banks, I. (1995). *Whit*. London: Abacus.

Barker, P. (1994). *The Eye in the Door*. London: Penguin.

Bashiruddin, A., J. Edge and E. Hughes-Pélégrin (1991). Who speaks in seminars? Status, culture and gender at Durham University. In *Language and Power*, British Studies in Applied Linguistics, 5. BAAL in association with CILT.

Bauer, L. (1994). *Watching English Change*. Harlow: Longman.

Bell, R.T. (1976). *Sociolinguistics: goals, approaches and problems*. London: Butsford.

Bell, A. and P. Garrett (Eds.) (1998). *Approaches to Media Discourse*. Oxford: Blackwell.

Bell, J. and R. Gower (1992). *Upper Intermediate Matters*. London: Longman.

Bernstein, B. (1971). *Class, Codes and Control*. London: Routledge and Kegan Paul.

Biber, D., S. Johansson, G. Leech, S. Conrad and E. Finegan (1999). *Longman Grammar of Spoken and Written English*. London: Longman.

Bloomfield, L. (1935). *Language*. London: Allen and Unwin.

Blue, G. (Ed.) (1993). *Language Learning and Success: Studying Through English*. Review of ELT, 3/1, Modern English Publications and the British Council: Macmillan.

Bolinger, D. (1980). *Language – The Loaded Weapon*. London: Longman.

Bolitho, R. and B. Tomlinson (1995). *Discover English* (2nd Edition). Oxford: Heinemann.

Brazil, D., M. Coulthard and C. Johns (1980). *Discourse Intonation and Language Teaching*. London: Longman.

Broughton, G. (1968). *Success With English*. Harmondsworth: Penguin.

Brown, G. and G. Yule (1983). *Discourse Analysis*. Cambridge: Cambridge University Press.

Brown, K. (1995). World Englishes: to teach or not to teach? *World Englishes*, 14/2:233–245.

Brown, P. and S. Levinson (1987). *Politeness: Some Universals in Language Usage*. Cambridge: Cambridge University Press.

Butt, D., R. Fahey, S. Spinks and C. Yallop (1995). *Using Functional Grammar: An Explorer's Guide*. Macquarie University, Sydney: National Council for English Language Teaching and Research.

Bygate, M., A. Tonkyn and E. Williams (1994). *Grammar and the Language Teacher*. London: Prentice Hall.

Calvet, L-J. (1974). *Linguistique et Colonialisme: petit traite de Glottophagie*. Paris: Payot.

*Cambridge International Dictionary of English*. (1995). Cambridge: Cambridge University Press.

Cameron, D. (1985). *Feminism and Linguistic Theory*. Basingstoke: Macmillan.

Cameron, D. (1994). Problems of sexist and non-sexist language. In J. Sunderland. (1994). *Exploring Gender: Questions and Implications for English Language Education*. Hemel Hempstead: Prentice Hall.

Cameron, D. (1995). *Verbal Hygiene*. London: Routledge.

Canale, M. (1983). From communicative competence to communicative language pedagogy. In J. C. Richards and R. Schmidt (1983). *Language and Communication*. London: Longman.

Canale, M. and M. Swain (1980). Theoretical bases of communicative approaches to language learning and testing. *Applied Linguistics*, 1/1.

Carter, R. (1997). *Investigating English Discourse*. London: Routledge.

Carter, R. (1998). Orders of reality: CANCODE, communication, and culture. *ELTJ*, 52/1:43–56.

Carter, R. (Ed.) (1990). *Knowledge About Language and the Curriculum: the LINC Reader*. Sevenoaks: Hodder and Stoughton.

Carter, R. and M. McCarthy (1997). *Exploring Spoken English*. Cambridge: Cambridge University Press.

Central Office of Information. (1986). *Britain 1986: An Official Handbook*.

Chaudron, C. (1988). *Second Language Classrooms – Research on Teaching and Learning*. Cambridge: Cambridge University Press.

Christie, F. (1985). *Language Education*. Geelong: Deakin University Press.

Clark, H. H. and E. V. Clark (1977). *Psychology and Language: An Introduction to Psycholinguistics*. New York: Harcourt Brace Jovanovich.

Clark, R., A. Cottey, C. Constantinou and O. C. Yeoh (1991). Rights and obligations in student writing. In *Language and Power*, British Studies in Applied Linguistics, 5. BAAL in association with CILT.

Coates, J. (1993). *Women, Men and Language (2nd edition)*. London: Longman.

Coates, J. (1994). No gap, lots of overlap: turn-taking patterns in the talk of women friends. In D. Graddol, J. Maybin and B. Stierer. (1994).

Coates, J. (Ed.) (1998). *Language and Gender*. Oxford: Blackwell.

Coggle, P. (1993). *Do You Speak Estuary?* London: Bloomsbury.

Coles, M. and B. Lord (1974). *Access to English: Starting Out.* London: Oxford University Press.

*Collins COBUILD English Grammar.* (1990). London: Collins ELT.

*Collins COBUILD English Dictionary.* (1995). London: HarperCollins.

Connor, U. (1995). *Contrastive Rhetoric: Cross Cultural Aspects of Second Language Writing.* Cambridge: Cambridge University Press.

Connor, U. and R. B. Kaplan (Eds.) (1987). *Writing Across Languages: Analysis of L2 Text.* Reading, MA: Addison Wesley.

Cook, G. (1989). *Discourse.* Oxford: Oxford University Press.

Cook, G. (1998). The uses of reality: a reply to Ronald Carter. *ELTJ,* 52/1:57–63.

Coulthard, M. (1985). *An Introduction to Discourse Analysis: New Edition.* Harlow: Longman.

Coulthard, M. (Ed.) (1992). *Advances in Spoken Discourse Analysis.* London: Routledge.

Coulthard, M. (1992). Forensic discourse analysis. In M. Coulthard. 1994.

Coulthard, M. (Ed.) (1994). *Advances in Written Text Analysis.* London: Routledge.

Coulthard, M. (1997). A failed appeal. *Forensic Linguistics,* 4/2:287–302.

Coulthard, M. and M. Montgomery (Eds.) (1981). *Studies in Discourse Analysis.* London: Routledge and Kegan Paul.

Crystal, D. (1980). *A First Dictionary of Linguistics and Phonetics.* London: Andre Deutsch.

Crystal, D. (1984). *Who Cares About English Usage?* Harmondsworth: Penguin.

Crystal, D. (1986). *Listen to Your Child.* Harmondsworth: Penguin.

Crystal, D. (1987). *The Cambridge Encyclopedia of Language (1st edition).* Cambridge: Cambridge University Press.

Crystal, D. (1995). *Cambridge Encyclopedia of the English Language.* Cambridge: Cambridge University Press.

Crystal, D. (1997a). *The Cambridge Encyclopedia of Language (2nd edition).* Cambridge: Cambridge University Press.

Crystal, D. (1997b). *English as a Global Language.* Cambridge: Cambridge University Press.

Cullen, R. (1998). Teacher talk and the classroom context. *ELTJ,* 52/3:179–187.

Cutts, M. and C. Maher (1984). *Gobbledygook.* London: Allen and Unwin.

Day, R. (1980). ESL: a factor in linguistic genocide? In J. C. Fisher, M. A. Clarke, and J. Schachter (1980). *On TESOL Building Bridges: research and practice in teaching English as a second language.* TESOL, Washington.

Day, R. (1985). The ultimate inequality: linguistic genocide. In N. Wolfson and J. Manes (1985). *Language of Inequality.* Berlin: Mouton.

Department for Education and Employment. (1998). *National Literacy Strategy.* London: DEE.

Dickens, C. (1843/1994). *Martin Chuzzlewit.* London: Wordsworth Classics.

Dickens, C. (1848/1995). *Dombey and Son.* London: Wordsworth Classics.

Donald, J. and A. Rattansi (Eds.) (1992). *'Race', Culture and Difference.* Open University Press/Sage Publications.

Duff, P. A. and Y. Uchida (1997). The negotiation of teachers' sociocultural identities and practices in postsecondary EFL classrooms. *TESOL Quarterly,* 31/3:451–486.

Duranti, A. and C. Goodwin (Eds.) (1992). *Rethinking Context: Language as an Interactive Phenomenon.* Cambridge: Cambridge University Press.

Dyer, G. (1982). *Advertising as Communication.* London: Routledge.

Eckersley, C.E. (1938). *Essential English For Foreign Students. Book 1.* London: Longman.

Edwards, D. and N. Mercer (1987). *Common Knowledge: The Development of Understanding in the Classroom.* London: Methuen.

Ellis, G. and B. Sinclair (1989). *Learning to Learn English: A Course in Learner Training.* Cambridge: Cambridge University Press.

Fairclough, N. (1989). *Language and Power.* London: Longman.

Fairclough, N. (1991). Critical linguistics, new times and language education. In *Language and Power*, British Studies in Applied Linguistics, 5. BAAL in association with CILT.

Fairclough, N. (Ed.) (1992). *Critical Language Awareness.* London: Longman.

Flanders, N. (1970). *Analyzing Teaching Behavior.* New York: Addison Wesley.

Fowler, R., B. Hodge, G. Kress and T. Trew (1979). *Language and Control.* London: Routledge and Kegan Paul.

Giles, H. (1970). Evaluative reactions to accents. *Educational Review,* 22:211–227.

Grabe, W. and R. B. Kaplan (1996). *Theory and Practice of Writing: an Applied Linguistic Perspective.* London: Longman.

Graddol, D. (1997a). *The Future of English?* British Council.

Graddol, D. (1997b). Can English survive the new technologies? *IATEFL Newsletter*, Issue 138, August, 1997:16–17.

Graddol, D., J. Maybin and B. Stierer (Eds.) (1994). *Researching Language and Literacy in Social Context.* Clevedon: Multilingual Matters.

Gretz, S. (1986). *The bears who stayed indoors.* A and C Black.

Grice, H. P. (1975). Logic and conversation. In P. Cole and J. Morgan. *Speech Acts (Syntax and Semantics,* Volume 3). New York: Academic Press.

Grundy, P. (1995). *Doing Pragmatics.* London: Edward Arnold.

Gumperz, J. J. (1982). *Discourse Strategies.* Cambridge: Cambridge University Press.

Gumperz, J. J. (Ed.) (1982). *Language and Social Identity.* Cambridge: Cambridge University Press.

Hale, S. (1997). Clash of world perspectives: the discursive practices of the law, the witness and the interpreter. *Forensic Linguistics*: 4/2:197–209.

Halliday, M. A. K. (1978). *Language as Social Semiotic: the Social Interpretation of Language and Meaning.* London: Edward Arnold.

Halliday, M. A. K. (1994). *An Introduction to Functional Grammar.* London: Edward Arnold.

Halliday, M. A. K. and R. Hasan (1976). *Cohesion in English.* Harlow: Longman.

Halliday M. A. K. and R. Hasan (1985). *Language, Context and Text.* Geelong: Deakin University Press.

Hammond, J. (1987) *An Overview of the Genre-Based Approach to the*

*Teaching of Writing in Australia*. Unpublished paper, Centre for Literacy, Language and Cognition, Wollongong University, Australia.

Hammond, J. (1987). Process or genre in teaching ESL students to write? Paper presented at the 5th ATESOL Summer School, Sydney, January, 1987.

Harmer, J. 1987. *Teaching and Learning Grammar*. London: Longman.

Harris, R. and D. Thorp (1995). Language, culture and learning: some missing dimensions to EAP. In P. Skehan. *Thames Valley University Working Papers in ELT* Vol 3:19–47.

Harvey, K. (1997). 'Everybody loves a lover': gay men, straight men and a problem of lexical choice. In K. Harvey and C. Shalom (1997). *Language and Desire*. London: Routledge.

Hatch, E. (1992). *Discourse and Language Education*. Cambridge: Cambridge University Press.

Hawkins, E. (1987). *Awareness of Language: An Introduction*. Cambridge: Cambridge University Press.

Hedge, T. and N. Whitney (Eds.) 1996. *Power, Pedagogy and Practice*. Oxford: Oxford University Press.

Herring, S. C., D. A. Johnson and T. DiBenedetto (1998). Participation in electronic discourse in a 'feminist' field. In J. Coates, 1998:197–210.

Hinton, M. and R. Marsden (1985). *Options*. London: Nelson.

Hoey, M. (1983). *On the Surface of Discourse*. London: George Allen and Unwin.

Holder, R. W. (1996). *Oxford Dictionary of Euphemisms*. Oxford: Oxford University Press.

Hollett, V. (1997). Teaching culture – teaching the abnormal. *IATEFL Newsletter, 135*:18–19.

Honey, J. (1997). *Language is Power*. London: Faber and Faber.

Howard, P. (1986). *The State of the Language*. London: Penguin.

Hudson, R. (1992). *Teaching Grammar: A Guide for the National Curriculum*. Oxford: Blackwell.

Hudson, R. (1996). *Sociolinguistics*. Cambridge: Cambridge University Press.

Hymes, D. (1972). On communicative competence. In J. B. Pride and J. Holmes (1982). *Sociolinguistics*. Harmondsworth: Penguin.

Ivanic, R. (1990). Critical language awareness in action. In R. Carter, (1990):122–132.

Ivanic, R. and D. Roach (1991). Academic writing, power and disguise. In *Language and Power*, British Studies in Applied Linguistics, 5. BAAL in association with CILT.

James, C. and P. Garrett (Eds.) (1991). *Language Awareness in the Classroom*. London: Longman.

James, K., R. R. Jordan and A. J. Matthews (1979). *Listening Comprehension and Note-Taking Course*. London: Collins.

Jin, L. and M. Cortazzi (1993). Cultural orientation and academic language use. In *Language and Culture*, British Studies in Applied Linguistics, 7. BAAL in association with Multilingual Matters.

Jones, L. (1981). *Functions of English*. Cambridge: Cambridge University Press.

Jordan, R. (1992). *Academic Writing Course*. (New edition.) London: Nelson.

Kachru, B. B. (1985). Standards, codification and sociolinguistic realism: the English language in the outer circle. In R. Quirk and H. G. Widdowson (1985). *English in the World*. Cambridge: Cambridge University Press.

Kaplan, R. B. (1987). Cultural thought patterns revisited. In U. Connor and R. B. Kaplan, (1987):9–22.

Kaplan, R. B. (1988). Contrastive rhetoric and second language learning: notes towards a theory of contrastive rhetoric. In A. Purves (1988):275–304.

Kaye, P. (1989). Laughter, ladies and linguistics: a light-hearted quiz for language-lovers and language learners. *ELTJ*, 43/3:185–191.

Kinnell, M. (Ed.) (1990). *The Learning Experiences of Overseas Students*. Open University Press.

Kramarae, C., M. Schulz and W. M. O'Barr (1984). *Language and Power*. Beverly Hills, CA: Sage Publications.

Kramsch, C. (1993). *Context and Culture in Language Teaching*. Oxford: Oxford University Press.

Labov, W. (1972). *Sociolinguistic Patterns*. Philadelphia, PA: University of Pennsylvania Press.

Lakoff, R. (1973). The logic of politeness: or minding your p's and q's. In C. Corum *et al. Papers from the Ninth Regional Meeting*, Chicago Linguistic Society: University of Chicago.

Lee, I. (1998). Supporting greater autonomy in language learning. *ELTJ*, 52/4:282–289.

Leech, G. (1983). *Principles of Pragmatics*. London: Longman.

Leung, C., R. Harris and B. Rampton (1997). The idealised native speaker, reified ethnicities and classroom realities. *TESOL Quarterly*, 31/3:543–560.

Levinson, S. C. (1983). *Pragmatics*. Cambridge: Cambridge University Press.

Lewis, M. (1986). *The English Verb*. Hove: Language Teaching Publications.

Liu, Dilin. (1998). Ethnocentrism in TESOL: Teacher education and the neglected needs of international TESOL students. *ELTJ*, 52/1:3–9.

Lock, G. (1996). *Functional English Grammar: an introduction for second language teachers*. Cambridge: Cambridge University Press.

*Longman Dictionary of English*. (1984). Harlow: Longman.

Maley, A. (1992). English as an International Language. *IATEFL Newsletter*, Issue 115, May, 1992:18.

Maley, Y., C. Candlin, J. Crichton and P. Koster (1995). Orientations in lawyer-client interviews. *Forensic Linguistics*, 2/1:42–55.

Marenbon, J. (1987). *English our English*. London: Centre for Policy Studies.

Martin, J. R. (1985). *Factual Writing: Exploring and Challenging Social Reality*. Geelong: Deakin University Press.

Martin, J. R. and J. Rothery (1980). Writing Project Report No.1. *Working Papers in Linguistics No.1*. Linguistics Department: University of Sydney.

Martin, J. R. and J. Rothery (1981). Writing Project, Report No.2. *Working Papers in Linguistics No.2*. Linguistics Department: University of Sydney.

Maule, D. (1988). 'Sorry, but if he comes, I go': teaching conditionals. *ELTJ*, 42/2:117–124.

McCarthy, M. (1991). *Discourse Analysis for Language Teachers*. Cambridge: Cambridge University Press.

McCarthy, M. and R. Carter (1994). *Language As Discourse*. London: Longman.

McCarthy, M. and R. Carter (1995). Spoken grammar: what is it and how do we teach it? *ELTJ*, 49/3:207–18.

McCarthy, M. and F. O'Dell (1994). *English Vocabulary in Use*. Cambridge: Cambridge University Press.

McGregor, H. E. (1960). *English for the Upper School*. Sydney: Whitcombe and Tombs.

Medgyes, P. (1996). Native or non-native: who's worth more? In T. Hedge and N. Whitney (1996).

Mercer, N. (1995). *The Guided Construction of Knowledge: Talk Among Teachers and Learners*. Clevedon: Multilingual Matters.

Mercer, N. and J. Swann (Eds.) (1996). *Learning English: development and diversity*. London: Routledge and Open University.

Metcalfe, J. E. and C. Astle (1985). *Correct English*. Tadworth: Clarion.

Mills, S. (Ed.) (1995). *Language and Gender: Interdisciplinary Perspectives*. London: Longman.

Mobel, K. H. (1999). *A Study of the Teaching of Writing in English at Tertiary Level in Malaysia*. Unpublished PhD thesis: University of Exeter.

Montgomery, M. (1986). *An Introduction to Language and Society*. London: Methuen.

Munro, V. R. (1996). International graduate students and the spread of English. *World Englishes*, 15/3:337–345.

Murphy, R. (1994). *English Grammar in Use*. Cambridge: Cambridge University Press.

Nesfield, J. C. (1944) (1st edition, 1898). *English Grammar: Past and Present*. London: Macmillan.

Ng, S. H. and J. J. Bradac (1993). *Power in Language: Verbal Communication and Social Influence*. Newbury Park: Sage Publications.

Norton, B. (1997). Language, identity, and the ownership of English. *TESOL Quarterly*, 31/3:409–430.

*Oxford Companion to the English Language*. (1992). Oxford: Oxford University Press.

Pardoe, S. (1994). Writing in another culture: the value of students' KAL in writing pedagogy. In *Evaluating Language*, British Studies in Applied Linguistics, 8. BAAL in association with Multilingual Matters.

Pemberton, R., E. S. L. Li, W. W. F. Or and H. D. Pierson (Eds.) (1996). *Taking Control: Autonomy in Language Learning*. Hong Kong: Hong Kong University Press.

Pennycook, A. (1994). *The Cultural Politics of English as an International Language*. Harlow: Longman.

Phillipson, R. (1992). *Linguistic Imperialism*. Oxford: Oxford University Press.

Phillipson, R. (1996). ELT: the native-speaker's burden. In T. Hedge and N. Whitney (1996).

Pinker, S. (1994). *The Language Instinct*. Harmondsworth: Penguin.

Potter, J. and M. Wetherall (1987). *Discourse and Social Psychology: Beyond Attitudes and Behaviour*. London: Sage.

Purves, A. (Ed.) (1988). *Writing Across Languages and Cultures*. London: Sage.

Quirk, R., S. Greenbaum, G. Leech and J. Svartvik (1985). *A Comprehensive Grammar of English*. London: Longman.

Rampton, M. B. H. (1996). Displacing the 'native speaker': expertise, affiliation, and inheritance. In T. Hedge and N. Whitney (1996).

Rassias, J. 1967. A philosophy of language instruction. Hanover, New Hampshire: The Dartmouth Printing Company.

Rees, A. L. W. (1997). A closer look at classroom observation: An indictment. In I. McGrath. *Learning to Train: Perspectives on the Development of Language Teacher Trainers*. Papers from a Symposium held at the Institute for Applied Language Studies, University of Edinburgh, November 1995. Hemel Hempstead: Prentice Hall, pp. 89–98.

Richards, J. J. Hull and S. Proctor (1990). *Interchange. Student's Book 1*. Cambridge: Cambridge University Press.

Roach, P. (1991). *English Phonetics and Phonology* (2nd edition). Cambridge: Cambridge University Press.

Rosewarne, D. (1994). Estuary English: tomorrow's RP? *English Today 37*, 10/1:3–8.

Rothery, J. (1985). *Teaching Writing in the Primary School: A Genre-based Approach to the Development of Writing Abilities*. Department of Linguistics, Sydney University.

Sacks, H., E. Schegloff and G. Jefferson (1974). A simplest systematics for the organization of turn-taking in conversation. *Language, 50*:696–735.

Schegloff, E. and H. Sacks (1973). Opening up closings. *Semiotica, 7, 3/4*:289–327.

Schiffrin, D. (1987). *Discourse Markers*. Cambridge: Cambridge University Press.

Schiffrin, D. (1994). *Approaches to Discourse*. Oxford: Blackwell.

Scollon, R. and S. W. Scollon (1995). *Intercultural Communication: A Discourse Approach*. Oxford: Blackwell.

Shepherd, J. and F. Cox (1991). *The Sourcebook. Pre-intermediate Student's Book*. London: Longman.

Sinclair, J. (1991). *Corpus, Concordance, Collocation*. Oxford: Oxford University Press.

Sinclair, J. (1995). *Activate Your English*. Cambridge: Cambridge University Press.

Sinclair, J. and D. Brazil (1982). *Teacher Talk*. Oxford: Oxford University Press.

Sinclair, J. and M. Coulthard (1975). *Towards an Analysis of Discourse*. Oxford: Oxford University Press.

Smith, G. (1979). *Attitudes to language in a multilingual community in east London*. Unpublished London University dissertation.

Smith, L. E. (1987). *Discourse Across Cultures: Strategies in World Englishes*. New York: Prentice Hall.

Sperber, D. and D. Wilson (1995). *Relevance: Communication and Cognition*. (2nd edition). Oxford: Blackwell.

Sperling, D. (1998). *The Internet Guide* (2nd edition). Hemel Hemstead: Prentice Hall Regents.

Stannard Allen, W. (1974). *Living English Structure*. London: Longman.

Stubbs, M. (1983a). *Discourse Analysis: the Sociolinguistic Analysis of Natural Language*. Oxford: Blackwell.

Stubbs, M. (1983b). *Language, Schools and Classrooms*. (2nd edition). London: Methuen.

Swan, M. (1985a). A critical look at the Communicative Approach (1). *ELTJ*, 39/1:2–12.

Swan, M. (1985b). A critical look at the Communicative Approach (2). *ELTJ*, 39/2:76–87.

Swan, M. (1995). *Practical English Usage* (2nd Edition). Oxford: Oxford University Press.

Swan, M. and C. Walter (1985). *Cambridge English Course 2* (Student's Book). Cambridge: Cambridge University Press.

Swan, M. and C. Walter (1997). *How English Works*. Oxford: Oxford University Press.

Tannen, D. (1984a). *Conversational Style: Analyzing Talk Among Friends*. Norwood: Ablex.

Tannen, D. (Ed.) (1984b). *Coherence in Spoken and Written Discourse*. Norwood: Ablex.

*The Chambers Dictionary*. (1998). Edinburgh: Chambers Harrap.

Thomas, J. (1995). *Meaning in Interaction: An Introduction to Pragmatics*. Harlow: Addison Wesley Longman.

Thornbury, S. (1997). *About Language*. Cambridge: Cambridge University Press.

Trask, R. L. (1994). *Language Change*. London: Routledge.

Trask, R. L. (1995). *Language: The Basics*. London: Routledge.

Trudgill, P. (1983). *Sociolinguistics: An Introduction*. Harmondsworth: Penguin.

Tudor, I. (1996). *Learner-centredness as language education*. Cambridge: Cambridge University Press.

Valdes, J. M. (Ed.) (1986). *Culture Bound: Bridging the Cultural Gap in Language Teaching*. Cambridge: Cambridge University Press.

Van Lier, L. (1995). *Introducing Language Awareness*. London: Penguin.

Waksler, R. (1995). She's a mensch and he's a bitch: neutralizing gender in the 90s. *English Today 42*, 11/2:3–7.

Wardhaugh, R. (1985). *How Conversation Works*. Oxford: Blackwell.

Wardhaugh, R. (1992). *An Introduction to Sociolinguistics*. (2nd edition). Oxford: Blackwell.

Widdowson, H. (1978). *Teaching Language as Communication*. Oxford: Oxford University Press.

Widdowson, H. (1993). The ownership of English. *IATEFL Newsletter* 120:7.

Wilkinson, J. (1995). *Introducing Standard English*. Harmondsworth: Penguin.

Wiseman, R. L. and J. Koester (Eds.) (1993). *Intercultural Communication Competence*. Newbury Park: Sage Publications.

Wodak, R. (1996). *Disorders of Discourse*. London:Addison Wesley Longman.

Wong, I. (1982). Native-speaker English for the third world today? In J. Pride (1982). *New Englishes*. Rowley, MA: Newbury House.

Worsley, P. (Ed.) (1977). *Introducing Sociology*. Harmondsworth: Penguin.

Wright, T. (1994). *Investigating English*. London: Edward Arnold.

Young, D. J. (1984). *Introducing English Grammar*. London: Century Hutchinson.

Yule, G. (1996). *Pragmatics*. Oxford: Oxford University Press.

Zentella, A. C. (1997). *Growing Up Bilingual*. Malden, MA: Blackwell.

# Index

Page numbers in bold indicate definitions.